T0271849

Predictive Data Modelling for Biomedical Data and Imaging

RIVER PUBLISHERS SERIES IN BIOTECHNOLOGY AND MEDICAL RESEARCH

Series Editors:

PAOLO DI NARD
University of Rome Tor Vergata, Italy

PRANELA RAMESHWAR
Rutgers University, USA

ALAIN VERTES
London Business School, UK and NxR Biotechnologies, Switzerland

Aiming primarily at providing detailed snapshots of critical issues in biotechnology and medicine that are reaching a tipping point in financial investment or industrial deployment, the scope of the series encompasses various specialty areas including pharmaceutical sciences and healthcare, industrial biotechnology, and biomaterials. Areas of primary interest comprise immunology, virology, microbiology, molecular biology, stem cells, hematopoiesis, oncology, regenerative medicine, biologics, polymer science, formulation and drug delivery, renewable chemicals, manufacturing, and biorefineries.

Each volume presents comprehensive review and opinion articles covering all fundamental aspect of the focus topic. The editors/authors of each volume are experts in their respective fields and publications are peer-reviewed.

For a list of other books in this series, visit www.riverpublishers.com

Predictive Data Modelling for Biomedical Data and Imaging

Editors

Poonam Tanwar

Department of Computer Science & Engineering, Manav Rachna
International Institute of Research & Studies, Faridabad, India

Tapas Kumar

Department of Computer Science & Engineering, Manav Rachna
International Institute of Research & Studies, Faridabad, India

K. Kalaiselvi

Department of Data Analytics, Saveetha College
of Liberal Arts and Sciences, SIMATS, Chennai, India

Haider Raza

School of Computer Science and Electronics Engineering, University of
Essex United Kingdom

Seema Rawat

Amity School of Engineering and Technology, Amity University, India.

NEW YORK AND LONDON

Published 2024 by River Publishers
River Publishers
Alsbjergvej 10, 9260 Gistrup, Denmark
www.riverpublishers.com

Distributed exclusively by Routledge
605 Third Avenue, New York, NY 10017, USA
4 Park Square, Milton Park, Abingdon, Oxon OX14 4RN

Predictive Data Modelling for Biomedical Data and Imaging / by Poonam Tanwar, Tapas Kumar, K. Kalaiselvi, Haider Raza, Seema Rawat.

Routledge is an imprint of the Taylor & Francis Group, an informa business

ISBN 978-87-7004-077-8 (hardback)
ISBN 978-87-7004-190-4 (paperback)
ISBN 978-10-4012-416-1 (online)
ISBN 978-10-0351-685-9 (master ebook)

While every effort is made to provide dependable information, the publisher, authors, and editors cannot be held responsible for any errors or omissions.

Contents

2 Machine Learning Classification Algorithms for the Prediction of Diseases   **21**
Radhanath Patra and Bonomali Khuntia

I   Beginning of the Predictive Data Modeling for Biomedical Data and Imaging/Health Care   **45**

3 Biomedical Data Visualization and Data Representation   **47**
Subhranshu Mohapatra, Poonam Tanwar, and Shweta Sharma

Sachin Sharma, Madhulika Bhatiya, Anchal Garg, and Arun Yadav

5   Optimized Data Retrieval and Data Storage for Healthcare Applications   **107**
Pritam Ramesh Ahire, Rohini Hanchate, and K. Kalaiselvi

6   Computational Intelligence System for Healthcare   **127**
*M. Kiruthiga Devi, T. Nalini, Kamalakannan Machap,
and Rajan Kumar*

7 High-performance Intelligent Systems for Real-time Medical Imaging   **161**

V. Kanchana Devi, E. Umamaheswari, A. Karmel, Nebojsa Bacanin, David A. Maxim Gururaj, and R. Sreenivas

Preface

In this book, we embark on a journey into the realm of predictive data modeling for biomedical data and imaging/healthcare. Our aim is to explore the potential of predictive analytics in the field of medical science, utilizing various tools and techniques to unravel insights and enhance patient care.

It is divided into three sections, namely Section I - Beginning of Predictive Data Modeling for Biomedical Data and Imaging/Healthcare, Section II - Data Design and Analysis for Biomedical Data and Imaging/Healthcare, and Section III - Case Studies of Predictive Analytics for Biomedical Data and Imaging/Healthcare.

Chapter 1 serves as an introduction, offering a tour through the diverse array of tools available for predictive analytics in the realm of medical science. We delve into the foundations of this field, highlighting its significance and potential impact.

Chapter 2 delves into the application of machine learning classification algorithms in predicting diseases. By harnessing the power of these algorithms, we aim to develop accurate disease prediction models that can aid in early diagnosis and treatment.

In Chapter 3, we explore the crucial role of biomedical data visualization and data representation. Through visual techniques, we strive to effectively communicate complex medical data, facilitating a deeper understanding and informed decision-making.

Chapter 4 focuses on classification and clustering algorithms specifically designed for medical data. By employing these algorithms, we seek to uncover meaningful patterns and groupings within biomedical datasets, leading to improved diagnostic and treatment strategies.

Chapter 5 delves into optimized data retrieval and storage for healthcare applications. By developing efficient data management systems, we aim to enhance accessibility and facilitate seamless integration of healthcare data, leading to improved patient outcomes.

In Chapter 6, we explore the application of computational intelligence systems in healthcare. These systems leverage advanced algorithms to analyze complex medical data, enabling accurate decision-making and personalized patient care.

Chapter 7 explores the realm of high-performance intelligent systems for real-time medical imaging. By leveraging cutting-edge technologies, we aim to enhance the speed and accuracy of medical imaging processes, facilitating prompt diagnosis and treatment.

In Chapter 8, we present a real-time patient health monitoring system. By integrating various data streams and applying predictive analytics, we aim to develop a comprehensive monitoring solution that enables early detection and intervention for improved patient outcomes.

Chapter 9 delves into the development of an ensembled convolutional neural network for multi-class skin cancer detection. Through this case study, our main objective is to enhance the accuracy of skin cancer diagnosis, enabling early intervention and improved patient care.

Chapter 10 focuses on the identification and analysis of sitting postures in school kids. By applying similarity index retrieval techniques, we aim to identify optimal sitting postures and make recommendations to promote the well-being of school children.

In Chapter 11, we present a case study on fatty liver disease prediction using machine learning algorithms. By leveraging these algorithms, a novel prediction models that assist in early diagnosis and intervention has been proposed.

Chapter 12 explores the field of computer-aided drug design, specifically targeting the management of HIV. Using the application of advanced computational techniques, the main aim was to develop new chemical entities that hold promise in combating this challenging disease.

In Chapter 13, we delve into the detection of brain tumors using MRI images. By employing deep learning techniques and comparative analysis, researchers strive to improve the accuracy and efficiency of brain tumor detection, aiding in timely treatment decisions.

Chapter 14 focuses on the monitoring of footprints using footprint recognition, artificial intelligence, and machine learning. Through this case study, we aim to develop a robust system for foot health assessment and proactive interventions.

In Chapter 15, the detailed result of biomedical applications of footprint recognition using artificial intelligence and machine learning model for footprint recognition in biometric identification and authentication to enhance the security and convenience in hospitals and healthcare facilities is presented as a case study.

We hope this book will inspire further research and innovation in the field of predictive data modeling for biomedical data and imaging/healthcare. By exploring diverse case studies and methodologies, we aim to contribute to the advancement of healthcare practices, ultimately improving patient outcomes and well-being.

List of Figures

List of Tables

List of Contributors

Ahire, Pritam Ramesh, *Assistant Professor, Department of Computer Engineering, Nutan Maharashtra Institute of Engineering and Technology SPPU, Pune, Maharashtra*

Arya, Vaishali, *Ph.D Scholar, Faculty of Engineering and Technology, Manav Rachna International Institute of Research and Studies, Faridabad, 121004, Haryana, India; Faculty, School of Engineering and Sciences, GD Goenka University, Gurugram, 122103, Haryana, India*

Asgaonkar, Kalyani D., *All India Shri Shivaji Memorial Society's College of Pharmacy, India*

Bacanin, Nebojsa, *Singidunum University, Serbia*

Balakrishnan, C., *Department of Computer Science, Christ (Deemed to be University), India*

Balan, R. V. Siva, *Department of Computer Science, Christ (Deemed to be University), India*

Bansal, Devyanshi, *Amity University, India*

Bhardwaj, Aditya, *Amity University, India*

Bhatia, Madhulika, *Department of Computer Science and Engineering, Amity School of Engineering and Technology, Amity University, India*

Blessings, N. R. Wilfred, *IT Department, College of Computing and Information Sciences, University of Technology and Applied Sciences-Ibri, Oman*

Devi, M. Kiruthiga, *Department of Information Technology, Dr. MGR Educational and Research Institute, India*

Devi, V. Kanchana, *Vellore Institute of Technology, India*

Garg, Anchal, *University of Bolton, UK*

Gavande, Suraj, *Department of Pharmaceutical Sciences, Eugene Applebaum College of Pharmacy and Health Sciences (EACPHS), Wayne State*

University, USA; *Molecular Therapeutics Program, Barbara Ann Karmanos Cancer Institute, Wayne State University School of Medicine, USA*

Gupta, Munish, *Department of Computer Science and Engineering, Amity School of Engineering and Technology, India*

Gupta, Nikhil, *Department of Computer Electrical Engineering, GNIOT Engineering College, India*

Gururaj, David A. Maxim, *Vellore Institute of Technology, India*

Hanchate, Rohini, *Assistant Professor, Department of Computer Engineering, Nutan Maharashtra Institute of Engineering and Technology SPPU, Pune, Maharashtra*

Hooda, Madhurima, *National Health Services, UK*

Jayapriya, J., *Department of Computer Science, Christ (Deemed to be University), India*

Kalaiselvi, K., *Department of Data Analytics, Saveetha College of Liberal Arts and Sciences, SIMATS, Chennai, India*

Karmel, A., *Vellore Institute of Technology, India*

Khanzode, P. C., *Department of Computer Science & Engineering, Sipna College of Engineering & Technology, India*

Khuntia, Bonomali, *Department of CSE, Berhampur University, India*

Kohli, Neha, *Ph.D Scholar, Faculty of Engineering and Technology, Manav Rachna International Institute of Research and Studies, Faridabad, 121004, Haryana, India; Faculty, School of Engineering and Sciences, GD Goenka University, Gurugram, 122103, Haryana, India*

Kumar, Manoj, *University of Wollongong, UAE*

Kumar, Rajan, *Department of Information Technology, Dr. MGR Educational and Research Institute, India*

Kumari, V. Sheeja, *Department of Computational Intelligence-Institute of AI & ML, Saveetha School of Engineering, SIMATS University, India*

Machap, Kamalakannan, *School of Technology, Asia Pacific University, Technology Park Malaysia, Malaysia*

Mohapatra, Subhranshu, *Department of Computer Science & Engineering, School of Technology, Manav Rachna International Institute of Research & Studies, India*

Mohod, Anamika P., *Department of Computer Science & Engineering, Sipna College of Engineering & Technology, India*

Nalini, T., *Department of CSE, Saveetha Institute of Medical and Technical Sciences, India*

Nautiyal, Lata, *University of Bristol, UK*

Pathak, Shikhar, *Department of Computer Science and Engineering, Amity School of Engineering and Technology, India*

Patil, Shital M., *All India Shri Shivaji Memorial Society's College of Pharmacy, India*

Patra, Radhanath, *Department of ECE, Berhampur University, India*

Raheja, Supriya, *Amity University, India*

Raut, Prajal P., *Department of Computer Science & Engineering, Sipna College of Engineering & Technology, India*

Selvi, G. Vennira, *Department of Applied Machine Learning-Institute of AI & ML, Saveetha School of Engineering, SIMATS University, India*

Senthilnathan, T., *Department of Computer Science, Christ (Deemed to be University), India*

Sharma, Sachin, *Department of Computer Science and Engineering, Amity School of Engineering and Technology, Amity University, India*

Sharma, Shweta, *Department of Computer Science & Engineering, School of Technology, Manav Rachna International Institute of Research & Studies, India*

Sreenivas, R., *Vellore Institute of Technology, India*

Subburaj, Surender, *School of Engineering, Cardiff University, United Kingdom*

Sudha, I., *Department of Computer Science and Engineering, Saveetha School of Engineering, SIMATS University, India*

Tangirala, Suryakanthi

Tanwar, Poonam, *Department of Computer Science & Engineering, School of Technology, Manav Rachna International Institute of Research & Studies, India*

Umamaheswari, E., *Vellore Institute of Technology, India*

Yadav, Arun, *Department of Computer Science and Engineering, NIT Hamirpur, India*

List of Abbreviations

3D	Three-dimensional
ACO	Ant colony optimization
ADAS	Advanced driver assistance systems
ADDI	Alzheimer's disease data initiative
ADME	Absorption, distribution, metabolism and excretion
ADMET	Absorption, distribution, metabolism, excretion, and toxicity
ADNI	Alzheimer's disease neuroimaging initiative
AI	Artificial intelligence
ANN	Artificial neural network
ASIC	Application specific integrated circuits
ASM	Attribute selection measure
AWS	Amazon web services
BBB	Blood–brain barrier
BCD	Breast cancer diagnosis
BCP	Breast cancer prognostics
BIRCH	Balanced iterative reducing clustering using hierarchies
BMI	Body mass index
CAD	Computer aided drug
CADD	Computer-aided drug design
CART	Classification and regression trees
CI	Computational intelligence
CKD	Chronic kidney disease
CLARANS	Clustering large applications based upon randomized search
CLIQUE	Clustering in quest
CMU	Carnegie Mellon University
CNN	Convolutional neural network
CNS	Central nervous system
CPM	Convolutional pose machine
CPT	Current procedural terminology

CPTAC	Clinical proteomic tumor analysis consortium
CRD	Chronic renal disease
CSV	Comma separated values
CT	Computerized tomography
CTD	Cumulative traumatic disorder
CTS	Computer-generated tomography scanner
CURE	Clustering using representatives
CV	Computer vision
DA	Discriminant analysis
DBSCAN	Density-based spatial clustering of applications with noise
DCNN	Deep CNN
DH	Digital healthcare
DHI	Digital health intelligence
DKBS	Digital knowledge-based system
DL	Deep learning
DMDF	Department of Macro-Fiscal and development finance
DPPOS	Diabetes prevention program outcomes study
DQN	Deep Q-network
DT	Decision trees
DWH	Data warehouse
ECG	Electrocardiogram
EHRs	Electronic health records
eMERGE	Electronic medical records and genomics
EMG	Electromyography
EMR	Electronic medical record
ERFC	Emerging risk factors collaboration
ETA	Estimated time of arrival
ETL	Extract, transform, and load
FCN	Fully convolutional network
FCNN	Fully convolutional neural network
FLD	Fatty liver disease
FN	False negative
FNA	Fine needle aspirate
FP	False positive
GAN	Generative network
GANS	Generative adversarial networks
GB	Gigabyte

GDC	Genomic data commons
GENIE	Genetic epidemiology of diabetes
GEO	Gene expression omnibus
GFR	Glomerular filtration rate
GISAID	Global initiative on sharing all influenza data
GPS	Global positioning system
GPU	Graphics processing unit
HAM10000	Human against machine with 10,000 training images
HBA	Hydrogen bond acceptor
HBD	Hydrogen bond donor
hERG	Human Ether-a-go-go-related Gene
HIE	Health information exchange
HIPAA	Health insurance portability and accountability act
HITECH	Health information technology for economic and clinical health
HIV	Human immunodeficiency virus
HLC	Healthcare
HPIS	High-performance intelligent system
ICA	Integrated care assessment
ICGC	International cancer genome consortium
IDDO	Infectious diseases data observatory
IEDB	Immune epitope database
ILSVRC14	ImageNet huge scope visual acknowledgment challenge 2014
IoT	Internet of things
IR	Information retrieval
ISBI	International symposium on biomedical imaging
ISIC	International skin imaging collaboration
ISVM	Improved support vector machine
KNN	K-nearest neighbors
LFW	Labeled faces in the wild
LR	Logistic regression
LSTM	Long short-term memory
MDS	Molecular design suite
MeSH	Medical subject headings
ML	Machine learning
MLIOT	Machine learning internet of things

MLP	Multi-layer perceptron
MLPA	Machine-learning-based predictive analytics
MMFF	Merck molecular force field
MR	Molar refractivity
MRI	Magnetic resonance imaging
MSA	Multiple sequence alignment
MSCCA	Multi-class skin cancer classification algorithm
MSD	Musculoskeletal disorder
MW	Molecular weight
NACC	National Alzheimer's coordinating center
NAS	Network-attached storage
NHANES	National health and nutrition examination survey
NIAGADS	Genetics of Alzheimer's disease data storage site
NLP	Natural language processing
NMR	Nuclear magnetic resonance
NNRTI	Non-nucleoside reverse transcriptase inhibitor
NRB	Number of rotatable bonds
NRT	Nucleoside reverse transcriptase
OPTICS	Ordering points to identify clustering structure
OSDI	Ocular surface disease index
PAF	Part affinity fields
PCA	Principal component analysis
PCI DSS	Payment card industry data security standard
PDA	Personal digital assistant
PDB	Protein data bank
PDBQT	Protein data bank, partial charge (Q), & atom type (T)
PET	Positron emission tomography
PHI	Protected health information
PIDD	Pima Indian diabetes dataset
PNN	Probabilistic neural network
PRISMA	Favored revealing things for precise surveys and meta analyses
PSC	Pluviograph strip charts
PSO	Particle swam optimization
QT	Partial charge (Q), & atom type (T)
RAM	Random access memory
RAT	Rapid antigen test
RBF	Radial basis function

RCNN	Region based convolutional neural networks
RCSB	Research collaboratory for structural bioinformatics
REP	Reduced error pruning
ResNet	Residual network
RF	Random forest
RFID	Radio-frequency identification
RL	Reinforcement learning
RMSD	Root mean square deviation
RMSE	Root mean squared error
RNN	Recurrent neural network
RPA	Robotic process automation
RPHMS	Real-time patient health monitoring system
RSI	Repetitive strain injury
RST	Rough set theory
RTPCR	Reverse transcription-polymerase chain reaction
SAN	Storage network systems
SL	Supervised learning
Spo2	Oxygen saturation
SPP-Net	Spatial pyramid pooling layer network
STING	Statistical information grid
SVM	Support vector machine
TB	Tuberculosis
TCGA	The cancer genome atlas
TFLL	Tear film lipid layer
TGMLP	Triple gate multi-layer perceptron
TN	True negative
TP	True positive
TPU	Tensor processing unit
TSA	Topological surface area
UCI	University of California Irvine machine learning repository
VGG	Visual geometry group
ViPR	Virus pathogen resource
WBC	Wisconsin breast cancer
WBCD	Wisconsin diagnostics breast cancer dataset
WHO	World health organization

1

Introduction and Tour towards Various Tools of Predictive Analytics for Medical Science

Neha Kohli[1,2], Vaishali Arya[1,2], and Suryakanthi Tangirala

[1]Ph.D Scholar, Faculty of Engineering and Technology, Manav Rachna International Institute of Research and Studies, Faridabad, 121004, Haryana, India
[2]Faculty, School of Engineering and Sciences, GD Goenka University, Gurugram, 122103, Haryana, India
E-mail: nehaakohli@gmail.com; vaishali.arya05@gmail.com; ch.kanthi@gmail.com

Abstract

Almost every business is being transformed by improvements in machine learning and predictive analytics, which are underpinned by an ever-growing amount of data. During the past several years, predictive analytics' accuracy and precision have considerably improved and are continuing to advance at an exponential rate. Predictive analytics has made great strides in the healthcare industry, where it is regarded as the cornerstone of precision medicine. The most recent technological advancements are creating new opportunities for utilizing big data in healthcare to provide better services. Using mobile devices and internet services like sensor networks and smart monitors, the advancing new technologies have altered this situation, improving practical healthcare by employing predictive modeling and getting a deeper understanding of individual measurements. The use of predictive analytics tools in the healthcare industry opens up a variety of opportunities for researchers to examine the vast amount of data, spot patterns, and trends and provide solutions that improve medical treatment while lowering costs, managing health admissions, and assuring the safety of people.

Keywords: Analytics, predictive modelling, healthcare, bigdata.

1.1 Introduction

Medical science produces a huge amount of data, which is proven to be beneficial from collaborative and dynamic platforms like big data that have innovative tools and technology to progress the care of a patient [1]. The EHRs are one of the clinical and operative information methods that help to provide the healthcare sector with daily access to a large quantity of data [2]. Practitioners are creating new apps to help stakeholders in the healthcare industry take advantage of more prospects for higher value. Technology advancements and the creation of effective analytical tools have made it possible to dissect big data in healthcare and derive significant insights [3].

Business analytics refers to the methods, tools, procedures, and software used by firms to analyze massive amounts of data and improve their understanding of their industry, market, and ability to make quick choices [4, 5]. The digitization of healthcare data has made it possible to use it to raise the standard of treatment. When it comes to patient health and wellbeing, big data analytics in medical science denote the practices for analyzing the enormous volume of e-data. The healthcare data gathered from various sources can be used in a variety of contexts to improve performance management. Since this data is so varied, conventional software or hardware cannot easily analyze it. Health data can take many different forms, including lab data, health notes, clinical data, data from medical equipment or home-based monitoring sensors, financial data related to health amenities, clinical bills, social media columns about health-related topics, data from medicinal journals, etc. These documents may be available through a variety of sources like EHRs, Laboratory Information Library Systems, government, pharmacies, and insurance databases [6]. The process of predictive analytics is depicted in Figure 1.1.

Big data has four characteristics called the 4Vs: (i) volume - because of the huge amount of data, (ii) velocity - because of the quick accumulation in actual time, (iii) variety - because of the various formats of data in structured, semi-structured, and/or unstructured form, (iv) veracity - specifies to give a certain reliability [7]. Big Data Analytics methods refer to techniques such as prediction, simulation, optimization, and other approaches that facilitate verdict building and provide information to the decision-makers [8].

The researchers are constantly developing innovative applications for the healthcare stakeholders. The organizations are also working on creating all the possible big-data-enabled infrastructure that can help improvise

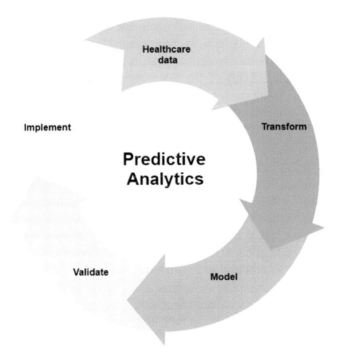

Figure 1.1 Healthcare Analytics.

decision-making by the management [3]. Nearly 80% of the information and communications technology's growth comes from sources that include big data analytics, cloud services, social media, and mobile technologies [9]. Big data analytics has the enormous potential to revolutionize healthcare as it develops into the next big thing in information technology. The outcomes of the increasing capacity to analyze complex datasets not only promise process optimization but also provide numerous ways to raise the standard of medical treatment and, therefore, patient happiness. The application of big data analytics in healthcare also helps rapid decision-making and, as a result, plays a key role in saving lives in situations where every second counts.

A rise in the long-term outlay in creating new tools with artificial intelligence and machine learning that can foresee upcoming occurrences to improve a person's health reflects the present concern of predictive analytics to advance the sector of healthcare. For the purposes of diagnosis and prognosis, predictive algorithms—or clinical prediction models, as they have historically been referred to—help identify those who have a higher risk of contracting a disease [10]. Predictive algorithms are employed in the era of personalized medicine to make clinical treatment decisions based on unique patient features and to provide patient counseling [11, 12, 13]. The number of new algorithm publications does not appear to be slowing down, especially with the growing accessibility of Big Data, medical imaging, and routinely gathered electronic health information [14, 15].

1.2 Literature Review

The potential impact of precision medicine on the development of more effective and personalized medical care is discussed by Zeeshan et al. by using AI to predict lifestyle and health outcomes, thus improving diagnostics and prognosis of some diseases. By enabling early interventions and individualized therapies, precision medicine promises to enhance conventional symptom-driven medical care. Better healthcare and precise medicine may be developed using AI and multipurpose ML systems. These platforms may be used to find the best routes to customize and affordable therapies [16].

S. Bhavya studies and examines various deep learning models for predictive analytics and modeling in the healthcare domain. Deep learning models like CNN, Gated Recurrent Unit, Long Short-Term Memory/Bi-directional LSTM, Restricted Boltzmann Machine, Recurrent Neural Network are the most effective techniques used. Medical time-series data frequently utilize the Long Short-Term Memory/Bi-Long Short-Term Memory model, and data generated from medical images often employ CNN [17].

A cluster of tools was created to help data scientists design predictive models in the context of telehealth. For this purpose, firstly a list of user needs was created. Then based on the data model of the telehealth programme "HcrzMobil Tirol," a viewer idea was created. The viewer idea and its application make it easier to have a greater knowledge of how predictive models are created in the context of telehealth [18].

In medical research, predictive models, which are probabilistic in nature, can offer an appropriate fit to data. In order to make predictions, linear and non-linear models are frequently utilised in medical research [19].

Using recorded data, operational processes in healthcare may be modeled using process mining approaches. Healthcare practitioners can use modeling to find inconsistencies between the planned and actual execution of a procedure [20].

The application of clinical prediction models can promote individualized clinical decision-making and enhance patient outcomes. For the purpose of creating prediction models for binary outcomes, logistic regression is a valuable tool. Clinicians can use published guidelines and heuristics to create prediction models based on logistic regression [21].

Tran et al. introduce a deep-learning-based prediction model including an autoencoder and a predictor for healthcare analytics. The model may generate multi-label predictions or binary predictions after learning from a lesser sample of earlier medical data. Test findings on the real-life datasets illustrate that the prediction model based on deep learning backs the healthcare analytics to a certain extent efficiently [22].

Algorithms for machine learning and artificial intelligence are extensively applied to medical research. Predictive modeling in healthcare has been found to benefit from machine learning techniques like deep learning that can take into consideration complicated relationships between features. Explainable AI is proving to be more dominant in helping the communication between internal choices, actions, and conduct to medical practitioners [23].

Prediction models can be used to determine the undetermined values of target variables. Prediction difficulty is determined by the relationship between the target variable and other relevant factors; with a linear relationship, we may utilize straightforward strategies such Simple linear regression. Although more powerful approaches are required for complex relations [24, 25, 26].

Dimitris et al. used contemporary data mining techniques to categorize claims data from various sources and estimate health care expenditures using performance metrics including hit ratio, penalty error, and R2 [27].

Duana et al. developed a recommended nursing clinical system that assists in making correct decisions and refining medical quality control. The system worked on the item sets of the provided dataset and employed Association Rules to discover patterns in the item sets of community hospitals of the specified region [28].

Santhanam et al. made use of a classification system that classified the donors of blood. The donors were classified into safe and unsafe donors by using the CART algorithm, which offers the capacity to effortlessly comprehend the classifier rules with the help of dataset of blood transfusion and then assess results using metrics of Precision and Recall [29].

Xiang et al. employed SVM, Regression tree, Random forest, and Boosting Ensemble along with Dataset of HPN 2011 to decrease hospitalizations. Predictions for the upcoming year were made by analyzing the past hospitalization record of the patients [30].

On the Cleveland Heart Disease database, Jyoti et al. compared the effectiveness of techniques of predictive data mining like Decision Trees,

KNN, Bayesian, and Neural Networks. They then used genetic algorithms to shrink the original data size and obtain the ideal subset of attributes necessary for prediction of heart diseases [31].

A decision tree model was developed by Sung et al. which helps in uncovering patterns in smoking behavior and factors to decrease heavy smoking habits among the elder population. The model was then compared to a logistic regression model using an accuracy performance measure [32].

Nichol et al. studied available MLPA health care products used in US health care settings. 106 MLPA products that attempt to improve health care efficiency by enhancing quality of care while lowering costs were examined. Based on publicly accessible product marketing materials, five types of predictions were provided by MLPA products, namely disease onset, treatment, cost, admissions and readmissions, and adverse events [33].

Soni et al. did a comparative study of various data mining techniques like Decision Tree, KNN, Neural Network, Bayesian Classification, and Classification Based on Clustering for prediction of heart diseases. It was reported that results of Bayesian Classification and Decision Tree surpass Neural Networks, KNN, and Classification Based on Clustering. After using the Genetic Algorithm to reduce the real data size in order to obtain the ideal subset of characteristics, the accuracy of Decision Tree and Bayesian Classification improves even further [34].

A study conducted by Bellazzi et al. explains the importance of predictive data mining in clinical medicine. For medical researchers and physicians, predictive data mining is increasingly becoming a vital tool. Understanding the primary problems underlying these approaches, as well as adhering to agreed-upon and established norms, is necessary for their application and dissemination of results. The recent integration of molecular and clinical data in genomic medicine has given the field a new impetus and a new set of hard issues to address [35].

1.3 Prediction Techniques

In artificial intelligence, machine learning combines computer science and the data statistics to create algorithms that generate effective results when subjected to appropriate data. In a wide-ranging capacity of applications, machine learning algorithms are being used where traditional algorithms face difficulty to implement desired functions. These algorithms work on various parameters of disease after preprocessing of the initial dataset, finally leading to prediction analysis as shown in Figure 1.2.

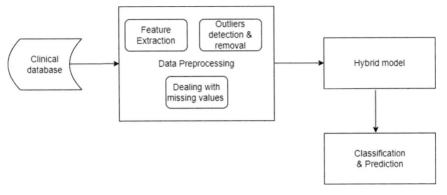

Figure 1.2 Experimental technique.

Below mentioned are few of the prediction techniques used in machine learning.

1.3.1 Decision tree

Decision tree algorithms belong to the category of supervised learning. The main objective of a decision-tree-based technique is to obtain a Boolean result at the leaf node. The tree-based approach describes a path starting from the root by a data separating sequence till the leaf node [36]. The decision tree classification technique categorizes datasets by applying particular conditions during the decision-making process. Decision trees are a convenient tool to assist in clinical decision-making, patient monitoring, and determine health outcome predictors [16].

1.3.2 SVM

Support Vector Machine states a supervised form of machine learning. SVM does the analysis and identification of the patterns from input data to achieve regression and classification analysis. The algorithms are widely used in applications that consist of face detection, hand-writing recognition, and digit identification, to name a few [37].

1.3.3 Neural networks

Deep learning algorithms focus on inducement of alike conclusions as human beings ensure by incessantly examining data conferring to a specified rational structure. It allows for machines to work on different images, audio files, and text to achieve human-like tasks. Therefore, in order to accomplish it, deep learning practices neural networks, which is a multi-layered structure of algorithms [38]

1.3.4 Artificial neural networks

ANN emphasize the concept of neurons. These neurons function in the same manner as the neurons in the human brain, which establish the foundation of deep learning. An artificial neuron mimics a neuron by providing a set of inputs, each having a certain weight. The neuron then calculates a function and yields an output centered on the weighted inputs. The neuron obtains n inputs. Subsequently, it adds the inputs and implements activation and then produces the output [38].

1.3.5 Linear regression

Linear regression is a tremendously resourceful method, which can be used to solve a range of research queries. Linear regression estimates the relationship of ≥ 1 independent variables with a constant dependent variable. It can also model curved associations [39].

1.3.6 Genetic algorithm

A Genetic Algorithm is made from a number of dissimilar components. It thus provides the flexibility to reuse the standard components with slight alteration in countless diverse genetic algorithms, making it easy to implement [42]. The algorithm has proven to be a global search approach studies from the development manner of natural entities. The algorithm defining the course of organic evolution is made, which is simulated on the computer that solves the optimization complications of the real world. The algorithm based on Darwin's theory of evolution makes the use of the principle of survival of the fittest [47]. It randomly generates various problem solutions and then selects the most favorable option. The iterations are completed and solution optimization is done just like biological evolution of nature.

1.3.7 Deep learning

A deep learning computational technique is provided with raw data, and based on the pattern recognition, multi-layered representations are created on its own. The sequentially arranged layers are composed of huge amounts of nascent, non-linear processes in a way that the initial layer having raw input data is given to the next subsequent layer, which is then converted into a further abstract representation [48].

1.3.8 Discriminant analysis

DA is a multivariate approach used to split multiple sets of observations based on variables evaluated on each sample and to determine the influence of each parameter on grouping. This technique can aid in identification, prediction, and symptoms recognition of diseases while also determining surgical and operative criteria in order to recognize patients for surgical procedures [16].

1.3.9 Random forest

Random Forest is a classification technique that generates output from a combination of decision trees operating on different subsets of a dataset. It can help to monitor and manage data from medical sensors and EHRs, provide distinction between variants of the same disease, forecast ICU patients' morality, analyzing social and economic elements in order to investigate the social factors that affect health, and predict treatment expenses [16].

1.3.10 Naive bayes

Naive Bayes classifiers founded on the Bayesian theorem are a group of classification algorithms. It is a class of algorithms in which every algorithm has a common goal with each pair of features that are classified is independent of one another [49].

1.3.11 K-Means clustering

K-means clustering is an unsupervised form of learning algorithm. It groups an unlabelled dataset into clusters with a goal to minimize the summation of distances among the data points and their equivalent clusters.

1.3.12 K-nearest neighbor

The KNN classification technique mostly comes to use when there is very less or almost no prior knowledge of data distribution. The classifier is based upon the Euclidean distance of a test sample and stated training samples [50].

1.3.13 Convolution neural network

CNNs have gained resurgence in the past few times in the field of image processing, speech, and pattern recognition. In comparison to ANN, it has reduced the number of parameters, which therefore has increased the popularity of this algorithm among the researchers. CNN performs with an assumption of features not spatially dependent [51].

1.4 Predictive Analytics Methodology

The medical science sector has witnessed inordinate evolution after the development of computational techniques. Along with this, a huge amount of medical data is being generated, that must be utilized in a way to extract maximum knowledge. This has prompted researchers to apply the new-age computational techniques like big data analytics, predictive analytics, machine learning, and deep learning algorithms to predict diseases and anticipate the cure. Predictive analytics has the capacity to reveal links and patterns inside huge amounts of data. By analyzing the symptoms, this technique may be utilized to predict illnesses and health situations.

Most of the methods for generating predictive models integrate the subsequent steps: (as shown in Figure 1.3):

1. **Definition:** Establish the research's aims and desired outcomes. It then requires translating them into predictive analytics tasks.
2. **Assessment:** Study data input to decide the most fitting model building technique.
3. **Data Preparation:** Select and extract input data before transforming it to construct a model.
4. **Model Building:** Create and test models to see if they will achieve the study objectives.
5. **Model Deployment:** Deploy the results of the model into applications. This can include providing insights with end users to inserting models into applications.
6. **Management:** Manage the models to increase performance, indorse re-use, regulate tool-sets, and minimize redundant actions.

1.5 Benefits of Predictive Tools in Healthcare

Predictive Analytics models are being used by healthcare organisations to detect the possibility for development. In recent years, accurate information has been obtained by gathering medical data from patients, converting it to

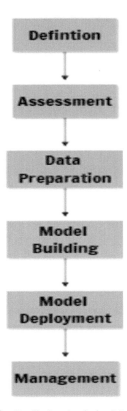

Figure 1.3 Predictive Analytics Methodology.

Big Data, and employing suitable algorithms to assist patients, physicians, and healthcare stakeholders in identifying values and prospects [40]. Digitization and use of Big Data will be advantageous and profitable for all involved. Moreover, modern analytical tools enable the analysis of data from all conceivable sources as well as cross-analyses to deliver superior data insights [26]. A cross-analysis, for example, can mean an amalgamation of patient demographics, costs, and treatment results to help discover the best, in medical terms, and most cost-effective therapy or therapies, and this may allow for a better modification of the service provider's offer [44].

1.5.1 Enhancing healthcare service quality

- Doctors' diagnosis and the treatment of illnesses indicated by them are evaluated using a Big Data based Decision Support System.

- Recognising patterns that lead to societal improvements in health and lifestyle.
- Forecast of the onset of diseases.
- Personalized treatment plans based on the analysis of the human genome.
- Offering innovative health services, avoiding and resolving crises.

1.5.2 Assisting medical workers in their tasks

- Doctors' would be able to provide a better diagnosis by comparing current medical cases to previous ones and also identify high risk patients.
- Diseases can be identified at earlier stages, which would lead to early cure.
- Personalized patient health management would be feasible.
- Data capture and analysis from hospitals, life monitoring devices in real time to forecast adverse occurrences.
- The capacity to forecast the onset of certain illnesses based on patient profiles, lifestyle changes, or precautionary care approaches.
- Recognizing epidemiological hazards and enhancing the management of pathogenic areas.
- Improved identification of disease progression and its drivers.

1.5.3 Contributing to the advancement of scientific and research activities

The discovery of novel medications is a difficult process, including over 90% of chemical entities studied failing to reach the market [45]. This process starts with the recognition of disease-relevant characteristics and continues through fundamental research, target identification and verification, preclinical testing, human clinical trials, and regulatory approval.

The conventional pharmaceutical industry's screening procedure for identifying new drug candidates is expensive and time-consuming, with a high dropout rate [45]. As a result, there is an urgent need for novel ways to drug research in which people will serve as future model organisms [46].

The prediction models will assist in the development of superior drugs and treatments by identifying patients with distinct biological features to participate in specialized clinical trials and drugs being developed to treat those specific sets of patients with minimum side effects.

1.5.4 Business and administration

Tools for prediction will help in cutting costs as well as thwart abuse practices by effectively detecting improper or illegal financial activities. Identification of duplicate and unnecessary medical procedures and tests would be possible and hence averted. These decisions will boost the overall profitability by recognising high-cost incurring patients or identifying doctors whose work, procedures, and treatment approaches are of high budget and providing them with economical solutions.

1.5.5 Operational assistance

- Faster data process rates.
- Enhanced quality and precision of clinical judgements.
- Instant access to clinical data for analysis.
- Reduced duration of diagnostic tests.
- Virtual consultations are cost-effective and time-efficient.

1.5.6 Organizational benefits

- Recognizing interoperability issues much more rapidly than conventional manual strategies.
- Facilitating data exchange with different institutions while adding new services, database sources, and research collaborators.
- Better cross-functional communication among all stakeholders.

1.5.7 Strategic growth

- Acquiring quick insights about ever-evolving healthcare market trends.
- Providing managerial positions with sound decision-support knowledge on a day-to-day clinical phenomenon.
- Maximizing business growth-related decisions.
- Giving a comprehensive perspective of treatment delivery in order to satisfy future needs.
- Establishing highly competitive health-care services [41].

To summarize, predictive tools have enormous promise for transforming healthcare by improving patient outcomes, predicting epidemic breakouts, providing important insights, avoiding avoidable diseases, lowering health-care delivery costs, and improving overall quality of life [43].

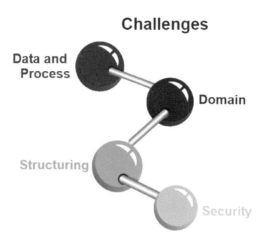

Figure 1.4   Challenges in Predictive Analytics.

1.6 Challenges

A major challenge faced in the medical science field while applying predictive analytics is to exploit the data intelligently and extract the knowledge effectively. Another challenge that impacts the performance results of models is transforming unstructured medical data into knowledge. Identification of patterns/dependencies in a multi-modal data demands structuring, which, in the case of medical image processing, is difficult at times. The challenge of ensuring the anonymity of any patient's information is also a major concern. To avoid the use or disclosing of patient data when limiting data access is applied, it reduces important information content at times. These challenges as shown in Figure 1.4 drive the researchers to increase the efforts to develop excellent predictive analytics techniques that can work on voluminous medical data.

1.7 Conclusions and Future Work

In conclusion, the application of predictive analytics is very significant in the medical science field as it gives us the opportunity to predict diseases earlier across all age groups. Through the anticipation of medication and treatment, predictive analytics can help in the decision-making process. The classifiers used in the computational techniques predict best results in terms of minimum execution time and maximum precision. Future research topics of predictive analytics in medical science are: aggregating and studying unstructured or semi-structured medical science data, indexing and processing data in real time, acclimating deep learning to stream complicated medical data, etc.

Acknowledgement

We would like to thank our supervisor Prof. Dr. Tapas Kumar for giving us the opportunity to present our work. This chapter would not be possible without his invaluable input and constant encouragement throughout the research process. His insights and expertise were instrumental in shaping the direction of this book chapter.

In addition, we would like to extend our sincere thanks to Dr. Poonam Tanwar for sharing her valuable time and providing insights and suggestions to us.

References

[1] Ali, O., Shrestha, A., Soar, J., & Wamba, S. F. (2018). Cloud computing-enabled healthcare opportunities, issues, and applications: A systematic review. International Journal of Information Management, 43, 146–158.

[2] Brooks, P., El-Gayar, O., &Sarnikar, S. (2015). A framework for developing a domain specific business intelligence maturity model: Application to healthcare. International Journal of Information Management, 35(3), 337–345.

[3] Groves, P., Kayyali, B., Knott, D., & Van Kuiken, S. (2013). The 'big data' revolution in healthcare. McKinsey Quarterly, 2, 3.

[4] Chen, H., Chiang, R. H. L., &Storey, V. C. (2012). Business intelligence and analytics: From big data to big impact. MIS Quarterly, 36(4), 1165–1188.

[5] Srinivasan, R., & Swink, M. (2018). An investigation of visibility and flexibility as complements to supply chain analytics: An organizational information processing theory perspective. Production and Operations Management, 27(10), 1849–1867.

[6] Raghupathi, W., &Raghupathi, V. (2013). An overview of health analytics. Journal of Health Medical Information, 4(132), 2.

[7] Gandomi, A., & Haider, M. (2015). Beyond the hype: Big data concepts, methods, and analytics. International Journal of Information Management, 35(2), 137–144.

[8] Duan, Y., Edwards, J. S., & Dwivedi, Y. K. (2019). Artificial intelligence for decision making in the era of Big Data–evolution, challenges and

research agenda. International Journal of Information Management, 48, 63–71.

[9] Andreu-Perez, J., Poon, C. C., Merrifield, R. D., Wong, S. T., & Yang, G. Z. (2015). Big data for health. IEEE Journal of Biomedical and Health Informatics, 19(4), 1193–1208.

[10] Steyerberg EW. Clinical Prediction Models. New York: Springer; 2009.

[11] Shah ND, Steyerberg EW, Kent DM. Big data and predictive analytics: recalibrating expectations. JAMA 2018; 320 (1): 27–8.

[12] Beam AL, Kohane IS. Big data and machine learning in health care. JAMA 2018; 319 (13): 1317–8.

[13] Hripcsak G, Albers DJ. Next-generation phenotyping of electronic health records. J Am Med Inform Assoc 2013; 20 (1): 117–21.

[14] Iqbal SA, Wallach JD, Khoury MJ, Schully SD, Ioannidis JPA. Reproducible research practices and transparency across the biomedical literature. PLoS Biol 2016; 14 (1): e1002333.

[15] Nosek BA, Alter G, Banks GC, et al. Promoting an open research culture.Science 2015; 348 (6242): 1422–5.

[16] Ahmed, Z., Mohamed, K., Zeeshan, S., & Dong, X. (2020). Artificial intelligence with multi-functional machine learning platform development for better healthcare and precision medicine. *Database : the journal of biological databases and curation, 2020*, baaa010.

[17] Bhavya, S., Pillai, A.S. (2021). Prediction Models in Healthcare Using Deep Learning. In: Abraham, A., Jabbar, M., Tiwari, S., Jesus, I. (eds) Proceedings of the 11th International Conference on Soft Computing and Pattern Recognition (SoCPaR 2019). SoCPaR 2019. Advances in Intelligent Systems and Computing, vol 1182. Springer, Cham.

[18] Sams, M., Eggerth, A., Hayn, D., Veeranki, S., & Schreier, G. (2019). Predictive Modelling and Its Visualization for Telehealth Data - Concept and Implementation of an Interactive Viewer. *Studies in health technology and informatics, 260*, 234–241.

[19] Panda, N. R., Pati, J. K., &Bhuyan, R. (2022). Role of Predictive Modeling in Healthcare Research: A Scoping Review. *International Journal of Statistics in Medical Research, 11*, 77–81.

[20] M.V. Manoj Kumar, Pradeep N, H.A. Sanjay,Chapter 4 - Predictive analysis and modeling in healthcare systems, Editor(s): Pradeep N, Sandeep Kautish, Sheng-Lung Peng, Demystifying Big Data, Machine Learning, and Deep Learning for Healthcare Analytics, Academic Press,2021, Pages 57-83.

[21] Shipe, M., Deppen, S., Farjah, F., & Grogan, E. (2019). Developing prediction models for clinical use using logistic regression: an overview. *Journal Of Thoracic Disease, 11*(Suppl 4), S574-S584. doi:10.21037/j td.2019.01.25

[22] N. D. Thong Tran, C. K. Leung, E. W. R. Madill and P. T. Binh, "A Deep Learning Based Predictive Model for Healthcare Analytics," *2022 IEEE 10th International Conference on Healthcare Informatics (ICHI)*, Rochester, MN, USA, 2022, pp. 547-549, doi:10.1109/ICHI54592.20 22.00106.

[23] Yang, C.C. Explainable Artificial Intelligence for Predictive Modeling in Healthcare. *J Healthc Inform Res* 6, 228–239 (2022).

[24] Wu, X., Kumar, V. and others, Top 10 algorithms in data mining, Knowl. Inf. Syst. (2008)

[25] Timofeev, R.: Classification and Regression Trees (CART) Theory and Applications Master thesis, Humboldt University, Berlin (2004)

[26] 16. Al-Janabi, S.: Pragmatic miner to risk analysis for intrusion detection (PMRA-ID). In: Mohamed, A., Berry, M.W., Yap, B.W. (eds.) SCDS 2017. CCIS, vol. 788, pp. 263–277.

[27] Al_Janabi, S., Abaid Mahdi, M.: Evaluation Prediction Techniques to Achievement an Optimal Biomedical Analysis, International Journal of Grid and Utility Computing (2019)

[28] Duana, L., Streeta, W.N., Xu, E.: Healthcare information systems: data mining methods in the creation of a clinical recommender system. Enterp. Inf. Syst. 5(2), 169–181 (2011)

[29] Santhanam, T., Sundaram, S.: Application of CART algorithm in blood donors classification. J. Comput. Sci. 6(5), 548–552 (2011)

[30] Peng, X., Wu, W., Xu, J.: Leveraging machine learning in improving healthcare, Association for the Advancement of Artificial Intelligence (2011)

[31] Soni, J., Ansari, U., Sharma, D., Soni, S.: Predictive data mining for medical diagnosis: an overview of heart disease prediction. Int. J. Comput. Appl. 17(8), 975–8887 (2011)

[32] Moon, S.S., Kang, S.-Y., Jitpitaklert, W., Kim, S.B.: Decision tree models for characterizing smoking patterns of older adults. Expert Syst. Appl. 39(1), 445–451 (2012)

[33] Nichol AA, Batten JN, Halley MC, Axelrod JK, Sankar PL, Cho MK A Typology of Existing Machine Learning–Based Predictive Analytic Tools Focused on Reducing Costs and Improving Quality in Health

Care: Systematic Search and Content Analysis J Med Internet Res 2021;23(6):e26391

[34] Soni, Jyoti & Ansari, Ujma& Sharma, Dipesh & Soni, Sunita. (2011). Predictive Data Mining for Medical Diagnosis: An Overview of Heart Disease Prediction. International Journal of Computer Applications. 17. 43-48. 10.5120/2237-2860.

[35] Riccardo Bellazzi, BlazZupan,Predictive data mining in clinical medicine: Current issues and guidelines, International Journal of Medical Informatics,Volume 77, Issue 2,2008,Pages 81-97,ISSN 1386-5056

[36] Jijo, B. T., &Abdulazeez, A. M. (2021). Classification based on decision tree algorithm for machine learning. *evaluation*, *6*(7).

[37] Behera, M. P., Sarangi, A., Mishra, D., & Sarangi, S. K. (2023). A Hybrid Machine Learning algorithm for Heart and Liver Disease Prediction Using Modified Particle Swarm Optimization with Support Vector Machine. *Procedia Computer Science*, *218*, 818-827.

[38] Abdel-Jaber, H., Devassy, D., Al Salam, A., Hidaytallah, L., & EL-Amir, M. (2022). A Review of Deep Learning Algorithms and Their Applications in Healthcare. *Algorithms*, *15*(2), 71. https://doi.org/10.3390/a15020071

[39] Schober, Patrick MD, PhD, MMedStat*; Vetter, Thomas R. MD, MPH†. Linear Regression in Medical Research. Anesthesia & Analgesia 132(1):p 108-109, January 2021. I DOI:10.1213/ANE.0000000000005206

[40] Hu H, Wen Y, Chua TS, Li X. Toward scalable systems for big data analytics: a technology tutorial. IEEE Access. 2014;2:652–87.

[41] Wang Y, Byrd TA. Business analytics-enabled decision-making effectiveness through knowledge absorptive capacity in health care. J Knowl-Manag. 2017;21(3):517–39.

[42] John McCall.Genetic algorithms for modelling and optimisation,Journal of Computational and Applied Mathematics,Volume 184, Issue 1,2005,Pages 205-222, ISSN 0377-0427, https://doi.org/10.1016/j.cam.2004.07.034.

[43] Chen H, Chiang RH, Storey VC. Business intelligence and analytics: from big data to big impact. MIS Q. 2012;36(4):1165–88.

[44] Raghupathi W, Raghupathi V. An overview of health analytics. J Health Med Inform. 2013;4:132.

[45] Brodniewicz, T. &Grynkiewicz, G. Preclinical drug development. Acta Pol. Pharm. 67, 578–585 (2010).

[46] FitzGerald, G. et al. Te future of humans as model organisms. Science 361, 552–553 (2018).

[47] An improved adaptive genetic algorithm, Shifen Han, Li Xiao, SHS Web Conf. 140 01044 (2022)

[48] Esteva, A., Robicquet, A., Ramsundar, B. *et al.* A guide to deep learning in healthcare. *Nat Med* 25, 24–29 (2019). https://doi.org/10.1038/s415 91-018-0316-z

[49] Rrmoku K, Selimi B, Ahmedi L. Application of Trust in Recommender Systems—Utilizing Naive Bayes Classifier. *Computation.* 2022; 10(1):6. https://doi.org/10.3390/computation10010006

[50] Peterson, L. E. (2009). K-nearest neighbor. *Scholarpedia*, 4(2), 1883.

[51] S. Albawi, T. A. Mohammed and S. Al-Zawi, "Understanding of a convolutional neural network," *2017 International Conference on Engineering and Technology (ICET)*, Antalya, Turkey, 2017, pp. 1-6, doi: 10.1109/ICEngTechnol.2017.8308186.

2

Machine Learning Classification Algorithms for the Prediction of Diseases

Radhanath Patra[1] and Bonomali Khuntia[2]

[1]Department of ECE, Berhampur University, India
[2]Department of CSE, Berhampur University, India

Abstract

Machine learning does a tremendous amount of work in the health sector. It analyzes medical data and does the early prediction of diseases, which helps health professionals to control morbidity and mortality rates effectively. In the proposed model, the importance of classifiers for the detection and prediction of various widespread diseases is addressed. Classifiers such as decision tree, logistic regression, random forest, support vector machine, and Naive Bayes are used to classify diabetes dataset with an accuracy of 80.73%, the lung cancer dataset with an accuracy of 100%, the breast cancer dataset with an accuracy of 97.14%, the kidney disease dataset with an accuracy of 100%, and the Cleveland heart disease dataset with an accuracy of 94.29%, respectively.

Keywords: Naïve Bayes (NB), decision tree (DT), *K*-nearest neighbor (KNN), support vector machine (SVM), random forest (RF), logistic regression (LR), Pima Indian diabetes dataset (PIDD).

2.1 Introduction

Nowadays, people suffer from various diseases. Doctors, hi-tech medical facilities, and advanced equipment are not enough to detect the disease correctly. Therefore, the role of machine intelligence toward the prediction of diseases is very important [1, 2]. Moreover, initial detection of disease is

21

also very crucial in some acute chronic diseases before the development of some critical conditions. Another major problem in the health sector is the origination of a high voluminous amount of medical data, which is difficult to manage and store [3].

In order to get over such type of problem, the application of machine learning computation is significant. The exploitation of various prominent machine learning algorithms has directed the utilization of such medical data in a better way by extracting useful information from specified data to help healthcare communities and biomedical fields in an effective way [4, 5]. The various techniques under machine learning help to extract the hidden data from the voluminous medical dataset in the easiest manner [6]. Nowadays, machine learning is used to detect chronic diseases such as breast cancer, heart diseases, diabetes, kidney disease, and lung cancer and analyze their symptoms and predict the severity of diseases effectively [7, 8].

The importance of our research is to analyze the chronic diseases and predict the output efficiently. In the present scenario, the mortality rate of breast cancer and lung cancer is quite high and the death rate due to heart diseases is also high in number [9, 10]. In addition to it, kidney disease and diabetes are also life-threatening diseases for human beings [11, 12]. So, exact data analysis is needed to predict the disease dataset accurately and promptly. The data analysis is done on disease datasets such as (1) lung cancer, (2) breast cancer, (3) diabetes, (4) heart disease, and (5) kidney disease. These datasets are accessed from the UCI machine learning repository dataset (open access). Cancer is one of the dangerous diseases, which needs to be properly detected and diagnosed in the preliminary stage [13]. Lung cancer and breast cancer are now considered dangerous for human beings. Lung cancer mostly affects the lungs, spread nearby the thoracic part and causes breathing problems. Lung cancer is now placed in the third position due to high mortality [14]. There are several reasons and factors that cause lung cancer, but some of the studies say that smoking, toxin absorption, and inhaled chemicals are responsible for the origin of the lung cancer. The lung cancer can be diagnosed with proper treatment [15]. It is divided into two categories, which are small cell lung cancer and non-small cell lung cancer. Similarly, breast cancer is the main cause of the highest death rate among females in the world [16]. Breast cancer causes breast cells to grow abnormally. Typically, breast cancer is found either in the ducts or in the fatty tissue of breast cancer [17, 18]. These cells are incontrollable and damage healthy cells near to chest and arms [19, 20]. People of all races are mostly affected by diabetes. Diabetes is well known as a silent killer. Diabetes imbalances glucose labels in blood blocks urine flow or causes the excess flow of urine [21]. The diabetes is divided into Type-1, Type-2, and gestational diabetes. In Type-1, patients depend on insulin to stay alive [22]. In Type-2 diabetes: produced insulin is not effectively utilized by the organs of the body [23]. Gestational diabetes: it is found in women during pregnancy and may affect the health condition of the baby [24, 25]. Heart disease: heart diseases are generally coronary heart diseases, congenital heart diseases, heart failures, and heart attacks [26]. Heavy body weight, smoking, high cholesterol level, and blood pressure are the major causes of heart diseases [27]. Kidney disease: the kidney generally removes toxins and waste from the blood. Due to kidney diseases, blood is not properly filtered and extra water labels in the blood are mixed along with toxins. This causes serious damage to the lungs, heart failure, and various organs of the body [28]. People die when kidney failure occurs. The study analyzes patients' datasets and performs effective computation to analyze the disease by applying supervised learning. The state-of-the-art focuses on a clear analysis of benchmark datasets in regard of classification accuracy, sensitivity, specificity, and false positive metrics comparison with high precision. Here, a supervised machine learning model for disease dataset analysis is proposed. The predictive model is employed to show better output for disease datasets such as breast cancer, lung cancer, kidney diseases, heart diseases, and Indian liver patient dataset analysis.

2.2 Literature Study

Lahoura et al. [29] have modeled a framework using extreme machine learning classifiers with cloud-based computing techniques to improve classification accuracy and speed. The gain ratio technique is used on the WBCD dataset to extract the best features, and the application of extreme machine learning methodologies in a cloud environment provides 98.8% classification accuracy. Dhahri et al. [30] have performed analysis on WBCD (Wisconsin diagnostics breast cancer dataset) using genetic programming and an ensemble machine learning classifier to classify benign and malignant. An analysis graph of the machine learning technique and classifier log loss is depicted to plot the performance and accuracy. AdaBoost classifier has shown a classification accuracy of 98.24% with the above-mentioned approach. Christo et al. [31] introduced a unique approach for breast cancer and hepatitis dataset classification. Here authors have introduced a wrapper approach by combining bioinspired algorithms and AdaBoost-SVM as classifiers. Their analysis showed a 98.47% classification accuracy with respect to WBCD dataset, and 95.51% classification accuracy for the hepatitis dataset. Osman et al. [32] have proposed an ensemble boosting classifier neural network to classify Wisconsin breast cancer (WBC) original, breast cancer diagnosis (BCD), breast cancer prognostics (BCP), and WBCD datasets with the latest accuracy of 97.45%, 98.4%, 97.7%, and 97.0%, respectively. Ed-daoudy et al. [33] have used the association rule to find out the best attributes from the WBCD dataset and applied an SVM classifier to find benign and malignant with an accuracy of 98% for eight attributes. Sakai et al. [34] enhanced the classification performance by integrating particle swam optimization (PSO) for feature selection in association with three machine learning classifiers such as *K*-nearest neighbor (KNN), Naive Bayes (NB), and reduced error pruning (REP) tree. The authors used a particle swarm optimization technique to select features from the WBCD of the UCI repository to give a classification accuracy of 81.3%, 80%, and 75% using Naive Bayes, REP tree, and *K*-nearest neighbor algorithms, respectively. Houssainy et al. [35] applied probabilistic neural network (PNN) and radial basis function (RBF) to classify stages of UCI learning repository chronic kidney diseases with an overall accuracy of 96.7%. Amansour et al. [36] have performed analysis on chronic kidney diseases of the UCI learning repository with the optimized parameter for designing artificial neural networks that predicted a classification accuracy of 99.75%. Kauar et al. [37] have introduced various classifiers such as linear Kernel SVM and RBF-SVM, KNN, artificial neural network (ANN), and multifactor dimensionality reduction technique on Pima Indian diabetes dataset (PIDD). Authors have suggested that linear Kernel SVM performs better and gives a classification accuracy of 89% and area under the curve of 0.90. Atik Mahbub [38] implemented a novel ensemble voting classifier, which is a combination of three classifiers. The author used a support vector classifier, multiplayer perceptron, and KNN to classify Pima Indian diabetes dataset (PIDD) with a classification accuracy of 86%. Sisodia et al. [39] used NB, SVM, and DT on Pima Indian diabetes dataset (PIDD) and concluded that Naive Bayes performed better and gives an accuracy of 76.3%. Escamilla et al. [40] have proposed the use of chi-square and principal component data reduction technique to improve the classifier performance. So, chi-square with principal component analysis and random forest classifier is used to predict the Cleveland heart dataset with 98.7% classification accuracy, the Hungarian dataset with 99% classification accuracy, and a mixture of the Cleveland heart dataset and Hungarian heart dataset with 99.4% classification accuracy. Tama et al. [41] proposed a two-tier ensemble architecture. In the first phase, a combination of correlation-based feature selection and PSO is applied to select the best features, and in the second phase, a classification model composed of random forest, gradient boosting technique, and XGBoost is framed to predict an accuracy of 93.55% for the Stat Log heart dataset, F1 score of 86.49% for the Cleveland heart dataset, 91.9% classification accuracy for the Hungarian heart dataset, and 98.3% for the Alizadeh Sani dataset. Mohan et al. [42] introduced a hybrid random forest and linear model and classified the Cleveland dataset with an accuracy of 88.4%. Shakeel et al. [43] used the wolf prey searching process for feature selection and ensemble learning generalized neural network, a novel approach of ANN to predict ELVIRA lung cancer data with a classification accuracy of 99.6%. Pian Li et al. [44] discussed various feature selection algorithms and proposed a conditional mutual information feature selection (FCMIM) algorithm to get the best features. The extracted features are applied to classifiers such as LR, KNN, ANN, SVM, and NB to classify the Cleveland heart disease dataset. It was observed that the FCMIM technique with SVM results in a classification accuracy of 92.37%.

2.3 Dataset Description

Datasets are available in Kaggle and UCI machine learning repositories. The dataset is having missing data that needs to be carefully handled before analysis; so data cleaning is required. The datasets used here are as follows.

Lung cancer dataset:

This dataset contains 60 rows and 7 columns, namely "Name," "Surname," "Age," "Smokes," "AreaQ," "Alcohol," and "Result." The "Result" column is the output in the form of either one or zero, which means whether the person has lung cancer or not. The first two attributes represent the patient's name and the other four attributes are numeric data types and the last column is the class label. Class labels are described as "0" for the absence of lung cancer and "1" for the presence of lung cancer.

Table 2.1 Demonstration of the lung cancer dataset.

Sl. no.	Name of the attribute	Data type	Min. range	Max. range
1	Age	Integer	18	77
2	Smokes	Integer	0	34
3	AreaQ	Integer	1	10
4	Alcohol	Integer	0	8
5	Result	Integer	0	1

Table 2.2   Demonstration of breast cancer dataset.

Sl. no.	Name of the attribute	Data type	Min. range	Max. range
1	Clump thickness	Integer	1	10
2	Uniformity of cell size	Integer	1	10
3	Uniformity of cell shape	Integer	1	10
4	Marginal adhesion	Integer	1	10
5	Single epithelial cell size	Integer	1	10
6	Bare nuclei	Integer	1	10
7	Bland chromatin	Integer	1	10
8	Normal nucleoli	Integer	1	10
9	Mitoses	Integer	1	10
10	Class	Integer	2	4

Breast cancer dataset:

This dataset contains 699 records and 11 attributes, namely "Sample Code Number: id number," "Clump Thickness," "Uniformity of Cell Size," "Uniformity of Cell Shape," "Marginal Adhesion," "Single Epithelial Cell Size," "Bare Nuclei," "Bland Chromatin," "Normal Nucleoli," "Mitoses," and "Class." The "Class" column is the output in the form of either class label 4 or class label 2. Class label 4 refers to malignant (cells are harmful/cancerous) and Class label 2 refers to benign (cells are unharmful/non-cancerous). It has 16 missing attributes. The benign value in total is 458 and the malignant is 241.

Pima Indians diabetes dataset (PIDD):

Pima Indian Diabetes contains 768 rows and 9 columns. Predictor variables are described as "No. of Pregnancies," "Glucose," "Blood Pressure," "Skin Thickness," "Insulin," "Body Mass Index (BMI)," "Diabetes Pedigree

Table 2.3   Demonstration of PIDD.

Sl. no.	Name of the attribute	Data type	Min. range	Max. range
1	No. of pregnancies	Integer	0	17
2	Glucose	Integer	0	199
3	Blood pressure	Integer	0	122
4	Skin thickness	Integer	0	99
5	Insulin	Integer	0	846
6	BMI	Integer	0	67.1
7	Diabetes pedigree function	Integer	0.078	2.42
8	Age	Integer	21	81
9	Outcome	Integer	0	1

Table 2.4 Demonstration of the heart disease dataset.

Sl. no.	Name of the attribute	Data type	Min. range	Max. range
1	Age	Integer	29	77
2	Sex	Integer	0	1
3	Cp	Integer	0	3
4	Trtbps	Integer	94	200
5	Chol	Integer	126	564
6	Fbs	Integer	0	1
7	Restecg	Integer	0	2
8	Thalachh	Integer	71	202
9	Exang	Integer	0	1
10	Oldpeak	Integer	0	6.2
11	Slope	Integer	1	3
12	Ca	Integer	0	3
13	Thal	Integer	3	7
14	Target	Integer	0	4

Function," "Age," and "Outcome." "Outcome" represents two class labels. Diabetes patients are 268 in number represented with a "1" class label, and non-diabetic patients are 500 in number represented with a "0" class label.

Heart disease dataset:

The dataset consists of 303 records and 144 attributes, namely "Age," "Sex," "Cp," "Trtbps," "Chol," "Fbs," "Restecg," "Thalachh," "Exhang," "Oldpeak," "Slope," "Ca," "Thal," and "Target," where the "Target" column is the output in the form of either one or zero, which means whether the person is suffering from heart disease or not. There are six records that have missing attributes. The "Target" column has class label 0 (164 in number) representing no heart disease, whereas class labels 1, 2, 3, and 4 represent the occurrence of heart disease.

Kidney disease:

This dataset contains 401 rows and 25columns, namely "id," "Age," "Blood Pressure(BP)," "Specific Gravity," "Albumin (Al)," "Sugar (Su)," "Red Blood Cells (RBC)," "Puscell (Pc)," "Puscell Clumps (PCC)," "Bacteria (Ba)," "Blood Glucose Random (BGR)," "Blood Urea (BU)," "Sodium (sod)," "Potassium (Pot)," "Hemoglobin (Hemo)," "Packed Cell Volume (PCV)," "White Blood Cell Count (WC)," "Red Blood Cell Count (Rc)," "Hypertension (Htn)," "Diabetes Mellitius (Dm)," "Coronary Artery

Table 2.5 Demonstration of the kidney disease dataset.

Sl. no.	Name of the attribute	Data type	Min. range	Max. range
1	Age	Integer	2	90
2	Blood pressure	Integer	50.0	180.0
3	Specific gravity	Nominal	1.005	1.025
4	Albumin	Nominal	0.0	5.0
5	Sugar	Nominal	0.0	5.0
6	Red blood cells	Nominal	0.0	1.0
7	Puscell	Nominal	0.0	1.0
8	Puscell clumps	Nominal	0.0	1.0
9	Bacteria	Nominal	0.0	1.0
10	Blood glucose random	Integer	22.0	490.0
11	Blood urea	Integer	1.5	391.0
12	Serum creatinine	Integer	0.4	76
13	Sodium	Integer	4.5	163.0
14	Potassium	Integer	2.5	47.0
15	Hemoglobin	Integer	3.1	17.8
16	Packed cell volume	Integer	9	54
17	White blood cell count	Integer	2200	26400
18	Red blood cell count	Integer	2.1	8.0
19	Hypertension	Nominal	0.0	1.0
20	Diabetes mellitus	Nominal	0.0	1.0
21	Coronary artery disease	Nominal	0.0	1.0
22	Appetite	Nominal	0.0	1.0
23	Pedal edema	Nominal	0.0	1.0
24	Anemia	Nominal	0.0	1.0
25	Class	Nominal	0	1

Diseases (CAD)," "Appetite (Appet)," "Pedal Edema (Pe)," "Anaemia (Ane)," and "Class." The "Class" column is the output in the form of "ckd" and "notckd" where "ckd" (250 in numbers) refers to chronic kidney disease and "notckd" (150 in numbers) refers to nonchronic kidney disease. Here are the 24 numbers of missing data.

2.4 Materials and Methods

The analysis of lung cancer, breast cancer, heart disease, kidney disease, and diabetes is done using a Python environment. Data pre-processing is needed prior to data analysis. It includes a series of steps: (1) collection of data; (2) pre-processing of data; and (3) classification as shown in Figure 2.1. Data pre-processing and feature engineering are applied to analyze the benchmark dataset. It makes data uniform and easy to access. Appropriate data analysis and choice of suitable classifier improves the output performance. Data

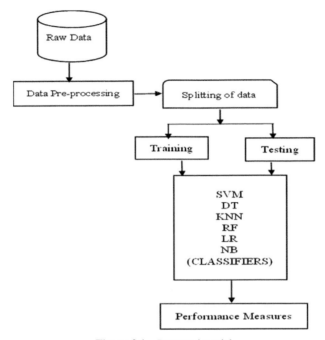

Figure 2.1 Proposed model.

pre-processing relies on a step-by-step process. It includes data cleaning: it replaces missing data entry with suitable means, i.e., either by null value or by data imputation mechanism [45]. In the proposed approach, the missing data values are replaced with most of the occurrence of column values using the imputer class in Python. The dataset is framed using a correlation matrix to extract suitable features of data [46]. Data preparation: data preparation is done using correlation matrix. The correlation matrix shows correlated tables between variables. Thus, suitable attributes are considered. This helps us to slice our data into dependent and independent variables. In machine learning, model predictors are known as causes, and responses are known as effects. Here in ML, when the dependent (or output variable *y*) and independent variables (or input variable *x*) give to a machine learning model, it gives a mapping function $y = f(x)$ splitting into training and test data. Scikit Learn library helps form training and test datasets. Dataset partition enables the user to reach the conclusion of the computation and performance of the machine learning classifier.

The model is based on a supervised machine-learning approach. It learns from the trained dataset and builds its own logic to predict the test dataset.

The system tries to learn from the previous data, builds the model, and predicts the future data. The training model is 80% of the original dataset and the remaining 20% is the testing dataset. The training dataset is analyzed with different machine learning models and performance is obtained from the test dataset. Classification is performed under supervised learning. For classification, predictors and responses are provided. These act as valid input data to train the model. The classifiers used in our paper are LR, SVM (linear and RBF classifier), NB, DT, and KNN. Logistic regression (LR): the most used classifier for binary classification is logistic regression. It develops a logic that predicts the probability of output based on inputs. The sigmoid function is explicitly used for LR. Support vector machine (SVM): the machine learning classifier is very popular for disease prediction. The objective of SVM is to optimize the hyperplane that helps to classify the dataset perfectly. In SVM, the support vector plays an important role to form a decision line, which clearly distinguishes the data into separate classes. The support vector machine performs well for linearly separable data for classification. In the proposed technique, datasets are linearly separable; so the use of an SVM classifier is preferred. Naive Bayes (NB): it is a sophisticated faster learning algorithm that performs well for both binary class and multi-class problems. It can predict the uncertainty of data using the Bayes theorem. Conditional probability is applied to predict the output from uncorrelated attributes. Random forest (RF): it is an ensemble machine learning classifier that uses decision trees and voting techniques to classify the disease of a dataset. It forms some subsamples and applies a decision tree to each subsample. The classification accuracy of each subsample is evaluated and the best value is selected by the voting concept for prediction.

K-nearest neighbor (KNN): KNN is a non-parametric learning algorithm, which is based on the Euclidean distance calculation. The dataset is divided into the training phase and the test phase. Data from test data is chosen and the Euclidean distance concept is applied in the training dataset to find the best neighbor. It assumes the k number of nearest neighbor values for prediction based on the maximum class label.

Result discussion:

Training accuracy:

The prediction of test dataset is done using confusion matrix. If the true positive represents positive true data values, false positive (FP) with false

Table 2.6 Demonstration of accuracy for training dataset values.

Diseases Algorithms	Diabetes	Lung cancer	Breast cancer	Kidney disease	Heart cancer
Logistic regression	76.69%	100.0%	97.13%	91.33%	87.56%
SVM (linear classifier)	76.56%	100.0%	96.94%	97.33%	87.05%
SVM (RBF classifier)	100.0%	100.0%	97.71%	66.33%	100.0%
Naive Bayes	76.56%	100.0%	96.18%	95.67%	83.42%
Decision tree	100.0%	100.0%	100.0%	100.0%	100.0%
KNN	78.65%	90.91%	97.51%	81.33%	73.58%
Random forest	98.44%	100.0%	99.81%	100.0%	99.48%

positive values, false negative (FN) with false negative values, and true negative (TN) with true negative values, then performance parameters are described as follows.

Testing accuracy:

After training the dataset, the model is used for test dataset to predict the accuracy and various classification parameters.

All the highlighted values show maximum accuracy with respect to various classifiers. So, the logistic regression model for diabetes prediction, random forest model for lung cancer detection, SVM (RBF classifier) for breast cancer, decision tree model for kidney disease prediction, and Naïve Bayes model for heart disease prediction give the highest accuracy as shown in Table 2.7.

Table 2.7 Demonstration of accuracy for testing dataset values.

Diseases Algorithms	Diabetes	Lung cancer	Breast cancer	Kidney disease	Heart cancer
Logistic regression	80.73%	100.0%	96.57%	95.0%	88.57%
SVM (linear classifier)	80.21%	100.0%	96.0%	95.0%	85.71%
SVM (RBF classifier)	67.71%	60.0%	97.14%	66.0%	68.57%
Naive Bayes	76.56%	100.0%	95.43%	95.0%	94.29%
Decision tree	77.6%	93.33%	95.43%	100.0%	85.71%
KNN	75.52%	93.33%	96.57%	72.0%	74.29%
Random forest	72.4%	100.0%	96.0%	98.0%	77.14%

AUC ROC:

The curve is plotted in between the true positive rate and false positive rate and signifies the performance of the model.

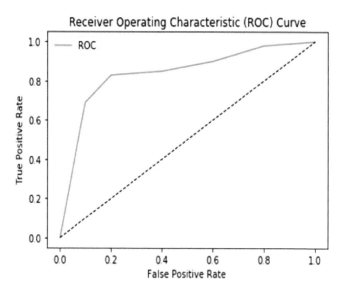

Figure 2.2   AUC ROC curve representation.

Table 2.8   Representation of various performance parameters for kidney diseases.

Algorithms	0/1	Precision	Recall	F1-score	ROC score (%)	AUC
Logistic regression	–	0.92	0.95	0.94	95.75	
	–	0.97	0.95	0.96		
KNN	0 –	0.59	0.89	0.71	75.38	
	1 –	0.90	0.61	0.73		
SVM (linear classifier)	0 –	0.90	0.97	0.94	95.45	
	1 –	0.98	0.94	0.96		
SVM (RBF classifier)	0 –	0.55	0.55	0.55	63.92	
	1 –	0.73	0.73	0.73		
Naive Bayes	0 –	0.92	0.95	0.94	94.0	
	1 –	0.97	0.95	0.96		
Decision tree	0 –	1.00	1.00	1.00	100.0	
	1 –	1.00	1.00	1.00		
Random forest	0 –	1.00	0.95	0.97	95.24	
	1 –	0.97	1.00	0.98		

Decision tree gives maximum accuracy, i.e., 100%; so the ROC curve is displayed as follows.

The ROC curve:

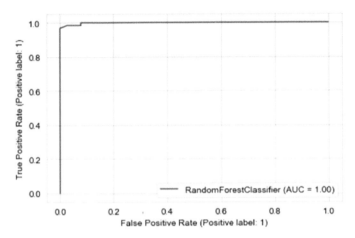

Figure 2.3 ROC curve representation of the decision tree classifier for kidney diseases.

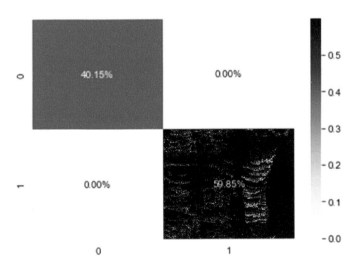

Figure 2.4 Confusion matrix for classification accuracy of 100% for kidney diseases.

Table 2.9   Representation of various performance parameters for breast cancer diseases.

Algorithms	2/4	Precision	Recall	F1-score	ROC AUC score (%)
Logistic regression	2-	0.97	0.97	0.97	96.37
	4-	0.96	0.96	0.96	
KNN	2-	0.97	0.97	0.97	96.37
	4-	0.96	0.96	0.96	
SVM (linear classifier)	2-	0.97	0.96	0.97	95.90
	4-	0.94	0.96	0.95	
SVM (RBF classifier)	2-	0.99	0.96	0.98	97.40
	4-	0.94	0.99	0.96	
Naive Bayes	2-	0.98	0.94	0.96	95.72
	4-	0.92	0.97	0.94	
Decision tree	2-	0.98	0.94	0.96	95.72
	4-	0.92	0.97	0.94	
Random forest	2-	0.99	0.94	0.97	96.47
	4-	0.92	0.99	0.95	

The ROC curve:

Here, SVM RBF classifier gives 97.14% accuracy; so it is used for model.

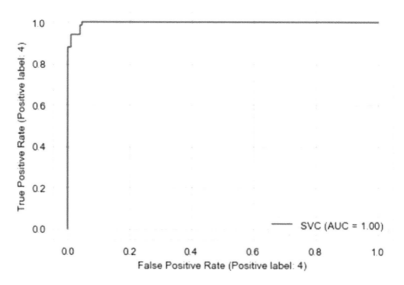

Figure 2.5   ROC curve representation of the decision tree classifier for breast cancer.

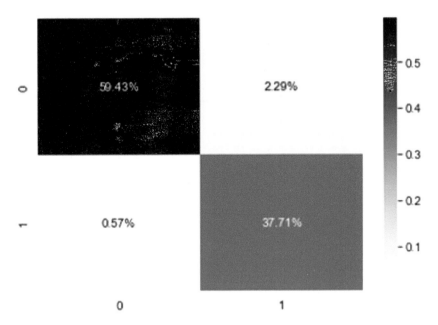

Figure 2.6 Confusion matrix for classification accuracy of 97.14% for breast cancer.

Table 2.10 Representation of various performance parameters for diabetes prediction.

Algorithms	0/1	Precision	Recall	F1-score	ROC AUC score (%)
Logistic	-	0.82	0.92	0.87	74.06
regression	-	0.77	0.58	0.66	
KNN	0 -	0.81	0.84	0.71	70.95
	1 -	0.63	0.58	0.73	
SVM (linear	0 -	0.82	0.90	0.86	74.83
classifier)	1 -	0.74	0.60	0.66	
SVM (RBF	0 -	0.68	1.00	0.81	69.15
classifier)	1 -	0.00	0.00	0.00	
Naive Bayes	0 -	0.80	0.88	0.84	70.45
	1 -	0.67	0.53	0.59	
Decision tree	0 -	0.85	0.81	0.83	75.86
	1 -	0.64	0.71	0.67	
Random forest	0 -	0.77	0.85	0.81	65.69
	1 -	0.59	0.47	0.52	

The ROC curve:

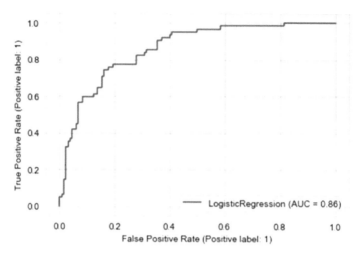

Figure 2.7   ROC curve representation of the decision tree classifier for PIDD dataset.

Logistic regression gives maximum accuracy of 80.72. The confusion matrix for the logistic.

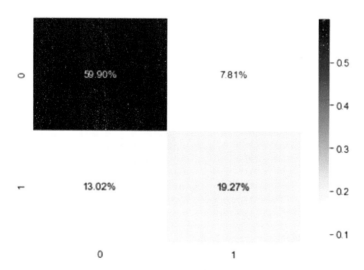

Figure 2.8   Confusion matrix for classification accuracy of 80.72% for PIDD dataset.

Table 2.11 Representation of various performance parameters for heart disease.

Algorithms	0/1	Precision	Recall	F1-score	ROC AUC score (%)
Logistic	-	0.82	0.82	0.82	86.74
regression	-	0.92	0.92	0.92	
KNN	0 -	0.60	0.55	0.57	68.93
	1 -	0.80	0.83	0.82	
SVM (linear	0 -	0.75	0.82	0.78	84.65
classifier)	1 -	0.91	0.88	0.89	
SVM (RBF	0 -	0.00	0.00	0.00	68.57
classifier)	1 -	0.69	1.00	0.81	
Naive Bayes	0 -	0.91	0.91	0.91	93.37
	1 -	0.96	0.96	0.96	
Decision tree	0 -	0.69	1.00	0.81	89.87
	1 -	1.00	0.79	0.88	
Random for-	0 -	0.59	0.91	0.71	80.87
est	1 -	0.94	0.71	0.81	

The ROC curve:

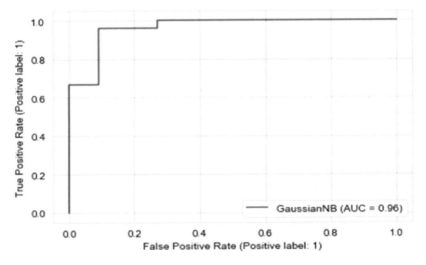

Figure 2.9 ROC curve for the heart dataset.

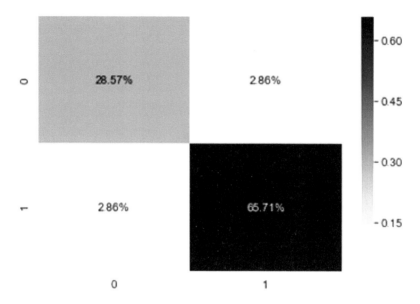

Figure 2.10 Confusion matrix for classification accuracy of 94.28% for the heart disease dataset.

Table 2.12 Representation of various performance parameters for lung cancer.

Algorithms	0/1	Precision	Recall	F1-score	ROC AUC score (%)
Logistic	-	1.00	1.00	1.00	100.0
regression	-	1.00	1.00	1.00	
KNN	0 -	1.00	0.90	0.95	95.0
	1 -	0.83	1.00	0.91	
SVM (linear	0 -	1.00	1.00	1.00	100.0
classifier)	1 -	1.00	1.00	1.00	
SVM (RBF	0 -	1.00	0.40	0.57	70.0
classifier)	1 -	0.45	1.00	0.62	
Naive Bayes	0 -	1.00	1.00	1.00	100.0
	1 -	1.00	1.00	1.00	
Decision tree	0 -	1.00	0.90	0.95	95.0
	1 -	0.83	1.00	0.91	
Random for-	0 -	1.00	1.00	1.00	100.0
est	1 -	1.00	1.00	1.00	

Logistic regression gives the accuracy of 100%.

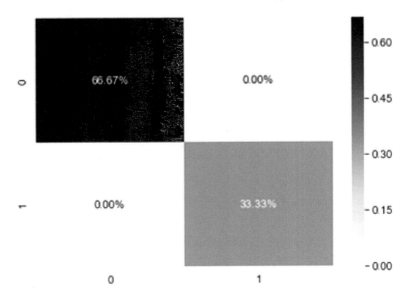

Figure 2.11 Confusion matrix for classification accuracy of 100% for lung cancer dataset.

The ROC curve:

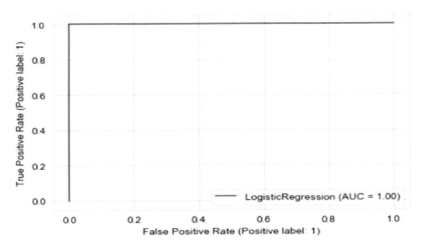

Figure 2.12 ROC curve for the lung cancer dataset.

2.5 Conclusion

From our analysis, we can conclude that there is a huge scope for researchers to use machine learning model for different disease predictions. The above-mentioned algorithm performs well in some dataset and poorly in some other cases for disease prediction. We have achieved 100% classification accuracy for lung cancer using logistic regression, Naïve Bayes, random forest, SVM (linear classifier), 97.14% classification accuracy for breast cancer using SVM (RBF classifier), 100% classification accuracy for kidney diseases using decision tree, 94.29% classification accuracy in case of Cleveland heart dataset, and 80.73% classification accuracy using logistic regression in case of PIDD.

Acknowledgement

It is our pleasure to express gratitude to all cited researchers for the contribution in the field of machine learning. I declare that the article is not copied from any other resources.

References

[1] Latif, J., Xiao, C., Tu, S., Rehman, S. U., Imran, A., & Bilal, A. (2020). Implementation and use of disease diagnosis systems for electronic medical records based on machine learning: A complete review. *IEEE Access*, *8*, 150489-150513.

[2] Chen, M., Hao, Y., Hwang, K., Wang, L., & Wang, L. (2017). Disease prediction by machine learning over big data from healthcare communities. *Ieee Access*, *5*, 8869-8879.

[3] Dash, S., Shakyawar, S.K., Sharma, M. *et al.* Big data in healthcare: management, analysis and future prospects. *J Big Data* **6,** 54 (2019). https://doi.org/10.1186/s40537-019-0217-0

[4] Ray, A., & Chaudhuri, A. K. (2021). Smart healthcare disease diagnosis and patient management: Innovation, improvement and skill development. *Machine Learning with Applications*, *3*, 100011.

[5] Lin, W. C., Chen, J. S., Chiang, M. F., &Hribar, M. R. (2020). Applications of artificial intelligence to electronic health record data in ophthalmology. *Translational vision science & technology*, *9*(2), 13-13.

[6] Jain, D., & Singh, V. (2018). Feature selection and classification systems for chronic disease prediction: A review. *Egyptian Informatics Journal*, *19*(3), 179-189.

[7] El Houby, E. M. (2018). A survey on applying machine learning techniques for management of diseases. *Journal of Applied Biomedicine*, *16*(3), 165-174.

[8] Uddin, S., Khan, A., Hossain, M. E., & Moni, M. A. (2019). Comparing different supervised machine learning algorithms for disease prediction. *BMC medical informatics and decision making*, *19*(1), 1-16.

[9] Haq, A. U., Li, J. P., Saboor, A., Khan, J., Wali, S., Ahmad, S., ... & Zhou, W. (2021). Detection of Breast Cancer Through Clinical Data Using Supervised and Unsupervised Feature Selection Techniques. *IEEE Access*, *9*, 22090-22105.

[10] Kancherla K., Mukkamala S. (2012) Feature Selection for Lung Cancer Detection Using SVM Based Recursive Feature Elimination Method. In: Giacobini M., Vanneschi L., Bush W.S. (eds) Evolutionary Computation, Machine Learning and Data Mining in Bioinformatics. EvoBIO 2012. Lecture Notes in Computer Science, vol 7246. Springer, Berlin, Heidelberg. https://doi.org/10.1007/978-3-642-29066-4_15

[11] Qin, J., Chen, L., Liu, Y., Liu, C., Feng, C., & Chen, B. (2019). A machine learning methodology for diagnosing chronic kidney disease. *IEEE Access*, *8*, 20991-21002.

[12] Kopitar, L., Kocbek, P., Cilar, L., Sheikh, A., &Stiglic, G. (2020). Early detection of type 2 diabetes mellitus using machine learning-based prediction models. *Scientific reports*, *10*(1), 1-12.

[13] Kourou, K., Exarchos, T. P., Exarchos, K. P., Karamouzis, M. V., & Fotiadis, D. I. (2015). Machine learning applications in cancer prognosis and prediction. *Computational and structural biotechnology journal*, *13*, 8-17.

[14] Patra, R. (2020, March). Prediction of Lung Cancer Using Machine Learning Classifier. In *International Conference on Computing Science, Communication and Security* (pp. 132-142). Springer, Singapore.

[15] Nasser, Ibrahim M. and Abu-Naser, Samy S., Lung Cancer Detection Using Artificial Neural Network (March 2019). International Journal of Engineering and Information Systems (IJEAIS), 3(3), 17-23, March 2019, Available at SSRN: https://ssrn.com/abstract=3369062

[16] Ganggayah, M. D., Taib, N. A., Har, Y. C., Lio, P., & Dhillon, S. K. (2019). Predicting factors for survival of breast cancer patients using machine learning techniques. *BMC medical informatics and decision making*, *19*(1), 1-17.

[17] Hosni, M., Abnane, I., Idri, A., de Gea, J. M. C., &Alemán, J. L. F. (2019). Reviewing ensemble classification methods in breast cancer. *Computer methods and programs in biomedicine*, *177*, 89-112.

[18] Ganggayah, M.D., Taib, N.A., Har, Y.C. *et al.* Predicting factors for survival of breast cancer patients using machine learning techniques. *BMC Med Inform DecisMak* **19,** 48 (2019). https://doi.org/10.1186/s12911-0 19-0801-4

[19] Kumar, M., Khatri, S. K., & Mohammadian, M. (2020). Breast cancer identification and prognosis with machine learning techniques-An elucidative review. *Journal of Interdisciplinary Mathematics*, *23*(2), 503-521.

[20] Dhahri, H., Al Maghayreh, E., Mahmood, A., Elkilani, W., & Faisal Nagi, M. (2019). Automated breast cancer diagnosis based on machine learning algorithms. *Journal of healthcare engineering*, *2019*.

[21] Zou, Q., Qu, K., Luo, Y., Yin, D., Ju, Y., & Tang, H. (2018). Predicting diabetes mellitus with machine learning techniques. *Frontiers in genetics*, *9*, 515.

[22] S. Perveen, M. Shahbaz, K. Keshavjee and A. Guergachi, "Metabolic Syndrome and Development of Diabetes Mellitus: Predictive Modeling Based on Machine Learning Techniques," in *IEEE Access*, vol. 7, pp. 1365-1375, 2019, doi: 10.1109/ACCESS.2018.2884249.

[23] Kopitar, L., Kocbek, P., Cilar, L., Sheikh, A., &Stiglic, G. (2020). Early detection of type 2 diabctes mellitus using machine learning-based prediction models. *Scientific reports*, *10*(1), 1-12

[24] Mercaldo, F., Nardone, V., &Santone, A. (2017). Diabetes mellitus affected patients classification and diagnosis through machine learning techniques. *Procedia computer science*, *112*, 2519-2528.

[25] Maniruzzaman, M., Kumar, N., Abedin, M. M., Islam, M. S., Suri, H. S., El-Baz, A. S., & Suri, J. S. (2017). Comparative approaches for classification of diabetes mellitus data: Machine learning paradigm. *Computer methods and programs in biomedicine*, *152*, 23-34.

[26] Li, J. P., Haq, A. U., Din, S. U., Khan, J., Khan, A., &Saboor, A. (2020). Heart Disease Identification Method Using Machine Learning Classification in E-Healthcare. *IEEE Access*, *8*, 107562-107582.

[27] Haq, A. U., Li, J. P., Memon, M. H., Nazir, S., & Sun, R. (2018). A hybrid intelligent system framework for the prediction of heart disease using machine learning algorithms. *Mobile Information Systems*, *2018*.

[28] Elhoseny, M., Shankar, K. &Uthayakumar, J. Intelligent Diagnostic Prediction and Classification System for Chronic Kidney Disease. *Sci Rep* **9**, 9583 (2019). https://doi.org/10.1038/s41598-019-46074-2

[29] Lahoura, V., Singh, H., Aggarwal, A., Sharma, B., Mohammed, M. A., Damaševičius, R., ... & Cengiz, K. (2021). Cloud Computing-Based Framework for Breast Cancer Diagnosis Using Extreme Learning Machine. *Diagnostics*, *11*(2), 241.

[30] Dhahri, H., Al Maghayreh, E., Mahmood, A., Elkilani, W., & Faisal Nagi, M. (2019). Automated breast cancer diagnosis based on machine learning algorithms. *Journal of healthcare engineering*, *2019*.

[31] Elgin Christo, V. R., Khanna Nehemiah, H., Minu, B., & Kannan, A. (2019). Correlation-based ensemble feature selection using bioinspired algorithms and classification using backpropagation neural network. *Computational and mathematical methods in medicine*, *2019*.

[32] Osman, A. H., &Aljahdali, H. M. A. (2020). An effective of ensemble boosting learning method for breast cancer virtual screening using neural network model. *IEEE Access*, *8*, 39165-39174.

[33] Ed-daoudy, A., &Maalmi, K. (2020). Breast cancer classification with reduced feature set using association rules and support vector machine. *Network Modeling Analysis in Health Informatics and Bioinformatics*, *9*, 1-10.

[34] Sakri, S. B., Rashid, N. B. A., & Zain, Z. M. (2018). Particle swarm optimization feature selection for breast cancer recurrence prediction. *IEEE Access*, *6*, 29637-29647.

[35] Rady, E. H. A., & Anwar, A. S. (2019). Prediction of kidney disease stages using data mining algorithms. *Informatics in Medicine Unlocked*, *15*, 100178.

[36] Almansour, N. A., Syed, H. F., Khayat, N. R., Altheeb, R. K., Juri, R. E., Alhiyafi, J., ... & Olatunji, S. O. (2019). Neural network and support vector machine for the prediction of chronic kidney disease: A comparative study. *Computers in biology and medicine*, *109*, 101-111.

[37] Kaur, H., & Kumari, V. (2020). Predictive modelling and analytics for diabetes using a machine learning approach. *Applied computing and informatics*.

[38] Mahabub, A. A robust voting approach for diabetes prediction using traditional machine learning techniques. *SN Appl. Sci.* **1,** 1667 (2019). https://doi.org/10.1007/s42452-019-1759-7

[39] Sisodia, D., & Sisodia, D. S. (2018). Prediction of diabetes using classification algorithms. *Procedia computer science*, *132*, 1578-1585.

[40] Gárate-Escamila, A. K., El Hassani, A. H., &Andrès, E. (2020). Classification models for heart disease prediction using feature selection and PCA. *Informatics in Medicine Unlocked*, *19*, 100330.

[41] Tama, B. A., Im, S., & Lee, S. (2020). Improving an intelligent detection system for coronary heart disease using a two-tier classifier ensemble. *BioMed Research International*, *2020*.

[42] Mohan, S., Thirumalai, C., & Srivastava, G. (2019). Effective heart disease prediction using hybrid machine learning techniques. *IEEE Access*, *7*, 81542-81554.

[43] Shakeel, P. M., Tolba, A., Al-Makhadmeh, Z., & Jaber, M. M. (2020). Automatic detection of lung cancer from biomedical data set using discrete AdaBoost optimized ensemble learning generalized neural networks. *Neural Computing and Applications*, *32*(3), 777-790.

[44] Li, J. P., Haq, A. U., Din, S. U., Khan, J., Khan, A., &Saboor, A. (2020). Heart Disease Identification Method Using Machine Learning Classification in E-Healthcare. *IEEE Access*, *8*, 107562-107582.

[45] Sarker, I.H. Machine Learning: Algorithms, Real-World Applications and Research Directions. *SN COMPUT. SCI.* **2,** 160 (2021). https://doi.org/10.1007/s42979-021-00592-x

[46] Tallón-Ballesteros A.J., Riquelme J.C. (2015) Data Cleansing Meets Feature Selection: A Supervised Machine Learning Approach. In: Ferrández Vicente J., Álvarez-Sánchez J., de la Paz López F., Toledo-Moreo F., Adeli H. (eds) Bioinspired Computation in Artificial Systems. IWINAC 2015. Lecture Notes in Computer Science, vol 9108. Springer, Cham. https://doi.org/10.1007/978-3-319-18833-1_39

Section I

Beginning of the Predictive Data Modeling for Biomedical Data and Imaging/Health Care

3

Biomedical Data Visualization and Data Representation

Subhranshu Mohapatra, Poonam Tanwar, and Shweta Sharma

Department of Computer Science & Engineering, School of Technology,
Manav Rachna International Institute of Research & Studies, India
E-mail: subhranshumohapatra143@gmail.com;
poonamtanwar.fet@mriu.edu.in; shwetasharma.fet@mriu.edu.in

Abstract

Biomedical research produces a large amount of complex data from sources like genomic sequencing, medical imaging, and electronic health records. Biomedical data visualization is critical for analyzing, interpreting, and communicating this data effectively, especially as the amount of data and technology advances. This chapter discusses the importance of biomedical data visualization, in biomedical research and clinical practice. It explores the role and applications of biomedical data, the significance of visualizing it to discover patterns and relationships for new insights, and popular visualization techniques like heatmaps for identifying co-expressed gene clusters. Overall, biomedical data visualization is an essential tool for informed decision-making and effective communication of findings to wider audiences. Visualizing biomedical data can reveal patterns and relationships, leading to new insights. It also discusses the use of heatmaps and other visualization techniques to cluster co-expressed genes. Ultimately, biomedical data visualization is essential for informed decision-making and communicating research findings to a wider audience.

Keywords: Data visualization, data representation, graph, histogram, biomedical data.

3.1 Introduction

The field of biomedical research generates a massive amount of complex data that requires efficient methods of visualization and representation to be accurately analyzed, interpreted, and communicated. In the current era of big data, the volume and diversity of biomedical data continue to expand, and the integration of multiple data sources is becoming increasingly common.

Biomedical data visualization has become a critical tool in both biomedical research and clinical practice, enabling researchers and clinicians to gain insights from the data and make informed decisions. Visualization methods enable researchers to recognize patterns and connections that would be challenging to observe through conventional statistical techniques or manual examination. Furthermore, visualization aids in communicating findings to a broader audience, including patients, policymakers, and the general public, facilitating the sharing of knowledge and promoting transparency.

To encourage the adoption of effective data visualization methods in biomedical research and clinical practice, an annual review journal will publish articles highlighting the latest advances in data visualization. These articles will cover new techniques, tools, and best practices, as well as successful examples of visualization applications in biomedical research and clinical practice. Additionally, the journal will provide guidance on how to avoid common pitfalls and biases in data visualization, such as the misuse of color scales or the incorrect interpretation of correlation as causation.

By fostering interdisciplinary collaborations between data visualization experts and biomedical researchers and clinicians, we aim to create a community of researchers and practitioners devoted to advancing the field of biomedical data visualization and representation. Ultimately, our objective is to accelerate the discovery of new biomedical knowledge, improve clinical decision-making, and enhance patient outcomes.

3.2 Biomedical Data Visualization

Data visualization helps biomedical researchers and practitioners to analyze, interpret, and communicate complex data from various sources, including genomic sequencing, medical imaging, and electronic health records. The amount of data generated in biomedicine can be overwhelming and difficult to comprehend without visual representations. Visualization techniques help researchers to identify patterns and relationships in the data, which can lead to new discoveries and insights. Furthermore, using visualization tools can assist in decision-making by presenting a user-friendly approach to analyze and handle data, which empowers researchers to make knowledgeable decisions [1, 2].

In clinical practice, data visualization can aid in the diagnosis and treatment of diseases. Clinicians can use visual representations of patient data, such as imaging scans, vital signs, and lab test results, to quickly identify abnormalities and develop treatment plans. Visualization tools can also help researchers to identify new drug targets and understand the molecular mechanisms underlying diseases, which can lead to the development of new therapies.

Data visualization can also aid in the communication of research findings to a broader audience, including policymakers and the general public. The use of visualization tools can simplify the presentation of intricate information in an interactive and compelling manner, facilitating the comprehension and appreciation of research outcomes by individuals who are not experts in the field. This can lead to increased public awareness and support for biomedical research, as well as better-informed healthcare decisions by patients and their families [3].

Contemporary datasets are frequently arduous and costly to obtain and scrutinize. This especially true for large-scale biomedical datasets [4], such as a very small dataset for diabetes becomes very hard for evaluation in normal form while it becomes easy with the help of different types of data representation such as histograms, heatmaps, and others.

```
   preg  plas  pres  skin  test  mass  pedi   age  class
0     6   148    72    35     0  33.6  0.627   50      1
1     1    85    66    29     0  26.6  0.351   31      0
2     8   183    64     0     0  23.3  0.672   32      1
3     1    89    66    23    94  28.1  0.167   21      0
4     0   137    40    35   168  43.1  2.288   33      1

Summary statistics of the dataset:

              preg         plas         pres         skin         test         mass
count   768.000000   768.000000   768.000000   768.000000   768.000000   768.000000
mean      3.845052   120.894531    69.105469    20.536458    79.799479    31.992578
std       3.369578    31.972618    19.355807    15.952218   115.244002     7.884160
min       0.000000     0.000000     0.000000     0.000000     0.000000     0.000000
25%       1.000000    99.000000    62.000000     0.000000     0.000000    27.300000
50%       3.000000   117.000000    72.000000    23.000000    30.500000    32.000000
75%       6.000000   140.250000    80.000000    32.000000   127.250000    36.600000
max      17.000000   199.000000   122.000000    99.000000   846.000000    67.100000

              pedi          age        class
count   768.000000   768.000000   768.000000
mean      0.471876    33.240885     0.348958
std       0.331329    11.760232     0.476951
min       0.078000    21.000000     0.000000
25%       0.243750    24.000000     0.000000
50%       0.372500    29.000000     0.000000
75%       0.626250    41.000000     1.000000
max       2.420000    81.000000     1.000000
```

Figure 3.1 Data available in normal form [10].

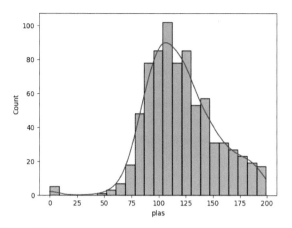

Figure 3.2   Representation of data in a histogram format [10].

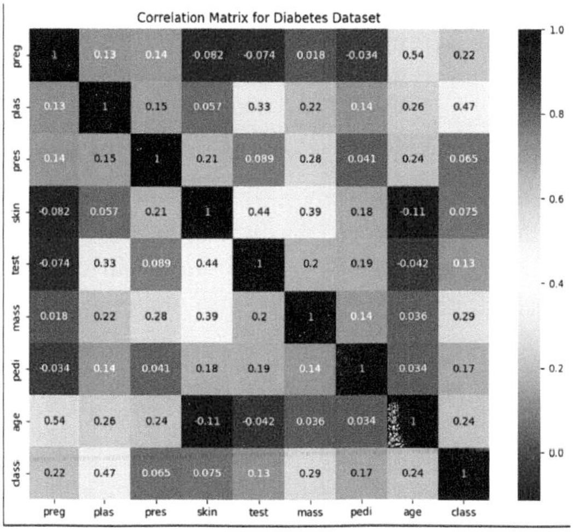

Figure 3.3   Heatmap representation ranging from blue-to-red gradient, where blue represents negative correlations and red represents positive correlations [10].

In this era, data visualization and representation can be done using machine learning and artificial intelligence in the field of biomedicine as this is an emerging field that aims to leverage advanced algorithms to help in better understanding these complex data [4]. The above pictures are generated with simple machine-level language that makes it easier for data visualization, but still some genomics or medical imaging data require specialized and expertized equipment and expertise to collect and analyze data.

As often as not, visualization can reveal unexpected patterns or outliers that would be missed by analytical methods, such that to get an increased number of pixels [5]. A visual system is capable of handling more information than is typically presented in scientific visualization. Visual patterns that are appropriately encoded can be detected within 250 milliseconds, even without concentrated attention. Employing higher resolution displays can aid in observing more details and increasing work efficiency. However, enlarging a visualization may impede pattern recognition.

Another possible solution to enhance the biomedical data visualization is to increase the efficiency and density of the data. A system with higher capacity can be utilized. Some visualization experts propose creating visualization with a high density of data.

Although this approach has its advantages, it also has its limitations. With increasing data density, visualizations may need to adopt particular and focused tactics to maintain their effectiveness.

3.3 Genomic Data

Genomic data refers to the information about an organism's DNA sequence. This data is often obtained through high-throughput sequencing technologies that generate vast amounts of genetic information. Genomic data can provide valuable insights into genetic variations, predisposition to certain diseases, and other biological processes that are relevant to health and disease. The analysis and interpretation of genomic data have become a critical component of biomedical research and have led to significant advances in our understanding of the genetic basis of disease [6].

Genomic data plays a crucial role in biomedical research and has numerous applications in clinical medicine. It provides insights into the genetic basis of diseases, including their underlying mechanisms and potential treatment options. By analyzing genomic data, researchers can identify genetic variations that may contribute to the development of certain diseases, allowing for the development of personalized therapies that target specific genetic mutations [3]. Additionally, genomic data can be used to develop new diagnostic tests and screening tools for genetic diseases. In cancer research, genomic data can help identify genetic mutations that drive tumor growth, which can inform treatment decisions and improve patient outcomes. In general, genomic data has drastically transformed our comprehension of human biology and holds the potential to revolutionize healthcare by facilitating more individualized and accurate treatments for a broad spectrum of illnesses.

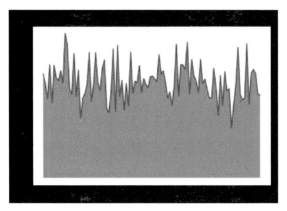

Figure 3.4   Scatter plot representation for the diabetes dataset [10].

Genomic data visualization plays an essential role in aiding researchers to scrutinize and decipher the copious amount of data produced by genomic research. The lucid and informative depiction of genomic data assists researchers in identifying intricate patterns and relationships that could be challenging to distinguish from raw data alone. Heatmaps are a popular visualization technique in genomics [9], as they provide a color-coded representation of gene expression levels across different samples or conditions [7]. Heatmaps are particularly useful for identifying clusters of genes that are co-expressed or have similar expression patterns, which can provide an insight into potential biological functions and pathways.

Scatterplots are another useful tool for visualizing genomic data. They allow researchers to explore the relationship between two genes or to compare gene expression levels across different samples or conditions. Scatterplots can also reveal patterns and correlations that might not be apparent for heatmaps and can be particularly useful for identifying regulatory relationships between genes [8]. By plotting gene expression levels against one another, researchers can identify genes that are positively or negatively correlated, which can provide an insight into potential regulatory networks and signaling pathways.

There are several other visualization techniques used in genomic data analysis. Circular plots are a popular method for visualizing genomic data, particularly for representing the organization and structure of chromosomes. Circular plots display the genomic data in a circular format, where the outer ring represents the chromosome, and the inner rings display additional information such as gene density, repeat regions, and chromosomal rearrangements.

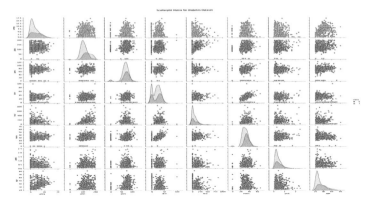

Figure 3.5 Various types of data representation and visualization of dataset available for diabetes [10].

Bar charts are another useful tool for visualizing genomic data. They are commonly used to represent the frequency of different genetic variants or mutations across different samples or populations. Bar charts provide a clear visual representation of the distribution of variants and can be useful in identifying common variants that may be associated with certain diseases.

Sankey diagrams are another type of visualization used in genomic data analysis. They are particularly useful for representing the flow of biological data or processes through a system. Sankey diagrams use arrows of different widths to represent the flow of data or processes between different components of a system, such as genes, proteins, or metabolic pathways.

Choosing a visualization method relies on the specific research query and the attributes of the data under examination. Every method has its advantages and drawbacks, and researchers must determine the most suitable method to visualize and construe the data effectively. Overall, the visualization of genomic data plays a critical role in facilitating the analysis and interpretation of complex biological data, ultimately leading to new insights into the genetic basis of disease and other biological processes.

3.4 Datasets

3.4.1 Cancer

The intricacies of cancer arise from mutations in genes and changes in gene expression. Gene expression data from cancer patients can be evaluated using different data visualization methods such as clustering analysis and heatmaps

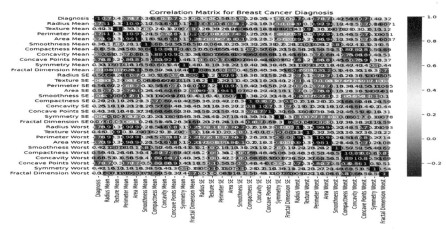

Figure 3.6   Correlation matrix for breast cancer diagnosis [10].

to detect gene expression patterns correlated with specific types of cancer or distinct stages of the disease.

There are multiple datasets that are publicly available for cancer research, which can be extremely useful for researchers to obtain a comprehensive view of the disease. For example, using a dataset available online, a matrix can be defined that can be used for the diagnosis of breast cancer.

One of these datasets is The Cancer Genome Atlas (TCGA), which is a vast dataset that includes genomic, epigenomic, transcriptomic, and proteomic data on various types of cancer.

Another dataset available is Genomic Data Commons (GDC), which serves as a repository of genomic and clinical data for cancer research.

The International Cancer Genome Consortium (ICGC) is yet another database that contains genomic data from over 25,000 cancer cases.

Moreover, the National Cancer Institute's Genomic Data Commons is a database that provides access to genomic and clinical data on more than 40 cancer types.

Gene Expression Omnibus (GEO) is a public repository of gene expression data that includes datasets related to cancer.

Finally, Clinical Proteomic Tumor Analysis Consortium (CPTAC) is a dataset containing proteomic and phosphoproteomic data on various types of cancer.

By utilizing these datasets, cancer researchers can conduct comprehensive analyses and explore the different aspects of cancer biology, which can ultimately lead to the development of improved cancer treatments. The vast amount of information available through these datasets can help researchers identify novel biomarkers for diagnosis and treatment, as well as uncover new therapeutic targets for various types of cancer. Overall, these publicly available datasets represent a valuable resource for cancer researchers seeking to better understand and combat the disease.

3.4.2 Alzheimer's disease

Alzheimer's is a type of progressive neurodegenerative disorder that is mainly characterized by the buildup of beta-amyloid plaques and neurofibrillary tangles in the brain. One of the most useful ways to study the disease progression of Alzheimer's and evaluate the efficacy of various treatments is through the utilization of structural data obtained from brain imaging studies. These imaging techniques can provide researchers with detailed insights into the changes that occur in the brain over time, including the areas that are affected by the disease, the patterns of damage, and the rate of progression. By analyzing these structural data, researchers can develop a better understanding of the disease and identify potential therapeutic targets to help treat or even prevent Alzheimer's disease.

There are several publicly accessible datasets available for Alzheimer's disease research, which includes the following.

The Alzheimer's Disease Neuroimaging Initiative (ADNI) is an all-encompassing dataset that comprises clinical, imaging, genetic, and bio-chemical data obtained from over 800 subjects, which includes individuals diagnosed with Alzheimer's disease, mild cognitive impairment, and healthy controls.

The National Alzheimer's Coordinating Center (NACC) is a repository that gathers and distributes clinical and neuropathological information regarding people who have Alzheimer's disease and similar conditions.

The Genetics of Alzheimer's Disease Data Storage Site (NIAGADS) is a database that comprises genomic and phenotypic data on individuals with Alzheimer's disease and related disorders.

The Human Brain Atlas is a dataset that offers brain imaging data for research on Alzheimer's disease and other neurological disorders.

The Alzheimer's Disease Data Initiative (ADDI) is a database that gives access to various Alzheimer's disease datasets, including imaging, genomic, and clinical data.

These datasets offer valuable resources for Alzheimer's disease researchers to explore and analyze disease-related data, which ultimately leads to a better understanding of the disease and enhanced treatment options.

3.4.3 Diabetes

Diabetes is a metabolic condition that is distinguished by elevated levels of blood sugar. By analyzing gene expression datasets from diabetic patients, researchers can identify specific genes involved in regulating blood sugar levels. These datasets can be represented through various data visualization techniques such as heatmaps. By examining these patterns, researchers can obtain a better understanding of how diabetes develops and how it affects the body's metabolic pathways. Ultimately, this knowledge can be used to develop better treatment options for diabetes.

Various publicly available datasets are available for conducting diabetes research.

These include the National Health and Nutrition Examination Survey (NHANES), which collects health and nutritional data on the US population, including diabetes and other chronic diseases.

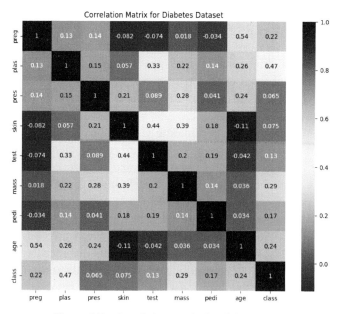

Figure 3.7   Correlation matrix for diabetes [10].

The Diabetes Prevention Program Outcomes Study (DPPOS) pro-vides information on the long-term outcomes of interventions for diabetes prevention.

The Emerging Risk Factors Collaboration (ERFC) dataset offers informa-tion on the risk factors for diabetes and other chronic diseases.

The Electronic Medical Records and Genomics (eMERGE) Network dataset combines electronic medical records with genomic data to study the genetics of diabetes and other diseases [9].

Finally, the Genetic Epidemiology of Diabetes (GENIE) Consortium dataset provides genetic and clinical data on individuals with diabetes.

These datasets are a valuable resource for researchers to explore and analyze diabetes-related data, ultimately leading to improved insights into the disease and better treatment options.

3.4.4 Infectious disease

Various biological datasets, including gene expression, protein–protein inter-action, and sequence data, can be employed to investigate the pathogenesis of infectious diseases such as COVID-19, Ebola, and HIV/AIDS. By analyz-ing these datasets, researchers can identify potential targets for therapeutic interventions, aiding in the development of effective treatments for these diseases.

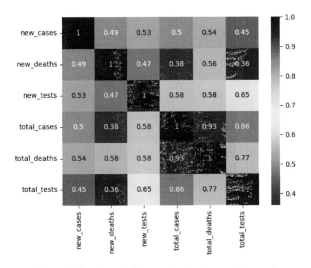

Figure 3.8 Correlation matrix for COVID-19 [12].

There are multiple datasets available for researchers studying infectious diseases, such as the following.

The Global Initiative on Sharing All Influenza Data (GISAID), which is a database containing genomic data on influenza viruses and other emerging infectious diseases including COVID-19.

The Virus Pathogen Resource (ViPR), which provides comprehensive data on viruses, including genomic sequences and protein structures, and also includes information on host−pathogen interactions.

The GenBank, which is a database that includes nucleotide sequences for viruses and other organisms, encompassing many infectious diseases.

The Immune Epitope Database (IEDB), which provides information on the immune response to infectious diseases and other diseases, including data on epitopes, antigens, and antibodies.

The Infectious Diseases Data Observatory (IDDO), which contains clinical, epidemiological, and molecular data on infectious diseases, including malaria, tuberculosis, and Ebola.

These datasets offer a wide range of data types, such as genomic sequences, protein structures, clinical data, and immune response information, which are valuable resources for infectious disease researchers to explore and analyze the data related to these diseases. By utilizing these datasets, researchers can achieve a better understanding of infectious diseases and identify potential targets for therapeutic interventions.

3.4.5 Diabetes data

To visualize diabetes-related data, a popular method is to use a line graph to plot the blood glucose levels over the time. Here *x*-axis represents time, while the *y*-axis represents the blood glucose levels. By analyzing the fluctuations in blood glucose levels, patterns or trends can be detected, such as spikes in blood glucose levels after meals or decreases during physical activity. This type of visualization can help identify factors that influence blood glucose levels, which can aid in managing and treating diabetes.

To monitor insulin levels over a certain time frame, a line graph can be used with the *y*-axis representing insulin levels and the *x*-axis representing time. Insulin, a hormone that plays a vital role in regulating blood glucose levels and analyzing its levels through this type of graph can uncover any recurring patterns or abnormalities in insulin secretion. Early detection of such patterns can help healthcare professionals identify potential issues with insulin regulation, leading to early intervention and better management of the condition.

Gene expression data can be analyzed to understand the patterns associated with diabetes. Heatmaps are a useful tool to identify these patterns, with the color scale indicating the level of gene expression. Clustering analysis can be used to identify the groups of genes that are co-regulated and associated with similar biological pathways. This approach helps to understand the gene expression patterns and potentially find targets for therapeutic interventions.

To illustrate the intricate connections between various factors contributing to the development of diabetes complications, diagrams such as network diagrams and flowcharts can be employed. Retinopathy, neuropathy, and nephropathy are a few examples of diabetes-related complications that can be depicted in these diagrams. By visually representing these relationships, these diagrams can help researchers and healthcare professionals better understand the underlying mechanisms of these complications and develop strategies for prevention and treatment.

3.5 Technique

3.5.1 Graphs

Visualizing biomedical data is essential for interpreting and communicating research findings. Graphs serve as a widely used tool for displaying quantitative data in biomedical research, especially data related to biomarkers or clinical outcomes. Various types of graphs are used in biomedical research, including line graphs, bar graphs, scatterplots, box plots, and heatmaps.

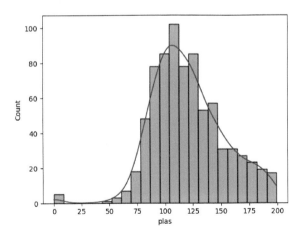

Figure 3.9 Graphical representation of the diabetes dataset [10].

Line graphs are commonly used to track changes in a variable over time, such as a patient's blood pressure throughout the day. On the other hand, bar graphs are useful for comparing data across different categories, such as incidence rates of a particular disease among different age groups. Scatterplots are useful for exploring the relationship between two variables, such as the correlation between a patient's age and cholesterol levels [8].

Box plots are useful for displaying the distribution of a dataset, allowing easy identification of any extreme values. They show the median, quartiles, and outliers of the data. Heatmaps are useful for visualizing large amounts of data in a visually appealing way, often used for gene expression data or protein–protein interactions.

Using these types of graphs, researchers can better understand and communicate their findings with others in the biomedical field. Graphs provide a clear visual representation of complex data and can help identify patterns, trends, and outliers. Incorporating effective data visualization techniques in biomedical research is crucial for making significant strides in understanding and addressing health issues.

3.5.2 Charts

Visualizing biomedical data is an essential aspect of biomedical research that facilitates the analysis, interpretation, and communication of complex

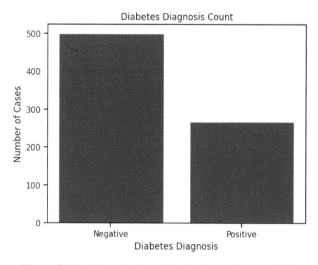

Figure 3.10   Chart showing diabetes diagnosis count [10].

data. Charts are a popular method of visualizing biomedical data as they offer a clear and concise way of presenting quantitative data. Different types of charts are used in biomedical research, including line charts that track changes in a variable over time, such as changes in blood pressure over the course of a day or biomarker changes during clinical trials.

Bar charts are useful for comparing data across different categories, such as incidence rates of a particular disease in different age groups or the frequency of a specific mutation in different populations. Scatterplots are utilized to investigate the association between two variables, such as the link between age and cholesterol levels, or the correlation between various biomarkers [8].

3.5.3 Boxplots

Boxplots show the distribution of a dataset and provide insight into extreme values, median, and quartiles and are useful for comparing the distribution of biomarkers in different patient populations. Heatmaps display large amounts of data in a visually appealing way and are often used to visualize gene expression data or protein—protein interactions. They offer insight into gene expression patterns in various tissues or interactions between different proteins.

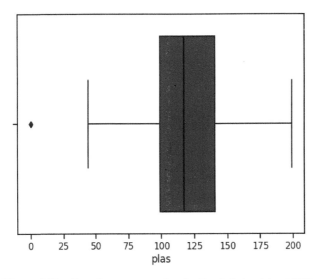

Figure 3.11   Box plot representation for the diabetes dataset [10].

By utilizing these chart types, researchers can give a better understanding of the data and effectively communicate their findings with peers in the biomedical field. Effective data visualization plays a critical role in advancing biomedical research and discovering new treatments and therapies for various diseases.

3.5.4 Heatmaps

Heatmaps are a popular tool for visualizing biomedical data due to their ability to display large amounts of information in a visually appealing way. Heatmaps use color to represent the intensity of a particular variable across a set of data. In biomedical research, heatmaps are often used to visualize gene expression data or protein−protein interactions.

In gene expression studies, heatmaps can be used to show the expression levels of many genes simultaneously across different tissues or experimental conditions. The colors in the heatmap represent the level of expression, with high expression shown in one color and low expression shown in another color. This allows researchers to easily identify patterns of gene expression and identify genes that are upregulated or downregulated under certain conditions.

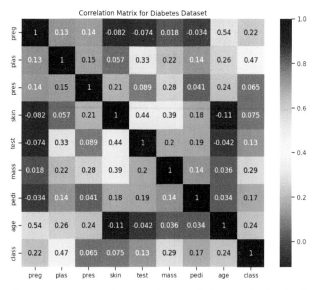

Figure 3.12   Heatmaps representation showing correlation matrix for the diabetes dataset [10].

Similarly, heatmaps can be used to visualize protein–protein interactions in biomedical research. In this case, the colors in the heatmap represent the strength of the interaction between two proteins. Heatmaps can show which proteins interact with each other and to what extent, allowing researchers to identify new protein–protein interactions and gain a better understanding of cellular signaling pathways.

Overall, heatmaps are a powerful tool for biomedical data visualization, enabling researchers to analyze and communicate complex data effectively. By using heatmaps, researchers can gain new insights into biological processes and develop new treatments and therapies for diseases.

3.5.5 Network

Network visualization has emerged as a popular technique for visualizing complex biomedical data, including disease pathways and protein–protein interactions. These visualizations rely on nodes to represent biological entities and edges to represent their relationships.

In protein–protein interaction networks, nodes represent proteins and edges represent the interactions between them. By mapping these interactions in a network, researchers can identify important proteins, pathways, and potential targets for drug development.

Similarly, in disease pathway networks, nodes represent genes or proteins, and edges represent their interactions. By visualizing these pathways in a network, researchers can identify key components involved in the disease process and potential targets for therapeutic intervention.

Network visualization is an interactive and intuitive way to explore complex data, allowing researchers to identify new hypotheses and insights into biological processes. It is becoming increasingly important in biomedical research and is expected to contribute significantly to the development of new treatments and therapies for diseases.

3.5.6 Tree

In biomedical research, trees are widely used for visualizing hierarchical relationships between entities. A tree visualization uses nodes and branches to represent the entities and their relationships, respectively.

One of the applications of tree visualization in biomedical research is the use of phylogenetic trees to study evolutionary relationships between organisms or genetic sequences. Phylogenetic trees display the shared ancestry among species or genetic sequences and allow researchers to examine the evolution of traits or identify new genetic markers.

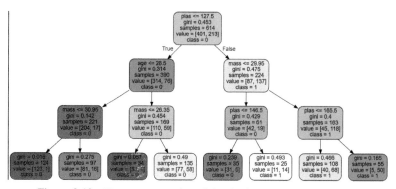

Figure 3.13   Tree representation of data in the diabetes dataset [10].

Another use case for tree visualization is in clinical decision-making. Decision trees can be employed to provide clinicians with a visual representation of the possible outcomes of various treatment options, enabling them to make more informed decisions about patient care and improve treatment results.

Tree visualizations are also commonly used in genomics to depict the structure of genetic data. Genealogical trees, for instance, show the relationships between individuals or families based on their genetic information. Such visualizations help researchers study inheritance patterns of genetic disorders or identify genetic variants linked to particular traits; it also allows researchers to investigate relationships between entities and identify new hypotheses for further study [4].

3.5.7 Sequence alignments

Sequence alignment is a frequently used technique for visualizing biomedical data, particularly in the comparison of genetic sequences. It involves aligning multiple sequences to identify similarities and differences between them.

In biomedical research, sequence alignment is often utilized to compare DNA or protein sequences from various species, identify genetic variations linked to diseases, or predict the function of unknown proteins.

To highlight similarities and differences between sequences, sequence alignment visualizations often incorporate color coding. By comparing aligned sequences, researchers can identify conserved regions crucial to protein function or evolution or identify mutations linked to disease processes.

Multiple sequence alignment (MSA) tools are a common type of sequence alignment visualization, aligning numerous sequences to detect conserved regions and gaps. MSA visualizations can assist researchers in identifying functional domains, protein families, or phylogenetic relationships among different organisms.

All in all, sequence alignment is a useful tool for analyzing and visualizing intricate biomedical data. By using sequence alignment, researchers can gain fresh perspectives into the structure, function, and evolution of genetic sequences and find new targets for developing drugs and treating diseases.

3.5.8 3D structure

Three-dimensional (3D) structure visualization is a valuable tool in biomedical research for analyzing and visualizing data related to the structure and function of biomolecules, including proteins, DNA, and RNA. It involves creating 3D models of molecules using software tools based on experimental data from techniques such as X-ray crystallography or nuclear magnetic resonance (NMR) spectroscopy.

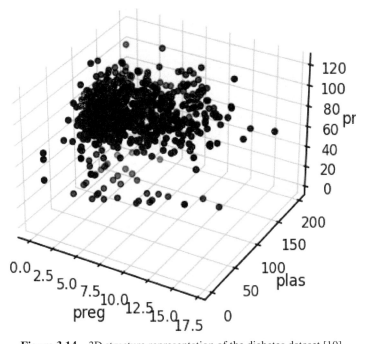

Figure 3.14   3D structure representation of the diabetes dataset [10].

By visualizing the 3D structure of proteins and biomolecules, researchers can gain an insight into their function, identify potential drug binding sites, and design new drugs or therapies to target specific structures. Popular tools for 3D structure visualization include PyMOL, Chimera, and VMD.

Visualizing the interactions between different molecules, such as protein–protein or protein–ligand interactions, is another application of 3D structure visualization. Researchers can identify key structural features important for the interaction and develop new drugs or therapies targeting these features.

Overall, 3D structure visualization is a powerful tool for analyzing complex biomedical data, allowing researchers to gain new insights into the structure and function of biomolecules and develop new treatments for diseases.

3.6 Application of Data Visualization and Representation

Understanding complex biological systems: Data visualization and representation are essential tools for understanding complex biological systems. Biomedical research generates large amounts of data, which can be difficult to interpret without proper visualizations. By using various visualization techniques, researchers can identify patterns and relationships in the data, gain insights into the underlying biological processes, and make informed decisions.

For example, protein–protein interaction networks can be visualized using nodes and edges to represent proteins and their interactions, respectively. This enables researchers to identify critical hubs and pathways in the network and gain insights into biological processes. Similarly, genetic data can be visualized using tools such as sequence alignment and phylogenetic trees, which help identify genetic variants and relationships between different genetic sequences. This can help to identify potential targets for drug discovery and the treatment of genetic disorders [13].

Additionally, data visualization and representation can be used to explore the structure and function of complex biomolecules, such as proteins and DNA. Creating 3D models of biomolecules can help researchers understand their function, identify potential drug-binding sites, and design new drugs to target specific structures.

In conclusion, data visualization and representation play a crucial role in biomedical research. They help researchers understand complex biological systems, identify new targets for drug discovery, and design more effective treatments and therapies for diseases.

3.6.1 Drug discovery and development

Data visualization and representation play a crucial role in drug discovery and development. Biomedical research generates an immense amount of data on potential drug targets, including genetic information, protein structures, and chemical compounds. By using visualization techniques, researchers can analyze the relationships between these data points and identify potential drug candidates.

Data visualization is commonly used in drug discovery to understand the interactions between chemical compounds and protein targets. By creating 3D models of the protein structure and the chemical compound, researchers can identify potential binding sites and design new compounds that target these sites.

Another example is the use of data visualization to explore the connections between genetic variants and drug response. By analyzing genetic data and drug response data together, researchers can identify genetic markers that are associated with drug response or resistance. Visualizing this data can help researchers to develop personalized treatments for patients and identify new drug targets.

In summary, data visualization and representation are essential in drug discovery and development, enabling researchers to comprehend complex datasets and identify new drug targets and therapies.

3.6.2 Clinical decision-making

Data visualization and representation are also valuable in clinical decision-making. In the biomedical field, patient data is generated, including medical images, laboratory test results, and electronic health records, which can be difficult to interpret without appropriate visualizations [14]. By using visualization techniques, clinicians can better understand the data and make informed decisions about patient care.

For instance, medical imaging data can be visualized to better understand the structure and function of organs and tissues. Using 3D modeling software, clinicians can create visualizations of patient anatomy to assist in surgical planning and diagnosis.

Likewise, laboratory test results can be visualized to identify trends and patterns in patient health. By creating visualizations of test results over time, clinicians can monitor disease progression, evaluate treatment efficacy, and make informed decisions regarding patient care.

In addition, electronic health records can be visualized to identify patterns and relationships in patient data. By creating visualizations of patient histories and clinical data, clinicians can identify potential risk factors, track disease progression, and develop personalized treatment plans for patients.

3.6.3 Education and communication

Data visualization and representation have additional uses in the biomedical field for education and communication purposes. Visual aids can be beneficial in enhancing the learning experience of students and improving the communication between researchers and the general public.

One example of this is the use of 3D models to visually demonstrate complex biological concepts, such as biomolecule structure and cellular processes, to students and the public. These visual aids can simplify the understanding of these concepts and also create interest and excitement for the field of biomedicine.

Moreover, visual aids can be employed to convey research findings to a broader audience. Infographics and data visualizations can present complicated data in a straightforward and concise way, allowing non-experts to comprehend and appreciate the research.

3.6.4 Personalized medicine

Data visualization and representation are becoming more prevalent in personalized medicine. This field involves customizing medical treatments based on an individual's unique genetic makeup, lifestyle, and medical history. Visualization techniques are useful in helping clinicians comprehend patient data and make informed decisions regarding individualized treatment plans.

One instance of this is the use of data visualization to analyze the relationship between genetic variants and disease susceptibility. By analyzing genetic and disease data in conjunction, researchers can determine genetic markers that are linked to a higher chance of developing certain diseases. Visualizing this data can aid clinicians in identifying high-risk patients and developing tailored prevention strategies.

Moreover, visualization methods can be utilized to monitor disease progression and the effectiveness of treatment in individual patients. By visualizing patient data over a period, clinicians can track the effectiveness of treatment and make informed decisions about changes to the treatment plan.

3.7 Advantages of Biomedical Data Visualization and Representation

3.7.1 Improved understanding

The use of data visualization and representation can enhance the understanding of complex biomedical data. Through the aid of visual aids, researchers and clinicians can easily identify patterns and relationships that may be difficult to discern through numerical analysis alone, leading to new insights and discoveries that may have been previously impossible.

Visual aids also have the potential to simplify complex concepts and make them more accessible to a broader audience. By presenting data in a clear and concise manner, visual aids can bridge the gap between technical jargon and everyday language, making it easier for non-experts to comprehend and appreciate the research.

Moreover, data visualization can promote communication and collaboration between researchers, clinicians, and patients. By presenting data in a visually attractive and easy-to-understand format, researchers can effectively communicate their findings to a broader audience, including patients and their families, resulting in increased patient engagement and participation in their healthcare, ultimately leading to better health outcomes.

3.7.2 Better communication

Biomedical data visualization and representation can enhance communication in multiple ways. Firstly, visual aids can assist researchers and clinicians in communicating complex data and discoveries in a more easily understandable manner. By presenting information visually, they can convey it more effectively and make it simpler for others to interpret and comprehend.

Moreover, visual aids can foster communication and collaboration among researchers, clinicians, and patients. Patients and their families may lack a background in biomedical research or may not have a comprehensive understanding of technical terminology, but visual aids can help bridge the gap and facilitate communication. By presenting data in a clear and concise way, patients can gain a better understanding of their condition and beco

3.7.3 Increased efficiency

Biomedical data visualization and representation can increase efficiency in research and clinical settings. Visual aids can save time and resources by facilitating the analysis and interpretation of data. Researchers and clinicians can easily identify trends and patterns in data, enabling them to focus their efforts on areas of interest or concern. This can accelerate the research process and lead to the discovery of new treatments and therapies more quickly.

In the clinical setting, visual aids can streamline decision-making and improve patient outcomes. By presenting patient data visually, clinicians can quickly identify key information and make informed decisions about patient care. This can optimize healthcare resources and result in improved patient outcomes.

3.7.4 Personalized medicine

Visualizing biomedical data can greatly benefit personalized medicine as it allows clinicians to develop treatment plans based on an individual's unique genetic makeup, lifestyle, and medical history. Through visual aids, patterns and relationships in the data can be identified, which may not be apparent through numerical analysis alone. Monitoring disease progression and treatment response can also be made more informed with the help of data visualization.

Visual aids can also help patients to understand their condition and participate in their own healthcare. By presenting data in a clear and concise manner, patients can understand the reasoning behind treatment decisions, leading to improved outcomes and greater satisfaction with their healthcare experience [9].

The use of biomedical data visualization and representation can also be advantageous in the field of education for medicine and biomedical research. Through the application of visual aids, educators can simplify complex concepts and make them more understandable to students and trainees.

Visual aids can be utilized to illustrate intricate biological processes, such as cellular pathways or disease mechanisms, enabling easier comprehension and retention of essential concepts by students.

Moreover, visual aids can be used to teach essential data analysis and interpretation skills to students, which are necessary for researchers and clinicians. By using real-world datasets and visual aids, students can develop critical thinking and problem-solving skills that are highly valued in the field of medicine and biomedical research.

Lastly, visual aids can be employed to exhibit research findings and encourage scientific literacy. By presenting data in an esthetically appealing way, researchers can engage a broader audience and communicate the importance and relevance of their research to the general public. This can increase interest in science and medicine, inspiring future generations of researchers and healthcare professionals.

3.8 Future Scope

In the coming years, the field of biomedical data is set to witness significant growth and progress. Advancements in technology and increasing volumes of data are expected to revolutionize the way healthcare providers access and analyze medical information. With respect to visualization and representation, the development of more advanced and interactive techniques will offer greater insights into complex biomedical datasets. Virtual and augmented reality tools, for example, may enable healthcare providers to visualize and manipulate data in 3D, providing a more immersive and intuitive experience.

Moreover, the integration of biomedical data with electronic health records and other health information systems will lead to more comprehensive patient profiles and improve the accuracy of diagnosis and treatment plans. In the future, biomedical data is likely to play a vital role in artificial intelligence and machine learning models, which will be able to predict disease progression and outcomes, identify personalized treatment plans, and even discover new therapies.

However, ethical considerations such as data privacy and ownership will need to be addressed to ensure that patient rights are protected. Despite these challenges, the future of biomedical data holds immense promise in transforming the field of medicine and improving patient outcomes. Therefore, it is crucial that we continue to invest in research and development in this area to fully realize its potential.

3.9 Conclusion

In summary, biomedical data plays a critical role in comprehending diseases and their management. The visualization and representation of this data have multiple benefits, such as identifying complex patterns and trends. Different techniques, including graphs, charts, heatmaps, and trees, can effectively represent biomedical data, leading to informed decisions by healthcare providers and improved patient outcomes. Moreover, incorporating biomedical data into artificial intelligence and machine learning models could revolutionize disease diagnosis and treatment [10]. However, using biomedical data also raises ethical and legal concerns that need to be addressed. In conclusion, the appropriate use of biomedical data, including visualization and representation, can significantly enhance patient care and advance the field of medicine.

References

[1] Graber ML, Franklin N, Gordon R. 2005. Diagnostic error in internal medicine. *Arch. Intern. Med.* 165: 1493–99

[2] Pinto A, Brunese L. 2010. Spectrum of diagnostic errors in radiology. *World J. Radiol.* 2: 377–83

[3] Inselberg A. 1997. Multidimensional detective. Proc. IEEE Symp. Inf. Vis., Phoenix, Ariz., 21 Oct., pp. 100- 7. New York: IEEE

[4] Craft M, Dobrenz B, Dornbush E, Hunter M, Morris J, et al. 2015. An assessment of visualization tools for patient monitoring and medical decision making. Proc. Syst. Inf. Eng. Des. Symp., 24 Apr., Charlottesville, Va., pp. 212–17. New York: IEEE

[5] Card SK, Mackinlay JD, Shneiderman B. 1999. *Readings in Information Visualization: Using Vision to Think*. San Francisco: Morgan Kaufmann Definitive, annotated guide to classic papers on information visualization

[6] Porter M, Parks DH, Wang S, Churcher S, Blouin C, et al. 2009. GenGIS: a geospatial information system for genomic data. *Genome Res.* 19: 1896–904

[7] Myers RM, Levy SE 2016. Advancements in next-generation sequencing. Annu. Rev, Hum, Genom, Genet. 17:95-115

[8] Cleveland WS, Diaconis P, McGill R. 1982. Variables on scatterplots look more highly correlated when the scales are increased. *Science* 216: 1138–41

[9] Krzywinski M, Schein J, Birol I, Connors J, Gascoyne R, et al. 2009. Circos: an information aesthetic for comparative genomics. Genome Res. 19:1639-45

[10] Diabetes Data set https://raw.githubusercontent.com/jbrownlee/Datasets/master/pima-indians-diabetes.data.csv

[11] Cancer Data set https://archive.ics.uci.edu/ml/machine-learning-databases/breast-cancer-wisconsin/wdbc.data

[12] Covid-19 Data set https://raw.githubusercontent.com/owid/covid-19-da
ta/master/public/data/owid-covid-data.csv

[13] Chapman, C. (2019). A Complete Overviewof the Best Data Visualiza-
tionTools. https://www.toptal.com/designers/data-visualization/data-vis
ualizatoon

[14] Cromey DW. 2010. Avoiding twisted pixels: ethical guidelines for the
appropriate use and manipulation of scientific digital images. Sci. Eng.
Ethics 16: 639–67

4

Classification and Clustering Algorithms for Medical Data

Sachin Sharma[1], Madhulika Bhatiya[1], Anchal Garg[2], and Arun Yadav[3]

[1]Department of Computer Science and Engineering, Amity University, India
[2]University of Bolton, UK
[3]Department of Computer Science and Engineering, NIT Hamirpur, India
E-mail: sachina3010@gmail.com; drmadhulikabhatia@gmail.com;
garg.anchal@gmail.com; ayadav@nith.ac.in

Abstract

In recent years, there has been a substantial increase in the amount of attention paid to the use of machine learning strategies within the area of medical data. Classification and clustering algorithms are two major kinds of machine learning algorithms that are frequently utilized for a variety of tasks in medical data analysis. These algorithms are employed in a variety of different ways. Clustering algorithms are used to group data points that are similar together based on their similarity or distance metrics, while classification algorithms are used to predict the class or category of a new data point based on the patterns learned from labeled data. Classification methods may be found in machine learning software. We present an overview of classification and clustering algorithms for medical data in this article, covering its uses, problems, and future approaches, among other things.

Keywords: Algorithms, data, classification, machine, clustering, medical, learning, used, based, variety, medical data analysis, amount of attention, group data point, medical data analysis.

4.1 Introduction

The analysis of medical data is an extremely important part of the decision-making process in healthcare, as well as illness diagnosis, treatment planning, and monitoring patient outcomes. There has been a recent uptick in interest in the use of machine learning strategies for the purpose of analyzing medical information and deriving actionable insights. This coincides with the introduction of electronic health records (EHRs) and the accessibility of large-scale medical datasets. Classification and clustering algorithms are two important techniques in machine learning that have seen widespread usage in the analysis of medical data. Classification algorithms are used to organize data into categories.

The goal of classification algorithms is to organize data points into predetermined groups or classes using the patterns that are learned from labeled data. For instance, a classification algorithm may be used to a patient's medical history, clinical tests, and any other pertinent information in order to make an educated guess as to whether or not the patient is suffering from a certain condition. On the other hand, clustering algorithms collect data points that are comparable and group them together based on some measure of their similarity or distance rather than on any classes or labels that are predetermined. The use of clustering techniques, which may be used to recognize patterns or subgroups within a big dataset, can be beneficial in locating previously concealed links or trends in medical data. Clustering methods can be found here.

We present an overview of classification and clustering algorithms for medical data in this article, covering its uses, problems, and future approaches, among other things. We also discuss some of the recent break-throughs that have been made in this sector as well as some intriguing research avenues.

4.2 Main Text

4.2.1 Applications of classification and clustering algorithms in medical data analysis

Classification and clustering algorithms have been widely used in various applications in medical data analysis. Some of the common applications include:

1. **Disease diagnosis:** Based on patient data, such as symptoms, medical history, and clinical test results, classification algorithms are used to

make predictions about the presence or absence of a certain illness. These predictions might be positive or negative. For instance, algorithms for machine learning have been used to forecast the existence of a variety of ailments, including diabetes, cancer, heart disease, Alzheimer's disease, and others.

2. **Treatment planning:** Patients may be helped in picking the treatment plan that is most suited for them based on their features, such as their age, gender, genetic make-up, and stage of illness, with the use of classification algorithms. For instance, in the treatment of cancer, machine learning algorithms may be used to forecast the response to various treatment choices and to aid in the planning of personalized therapy.

3. **Patient monitoring:** Monitoring patient outcomes and making predictions about illness progression or treatment response are also possible applications for classification algorithms. In critical care units, for instance, machine learning algorithms may analyze patient data such as vital signs, laboratory findings, and medical history to forecast the probability of bad events such as sepsis or organ failure and trigger appropriate treatments. Other examples of these types of occurrences are cardiac arrest and stroke.

4. **Image analysis:** Image segmentation, object identification, and image classification are examples of the types of tasks that benefit greatly from the use of classification and clustering techniques in medical image analysis. For instance, in the field of radiology, machine learning algorithms may be used to categorize medical pictures like as X-rays, CT scans, and MRI scans in order to assist in the detection of illnesses such as cancer, pneumonia, or brain tumors. This can be accomplished by using imaging modalities such as X-rays, CT scans, and MRI scans.

5. **Drug discovery:** In the field of drug development, classification and clustering algorithms may be used to make predictions about the possible therapeutic qualities of chemical compounds and to locate prospective novel drug candidates. For instance, machine learning algorithms can analyze enormous chemical datasets in order to speed up the process of drug development by making accurate predictions about the activity, toxicity, and pharmacokinetics of various molecules.

4.2.2 Introduction to classification

Classification is a form of supervised learning that involves predicting the predetermined target class for each data sample [1]. It has garnered significant interest in medical applications, especially when dealing with imbalanced data [2]. Supervised learning is utilized to determine the category of new observations based on the information provided in the training data. The process entails training a program on a dataset or observations and subsequently classifying new observations into various groups or classes. Examples of classification tasks include distinguishing between "Yes" or "No," "0" or "1," "Spam" or "Not Spam," "Cat" or "Dog," and so on. These different terms, such as categories, objectives, and labels, all refer to the same concept: classes. In a classification algorithm, an input variable (x) is mapped to a discrete output function (y).

In classification algorithm, an input variable (x) is associated with a discrete output function (y), where y represents a categorical output.

$$y = f(x), \text{ where } y = \text{categorical output.}$$

An exemplary machine learning classification algorithm is an Email Spam Detector.

The primary objective of classification algorithms is to determine the category of a given dataset, particularly for predicting outputs in categorical data.

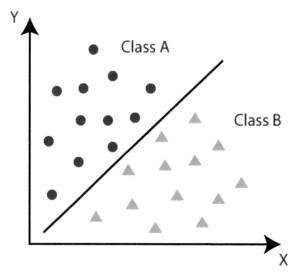

Figure 4.1   Classification Algorithm in Machine Learning - Javatpoint. Accessed: Dec. 13, 2023. [Online]. Available: https://www.javatpoint.com/classification-algorithm-in-machine-l earning

To better comprehend classification algorithms, consider the following diagram. It portrays two classes, Class A and Class B, which exhibit similar characteristics within each class but differ from other classes.

A classifier is the algorithm that applies the classification process to a dataset. There are two main types of classification methods:

⇒ **Binary classifier:** When a classification problem has only two possible outcomes, it is referred to as a binary classifier.
Examples: YES or NO, MALE or FEMALE, SPAM or NOT SPAM, CAT or DOG, etc.

⇒ **Multi-class classifier:** When a classification problem has more than two outcomes, then it is called as multi-class classifier.
Examples: Classifications of types of crops, classification of types of music, etc.

4.2.2.1 Types of ML classification algorithms

Machine learning (ML) is a branch of artificial intelligence (AI) that enables systems to learn from data and make predictions or decisions without explicit programming [3]. Classification algorithms can be categorized into two main types:

4.2.2.2 Logistic regression in machine learning

○ The logistic regression is somewhat like the linear regression, except for how each method is used. Logistic regression and artificial neural networks are the models of choice in many medical data classification tasks [4]. When trying to solve regression difficulties, linear regression is

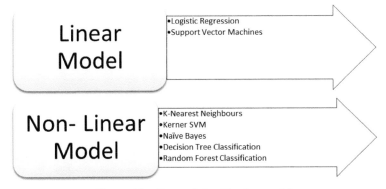

Figure 4.2 Types of classification model.

the method of choice, whilst logistic regression is used when attempting to solve classification issues.

o Logistic regression, which falls under the umbrella of the supervised learning approach, is widely regarded as one of the most successful machine learning algorithms. The categorical dependent variable may be predicted by utilizing it in conjunction with a predetermined group of independent factors.

o Logistic regression is used to make predictions about the outcome of a dependent variable that is categorical. As a result, the output needs to be a value that is either categorical or discrete. It is possible for it to be either Yes or No, 0 or 1, true or False, etc. But rather than reporting the precise value as 0 or 1, it offers the probability values that fall between 0 and 1.

o In logistic regression, rather than fitting a regression line, we fit an "S" shaped logistic function, which predicts two maximum values (0 or 1) for the dependent variable.

o The curve that results from the logistic function shows the probability of anything happening, such as whether the cells are malignant, whether a mouse is fat depending on its weight, and so on.

o Logistic regression is a major machine learning technique because of its ability to offer probabilities and classify new data using continuous and discrete datasets. This makes it suitable for both online and offline settings.

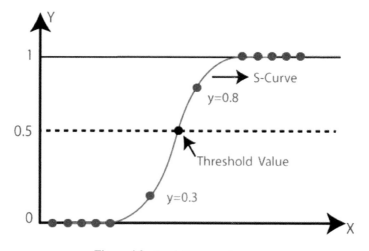

Figure 4.3   Logistic regression curve.

○ Logistic regression can readily discover which variables are the most useful for classifying observations and may be used to classify them using a variety of data formats. Logistic regression can also be used to classify observations. Figure 4.3 illustrates the logistic function.

4.2.2.3 Support vector machine in machine learning

Support vector machine (SVM) is a powerful machine learning method that utilizes the statistical learning theory and structural risk minimization principle to solve various pattern recognition problems [5]. It offers advantages in handling small sample sizes, nonlinearity, and high-dimensional data, effectively addressing challenges like the "curse of dimensionality" and overfitting [5]. The support vector machine (SVM), commonly referred to as SVM, is a highly popular supervised learning algorithm extensively utilized for both classification and regression tasks. While SVM can address problems related to classification and regression, its main application lies in the field of machine learning, particularly for addressing classification challenges. SVM is widely recognized for its effectiveness in creating optimal decision boundaries to separate different classes in a dataset. While it can also handle regression problems, SVM's widespread adoption and success primarily stem from its remarkable capabilities in tackling classification difficulties in various domains.

The main objective of SVM is to create an optimal decision boundary, often referred to as a hyperplane, which effectively separates classes in an *n*-dimensional space. This enables easy categorization of new data points in the future.

SVM selects extreme points and vectors, known as support vectors, which contribute to the construction of the hyperplane. These support vectors play a crucial role in the SVM algorithm. Figure 4.4 illustrates how a decision boundary or hyperplane can differentiate between two distinct groups.

Support vector machines, often known as SVMs, are frequently used in the field of medical data analysis for classification tasks. These tasks may include the diagnosis of illnesses based on patient data. A use of SVM in medical data is shown by the following example.

Imagine that you have access to a database containing information on patients and that this database contains attributes that characterize each patient, such as their age, blood pressure, cholesterol levels, and so on. You also have information on whether a certain illness is present in each individual patient.

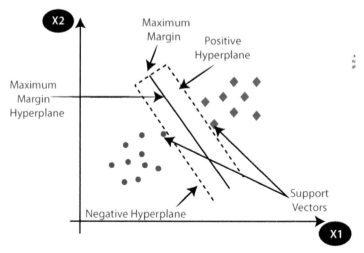

Figure 4.4   Support vector machine.

Your objective is to develop a classifier that, given a new patient's characteristics, can determine with high accuracy whether that patient is likely to have the condition. Figure 4.5 shows how to accomplish this goal with the help of SVM.

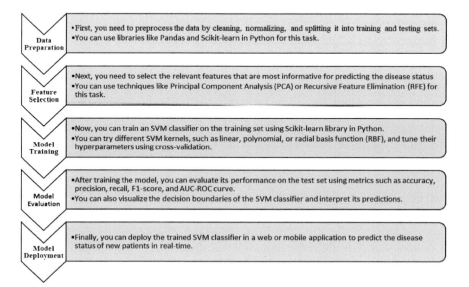

Figure 4.5   Goals of support vector machine.

In general, SVMs are useful tools for the analysis of medical data. This is particularly true when working with data that is both high-dimensional and complicated. The selection of the kernel and hyperparameters, on the other hand, may have a significant impact on the performance of the SVM; as a result, careful selection and tweaking are essential.

4.2.2.4 *K*-nearest neighbor (KNN) algorithm in machine learning

The *K*-nearest neighbor (KNN) algorithm is a machine learning technique utilized for solving classification and regression problems. It operates on the principle that if two data points are close in terms of their features, they are likely to belong to the same class. The simplicity of the KNN algorithm has led to its widespread application across various domains. However, the efficiency of the KNN algorithm for classification tasks can be significantly reduced when dealing with large sample sizes and a high number of feature attributes [6].

In KNN, the classification of a target data point is determined by examining the classes of its *K*-nearest neighbors in the feature space. The value

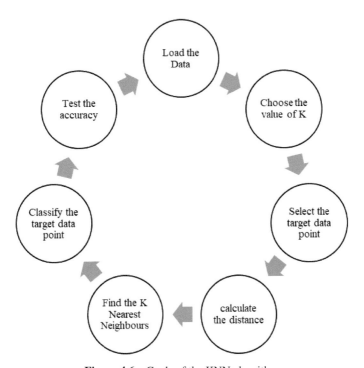

Figure 4.6 Goals of the KNN algorithm.

of K is a hyperparameter that can be adjusted to optimize the algorithm's performance.

The choice of distance metric plays a crucial role in the KNN algorithm and can be the Euclidean distance, Manhattan distance, or any other suitable distance metric based on the nature of the data being analyzed.

KNN is a straightforward and efficient technique for the analysis of medical data, particularly in situations in which there are a limited number of characteristics or the data itself is noisy. However, KNN may be computationally costly for big datasets or high-dimensional data. Additionally, the choice of K and the distance metric can have a significant impact on the performance of KNN.

4.2.2.5 The Naïve Bayes classifier algorithm in machine learning

The Naïve Bayes classifier is a probabilistic classifier that utilizes the Bayes theorem and incorporates the Naïve (strong) independence assumption. It operates under the assumption that the impact of a variable's value on a particular class is independent of the values of other variables, a condition referred to as class conditional independence. In other words, Naïve Bayes classifiers consider that each feature contributes to the classification process independently, without any correlation or influence from other features. This assumption simplifies the computational complexity of the algorithm and allows for efficient classification. By leveraging the Bayes theorem and assuming independence among variables, the Naïve Bayes classifiers provide a straightforward and efficient approach for various classification tasks [7]. Naïve Bayes is a probabilistic classification method that is used often in the area of machine learning for the goal of addressing binary and multi-class classification problems. This method was named after the inventor of the method. The approach is based on Bayes' theorem, which is a fundamental concept in probability theory that describes the link between conditional probabilities. It serves as the method's basis. Thomas Bayes was the one who came up with the Bayes' theorem. Naïve Bayesian models are probabilistic classifiers that make use of the renowned Bayesian theorem and make explicit assumptions about the independence of features in the data [7].

In the Naïve Bayes method, it is assumed that the characteristics that are used to predict the class labels are independent of one another, thus the name "Naïve." Despite this too simplistic assumption, Naïve Bayes has been found to perform very well in practice. This is particularly true when there are many characteristics, but the dataset itself is quite small.

The Bayes' theorem is used to the calculation process in order to calculate the probability of each class given the values of the attributes. The Naïve Bayes approach is responsible for this determination. In order to complete this phase, you will need to estimate not just the prior probability of each class but also the conditional probabilities of each feature, given each class. As soon as these probabilities have been computed, the algorithm will be able to make predictions for new instances by first calculating the likelihood of each class, given the feature values of the new instance, and then selecting the class that has the highest probability, given those feature values.

There are many more iterations of the Naïve Bayes approach, such as the Gaussian Naïve Bayes model, which assumes that the features are regularly distributed, and the multinomial Naïve Bayes model, which is useful for discrete data such as text classification. Both models require that the features are regularly distributed. Both models have positives and negatives associated with them. The Naïve Bayes technique is a basic and quick strategy that is often used as a baseline for assessing more complex modeling strategies.

Analyzing a patient's symptoms in addition to any other pertinent medical information may be done using the Naïve Bayes approach, which can be used in the context of medical data to estimate the likelihood that a patient suffers from a certain medical condition. This can be accomplished by using the method. The approach assumes that the attributes are conditionally independent, given the class name. This is where the phrase "Naïve" originates from.

The Naïve Bayes method is widely used for the categorization of medical data since it is efficient, easy to put into action, and can perform admirably with datasets ranging in size from small to larger. On the other hand, with huge and complicated datasets, it may not be as accurate as other, more complicated algorithms. In addition, the "Naïve" assumption of conditional independence could not hold true in certain circumstances, which would lead to outcomes that are less than ideal.

The Naïve Bayes algorithm is named as such due to the combination of the terms "Naïve" and "Bayes," which collectively describe its characteristics and approach:

o **Naïve**: The term "Naïve" in the Naïve Bayes algorithm stems from its assumption that the presence of one feature does not depend on the occurrence of other features. To illustrate, consider identifying a fruit based on its color, shape, and flavor. If a fruit is red, round, and sweet, it is considered an apple. In this case, each individual characteristic independently contributes to classifying the object as an apple, without relying on the other features.

○ **Bayes**: It is called Bayes because it depends on the principle of the Bayes' theorem.

○ Bayes' theorem, alternatively referred to as Bayes' rule or Bayes' law, is a mathematical principle employed to calculate the probability of a hypothesis, given prior knowledge or information. It relies on the concept of conditional probability, which involves determining the likelihood of an event or hypothesis occurring based on the occurrence of other related events or conditions. By applying Bayes' theorem, one can update the initial probability estimate (prior probability) of a hypothesis by incorporating additional evidence or observations (conditional probability), thus yielding a revised probability estimate known as the posterior probability.

○ The formula for Bayes' theorem is given as follows:

$$P(A|B) = \frac{P(B|A)P(A)}{P(B)}$$

where

P(A|B) **is the posterior probability**: The likelihood or probability of hypothesis A based on the occurrence of event B.

P(B|A) **is the likelihood probability**: The likelihood or probability of observing the evidence when the hypothesis is assumed to be true.

P(A) **is the prior probability**: The initial likelihood or probability assigned to the hypothesis in the absence of any observed evidence.

P(B) **is the marginal probability**: Probability of evidence.

4.2.2.6 Random forest algorithm in machine learning

Random forest (RF) is a highly popular ensemble learning method with numerous applications in medical data processing. This technique involves generating multiple classifiers and combining their results. In the case of RF, multiple classification and regression trees, also known as CART trees, are created. Each tree is trained on a bootstrap sample of the original training data and makes use of a random subset of input variables to determine the optimal split at each node [8]. By employing this approach, RF constructs a collection of decision trees by randomly selecting features at each node and utilizing bootstrap sampling from the original data. In the domain of medical data analysis, random forest finds various potential applications. Some examples include utilizing RF to predict disease outcomes, identify significant risk factors, classify medical images, detect anomalies in diagnostic tests, and assess the effectiveness of different treatment options. The versatility of random forest makes it a valuable tool for extracting meaningful insights from complex medical datasets, aiding in decision-making processes and improving patient care. In the field of medical data analysis, some possible uses of random forest include the following:

- disease diagnosis;
- risk assessment;
- treatment planning;
- drug discovery;
- patient

Overall, RF is a versatile algorithm, which can be applied to many different types of medical data analysis tasks, including disease diagnosis, risk assessment, treatment planning, drug discovery, and patient outcome prediction.

Random forest is a classification algorithm that derives its name from the fact that it consists of multiple decision trees created on different subsets of the given dataset, and the predictions of these trees are aggregated to enhance the overall predictive accuracy [9]. Rather than relying on a single decision tree, random forest combines the predictions from each tree and determines the final output based on the majority votes obtained.

Increasing the number of trees in the forest improves the accuracy of the model and mitigates the issue of overfitting.

The working of the random forest algorithm can be better understood through Figure 4.7.

Assumptions for random forest

The random forest algorithm leverages the collective predictions of multiple decision trees to determine the class of a dataset. As individual decision trees may yield correct or incorrect outputs, the combination of all trees ensures accurate predictions. Consequently, two assumptions contribute to the efficacy of a random forest classifier:

○ It is crucial to have genuine values in the feature variables of the dataset, enabling the classifier to generate precise results rather than relying on speculative guesses.

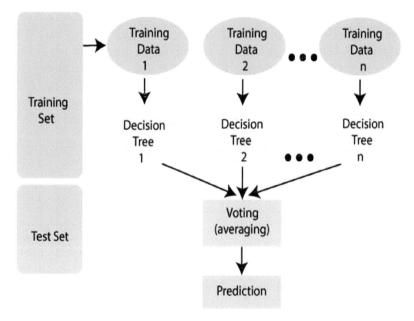

Figure 4.7   Model of random forest.

○ Secondly, to enhance the performance of the random forest classifier, it is essential for the predictions made by each tree to exhibit minimal correlation with one another.

By fulfilling these assumptions, the random forest algorithm can optimize its predictive power and provide more reliable and robust classification outcomes.

Why use random forest?

The random forest algorithm is widely recognized and favored for medical data analysis primarily due to its exceptional capability to effectively handle extensive and intricate datasets encountered in the medical field. Its unique strength lies in its capacity to efficiently process and derive insights from complex data structures commonly found in medical data. Furthermore, random forest demonstrates proficiency in handling data quality issues prevalent in real-world medical datasets, such as missing values and noisy data. By effectively addressing these challenges, random forest ensures reliable and accurate analyses, providing valuable insights for medical practitioners and researchers. Its robustness in managing large-scale data and its adaptability

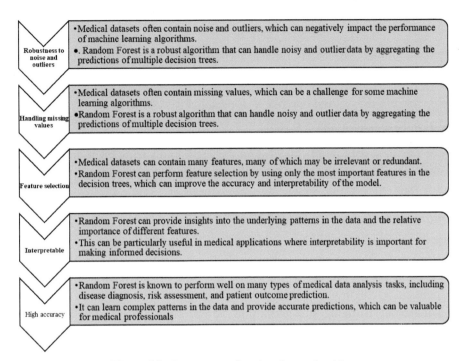

Figure 4.8   Importance of random forest algorithm.

to handle data imperfections make it an advantageous choice for medical data analysis tasks. Figure 4.8 shows some reasons why random forest may be a good choice for medical data analysis.

How does random forest algorithm work?

The random forest algorithm operates in two main phases. In the first phase, a random forest is created by combining multiple decision trees. Each decision tree is constructed using a subset of randomly selected data points from the training set. The process involves repeating the selection and building of decision trees N times, where N represents the desired number of decision trees in the random forest.

In the second phase, the random forest is utilized to make predictions. When presented with new data points, the algorithm calculates predictions for each decision tree within the random forest. Finally, the new data points are assigned to the category that receives the most votes from the decision trees.

To summarize the working process:

Step-1: Randomly select K data points from the training set.

Step-2: Build decision trees using the selected data points as subsets.

Step-3: Specify the desired number N of decision trees to be built.

Step-4: Repeat steps 1 and 2 N times.

Step-5: For new data points, determine the predictions from each decision tree and assign the new data points to the category that obtains the majority of votes from the decision trees.

Applications of random forest

There are mainly four sectors where random forest is mostly used:

1. **Banking:** The random forest algorithm is commonly employed in the banking sector to assess loan risks and aid in the identification of potential credit default or repayment challenges.
2. **Medicine:** Utilizing this algorithm, it becomes possible to identify disease trends and assess the risks associated with diseases by analyzing relevant data, enabling valuable insights for understanding and managing public health concerns.
3. **Land use:** This algorithm can be employed to identify regions with comparable land use patterns, assisting in the identification of areas characterized by similar types of land usage.
4. **Marketing:** The application of the random forest algorithm extends to the marketing domain, where it can be utilized to identify emerging marketing trends and patterns, enabling businesses to make informed decisions and develop effective marketing strategies.

4.2.2.7 Decision tree algorithm in machine learning

○ Decision tree is a versatile supervised learning technique applicable to both classification and regression problems, although it is primarily favored for solving classification tasks. Decision trees are among the most often used supervised machine learning algorithms, primarily due to their straightforward interpretation through rules they are composed of [10]. Visualizations of decision trees can help with the understanding of data and decision rules on top of them [10]. They represent a tree-like structure, where internal nodes correspond to dataset features, branches represent decision rules, and each leaf node signifies an outcome.

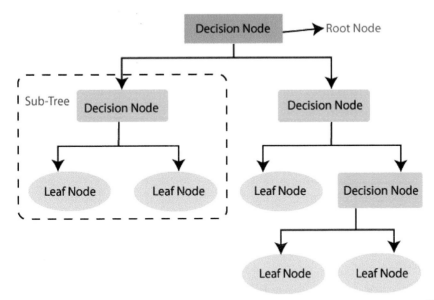

Figure 4.9 Decision Tree Algorithm in Machine Learning - Javatpoint,âĂİ www.javatpoint.com. Accessed: Dec. 13, 2023. [Online]. Available: https://www.java tpoint.com/machine-learning-decision-tree-classification-algorithm

○ In a decision tree, two types of nodes exist: Decision nodes and leaf nodes. Decision nodes facilitate decision-making and branch out into multiple paths, while leaf nodes serve as the final outputs without any further branches.

○ To construct a decision tree, the CART (classification and regression tree) algorithm is commonly employed. This algorithm recursively splits the tree based on the dataset's features, resulting in subtrees that are generated based on the answers to specific questions.

○ In essence, a decision tree poses questions and, depending on the answers (Yes/No), further divides the tree into subtrees, leading to a comprehensive and intuitive decision-making process.

Why use decision trees?

There are several reasons why decision trees can be a good choice for medical data analysis:

• **Easy to interpret:** Even non-experts may easily comprehend and make sense of the information presented in decision trees. The algorithm's decision-making process may be visualized as a flowchart, which can assist medical practitioners in gaining insights into the underlying patterns in the data. This visualization of the decision tree can be accomplished via the use of flowcharts.

- **Feature selection:** Decision trees can do feature selection, which involves determining which characteristics are the most significant for generating predictions. This may be especially helpful for medical datasets, which often consist of a huge number of attributes, the majority of which may either be superfluous or redundant.

- **Nonlinear relationships:** It is possible for decision trees to capture nonlinear correlations between the features and the goal variable. This capability might

- **Handling missing values:** It is possible for decision trees to deal with missing values by either substituting them with surrogate values or making predictions based on the data that is currently available.

- **Robustness to noise and outliers:** By recursively splitting the data into smaller subsets and making local judgments based on the information that is available, decision trees may be made to be resilient in the face of noisy and outlier data.

- **High accuracy:** When applied to medical datasets, decision trees have the potential to achieve extremely high levels of accuracy, particularly in situations in which the decision boundaries are nonlinear or when the connections between the characteristics and the target variable are intricate.

- **Treatment planning:** A patient's particular traits and medical history may be utilized in conjunction with decision trees to help determine which treatment plan will be most effective for that patient. The decision tree is able to create personalized therapy suggestions by learning from other instances that are comparable to them in the training data.

Decision tree terminologies

⇒ **Root node:** The starting node of the decision tree is known as the root node. It represents the entire dataset, which is subsequently divided into two or more sets with similar characteristics.

⇒ **Leaf node:** Terminal nodes, also referred to as leaf nodes, indicate the final output of the decision tree. Once a leaf node is reached, further segregation or division of the tree is not possible.

⇒ **Splitting:** Splitting refers to the process of dividing the decision node or root node into sub-nodes based on specific conditions provided.

⇒ **Branch/subtree:** A branch or subtree is formed as a result of the splitting process, creating a new section of the decision tree.

⇒ **Pruning:** Pruning involves the elimination of unwanted branches from the tree, streamlining and simplifying the structure.

⇒ **Parent/child node:** The root node of the tree is considered the parent node, while the remaining nodes are referred to as child nodes, forming the hierarchical structure of the decision tree.

How does the decision tree algorithm work?

In a decision tree, the algorithm begins at the root node to predict the class of a given dataset. It compares the attribute value of the root node with the corresponding attribute value in the dataset and follows the branch that corresponds to the comparison. The process continues as it moves to the next node, comparing attribute values and traversing through the tree until it reaches a leaf node.

The complete process can be better understood using the below algorithm:

- **Step-1:** Start with the root node, denoted as S, which contains the entire dataset.
- **Step-2:** Determine the best attribute by employing an attribute selection measure (ASM) to evaluate the dataset.
- **Step-3:** Divide the dataset into subsets based on the possible attribute values identified in step 2.
- **Step-4:** Create a decision tree node that represents the best attribute.
- **Step-5:** Recursively construct new decision trees using the subsets of the dataset created in step 3. This process continues until reaching a stage where further classification is not possible, resulting in the creation of leaf nodes.

By following these steps, the decision tree algorithm progressively constructs a tree structure that enables the classification of the given dataset.

Attribute selection measures:

During the implementation of a decision tree, a crucial challenge is selecting the optimal attribute for the root node and subsequent sub-nodes. To address this issue, the attribute selection measure (ASM) technique is employed. ASM assists in determining the most suitable attribute for each node in the tree, facilitating effective decision-making. ASM encompasses two widely adopted techniques for attribute selection. These techniques aid in identifying the attribute with the most significant impact on the classification process within the decision tree.

There are two popular techniques for ASM, which are:

○ Information gain
○ Gini index

1. Information gain:

○ Information gain serves as a metric for evaluating the alteration in entropy when a dataset is divided based on a specific attribute.
○ It quantifies the amount of information a feature contributes toward class determination.
○ By considering the information gain value, the decision tree algorithm determines the splitting of nodes and constructs the decision tree accordingly.
○ The objective is to maximize information gain, prioritizing the splitting of nodes/attributes with the highest information gain. It can be calculated using the below formula:

In formation Gain = Entropy (S) − [(Weighted Avg.) × Entropy (each feature)" is correct as set.Gain = Entropy (S) − [(Weighted Avg.) × Entropy (each feature)

Entropy: Entropy is a metric to measure the impurity in each attribute. It specifies randomness in data. Entropy can be calculated as follows:

Entropy (S) = −P(yes)log2 P(yes) − P(no) log2 P(no)

where

○ S = total number of samples
○ P(yes) = probability of yes
○ P(no) = probability of no

2. Gini index:

○ The Gini index, utilized within the CART (classification and regression tree) algorithm, serves as a measure to assess the impurity or purity of

a decision tree. In the CART algorithm, an attribute with a lower Gini index is favored over one with a higher Gini index.
o This index is employed for creating binary splits, as the CART algorithm utilizes it to generate such splits.
o The Gini index can be computed using the formula:
Gini index = $1 - \sum_j Pj{\wedge}2$.

Pruning: Pruning is a technique employed to obtain an optimal decision tree by removing unnecessary nodes. An excessively large tree increases the risk of overfitting, while a small tree may fail to capture essential dataset features. Therefore, pruning is a methodology aimed at reducing the size of the decision tree without sacrificing accuracy. Two primary pruning techniques are commonly used to achieve this objective.

There are mainly two types of trees that pruning technology used:

o Cost complexity pruning
o Reduced error pruning

Advantages of the decision tree

o Decision trees are easily comprehensible, as they follow a human-like decision-making process.
o They are highly valuable in solving decision-related problems and aid in exploring all potential outcomes.
o Decision trees facilitate thorough the consideration of various possibilities for a problem.
o Compared to other algorithms, decision trees require less data cleaning.

Disadvantages of the decision tree:

o Decision trees can become complex due to the presence of multiple layers.
o Overfitting can occur in decision trees, although this issue can be mitigated by employing the random forest algorithm.
o The computational complexity of decision trees may increase with a higher number of class labels.

4.2.3 Introduction to Clustering

Clustering is an attractive approach for finding similarities in data and putting similar data into groups [11]. The techniques of clustering are among the most valuable unsupervised machine learning approaches. These approaches are used to discover patterns of similarity and association across data samples and then cluster those samples into groups with comparable characteristics based on the qualities they share.

The significance of clustering lies in the fact that it reveals the natural divisions that exist within the currently unlabeled data. To determine the degree to which two sets of data are comparable, they simply speculate about certain data points. Each assumption will produce distinct clusters, but all of them will be equally legitimate.

4.2.3.1 Cluster formation methods

It is not necessary that clusters will be formed in a spherical form. Following are some other cluster formation methods.

Density-based

Cluster formation methods are not limited to spherical shapes; alternative methods exist. These include density-based methods, where clusters are identified as dense regions. These methods offer high accuracy and the ability to merge clusters effectively. Examples include density-based spatial clustering of applications with noise (DBSCAN) and ordering points to identify clustering structure (OPTICS).

Hierarchical-based

Hierarchical-based methods create clusters in a hierarchical tree structure. There are two categories: agglomerative (bottom-up approach) and divisive (top-down approach). Clustering using representatives (CURE) and balanced iterative reducing clustering using hierarchies (BIRCH) are examples of hierarchical-based methods.

Partitioning

Partitioning methods involve dividing objects into k clusters, with the number of clusters equal to the number of partitions. K-means and clustering large applications based upon randomized search (CLARANS) are examples of partitioning methods.

Grid:

Grid-based methods form clusters in a grid-like structure. These methods offer fast clustering operations that are independent of the number of data objects. Statistical information grid (STING) and clustering in quest (CLIQUE) are examples of grid-based methods.

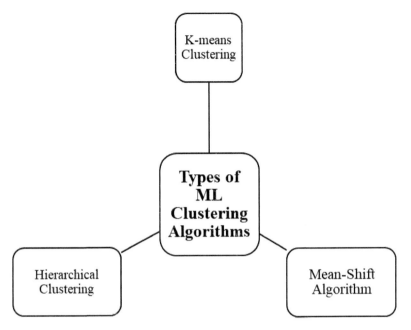

Figure 4.10 Types of clustering algorithms.

4.2.3.2 Types of machine learning clustering algorithms
The following are the most important and useful ML clustering algorithms.

4.2.3.2.1 Applications of clustering
We can find clustering useful in the following areas.

Data summarization and compression: Clustering aids in summarizing, compressing, and reducing data, with applications in image processing and vector quantization.

Collaborative systems and customer segmentation: Clustering is beneficial for identifying similar products or grouping users, enabling its use in collaborative systems and customer segmentation.

Intermediate step for other data mining tasks: Cluster analysis provides a concise data summary, which serves as a vital intermediate step for tasks like classification, testing, and hypothesis generation in data mining.

Trend detection in dynamic data: Clustering is useful for detecting trends in dynamic data by creating clusters of similar trends.

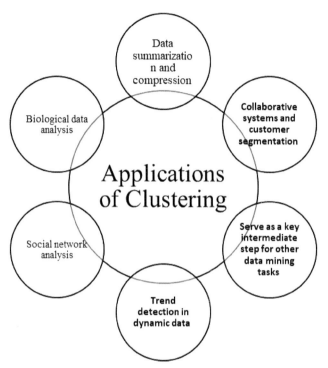

Figure 4.11   Application of clustering.

Social network analysis: Clustering techniques have applications in social network analysis, such as generating sequences in images, videos, or audios.

Biological data analysis: Clustering can be employed to group images or videos in biological data analysis, offering valuable insights in this domain.

4.2.3.3 K-means algorithm in machine learning

The K-means clustering algorithm is a straightforward method with low computational complexity and generates non-overlapping clusters [12]. It iteratively calculates centroids until an optimal solution is found, assuming the number of clusters is predetermined. This algorithm, known as a flat clustering algorithm, represents the number of clusters as "K" in K-means. It is also called flat clustering algorithm. The algorithm assigns data points to clusters by minimizing the sum of squared distances between the data points and centroids. A smaller variation within clusters results in a higher similarity among data points within the same cluster.

Working of K-means algorithm

The K-means clustering algorithm operates through the following steps:

Step 1: Determine the desired number of clusters, K, for the algorithm.
Step 2: Randomly select K data points and assign each point to a cluster.
Step 3: Calculate the cluster centroids.
Step 4: Iterate the following steps until an optimal centroid assignment is achieved:

- Compute the sum of squared distances between data points and centroids.
- Assign each data point to the closest cluster (centroid).
- Calculate new centroids by averaging the data points within each cluster.

K-means employs the expectation−maximization approach, where the expectation step assigns data points to the closest cluster, and the maximization step calculates the centroid for each cluster.

When using the K-means algorithm, it is recommended to standardize the data to ensure reliable results since the algorithm utilizes distance-based measurements. Additionally, due to the iterative nature and random initialization of centroids, K-means may converge to a local optimum rather than the global optimum. To mitigate this, different initializations of centroids can be tried.

Advantages:

The following are some advantages of K-means clustering algorithms:

- K-means is easy to understand and implement.
- It is faster than hierarchical clustering for datasets with many variables.
- Instances can change clusters upon re-computation of centroids.
- K-means tends to form tighter clusters compared to hierarchical clustering.

Disadvantages:

The following are some disadvantages of K-means clustering algorithms:

- Determining the appropriate number of clusters (K) can be challenging.
- The output is strongly influenced by the initial inputs, such as the number of clusters.
- The order of data can impact the final output.
- K-means is sensitive to rescaling, and changing the data scale can lead to different results.

- It may not perform well when clusters have complex geometric shapes.

Applications of K-means clustering algorithm:

Cluster analysis aims to achieve the following objectives:

- Obtain meaningful insights from the data under analysis.
- Enable cluster-specific predictions by building distinct models for different subgroups.

To fulfill these objectives, the K-means clustering algorithm is effective and finds utility in various applications, including:

- Market segmentation
- Document clustering
- Image segmentation
- Image compression
- Customer segmentation
- Analyzing trends in dynamic data

4.2.3.4 Mean-shift algorithm in machine learning

Mean shift is an iterative procedure that shifts each data point toward the average of the data points within its neighborhood [13]. It has been generalized, encompassing various k-means-like clustering algorithms. This technique operates as a mode-seeking process on a surface constructed using a "shadow kernel" [13]. The mean-shift method is a non-parametric clustering approach applicable to medical data, enabling the detection of clusters. The algorithm gradually moves the centroid of a cluster closer to the mean of the data points within a specified bandwidth, facilitating its functionality. Here is how the mean-shift algorithm can be applied to medical data.

Overall, the mean-shift method is valuable for clustering medical data and can aid in identifying subgroups with similar medical conditions or risk factors. However, it is crucial to carefully select the bandwidth parameter as it affects the performance of the algorithm. Additionally, for large datasets, the mean-shift method may not be as effective in achieving accurate clustering results.

Working of mean-shift algorithm

The mean-shift clustering algorithm operates through the following steps:

- Initially, each data point is assigned to its own cluster.
- The algorithm computes the centroids of these clusters.

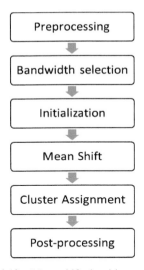

Figure 4.12 Mean-shift algorithm procedure.

- The centroids are updated to new positions.
- The process iterates, shifting toward higher density regions.
- The algorithm stops when the centroids reach positions where further movement is not possible.

Advantages

The following are some advantages of the mean-shift clustering algorithm:

- The mean-shift algorithm does not require any assumptions about the underlying model, unlike K-means or Gaussian mixture models.
- It can model complex clusters with non-convex shapes.
- The algorithm automatically determines the number of clusters based on a single parameter called bandwidth.
- There is no issue of local minima, as encountered in K-means.
- Outliers do not pose a problem.

Disadvantages

The following are some disadvantages of the mean-shift clustering algorithm:

- Mean-shift may not perform well in high-dimensional spaces where the number of clusters changes abruptly.

- It lacks direct control over the number of clusters, which can be problematic in certain applications that require a specific number of clusters.
- The algorithm may struggle to differentiate between meaningful and meaningless modes.

4.2.3.5 Hierarchical clustering in machine learning

A clustering method known as hierarchical clustering may be used to medical data points in order to put them together into clusters that are like one another. The method is designed to function by constructing a hierarchy of clusters, with the first step being the consolidation of individual data points into bigger groups. Hierarchical trees provide a view of the data at different levels of abstraction. Hierarchical clustering is another unsupervised learning algorithm that is used to group together the unlabeled data points having similar characteristics [14].

Hierarchical clustering is an unsupervised learning algorithm used to group unlabeled data points with similar characteristics. It can be categorized into two types: agglomerative hierarchical algorithms and divisive hierarchical algorithms.

Agglomerative hierarchical algorithms: Agglomerative hierarchical algorithms treat each data point as a separate cluster and gradually merge or agglomerate clusters from the bottom-up. The resulting hierarchy of clusters is represented as a dendrogram or tree structure.

Divisive hierarchical algorithms: Divisive hierarchical algorithms, on the other hand, start with all data points as one large cluster and proceed by dividing or splitting the big cluster into smaller clusters using a top-down approach.

Steps to perform agglomerative hierarchical clustering:

We will explain the widely used and important hierarchical clustering technique, specifically the agglomerative approach. The steps for performing agglomerative hierarchical clustering are as follows:

Step 1: Initially, each data point is treated as an individual cluster, resulting in K clusters, where K is the number of data points.

Step 2: Next, the two closest data points are merged to form a larger cluster, resulting in $K - 1$ clusters.

Step 3: To form additional clusters, the process continues by merging the two closest existing clusters, reducing the total number of clusters to $K - 2$.

Advantages	Disadvantages
• Interpretability • Flexibility • Scalability	• Computationally expensive • Sensitivity to the choice of linkage method • Difficulty in determining the number of clusters

Figure 4.13   Advantages and disadvantages of hierarchical clustering.

Step 4: This merging of clusters is repeated until only one big cluster remains, meaning K becomes 0 and no more data points are available to merge.

Step 5: Finally, dendrograms are used to divide the single big cluster into multiple clusters based on the specific problem requirements.

Advantages and disadvantages of hierarchical clustering:
When used in medical data, the common clustering method known as hierarchical clustering has both benefits and drawbacks, depending on the context. Using hierarchical clustering for medical data has several benefits and drawbacks, the most important of which are detailed in Figure 4.13.

4.3 Conclusion

Hierarchical clustering is a technology that is both effective and adaptable for the clustering of medical data. However, the outcomes of the clustering might be impacted by the distance measure, linking technique, and the number of clusters that are used. Additionally, the procedure may be computationally costly for big datasets.

References

[1] R. Sharma, S. N. Singh, and S. Khatri, "Medical Data Mining Using Different Classification and Clustering Techniques: A Critical Survey," in 2016 Second International Conference on Computational Intelligence

& Communication Technology (CICT), Ghaziabad, India: IEEE, Feb. 2016, pp. 687–691. doi: 10.1109/CICT.2016.142.

[2] M. Zhu et al., "Class Weights Random Forest Algorithm for Processing Class Imbalanced Medical Data," IEEE Access, vol. 6, pp. 4641–4652, 2018, doi: 10.1109/ACCESS.2018.2789428.

[3] M. Puttagunta and S. Ravi, "Medical image analysis based on deep learning approach," Multimed. Tools Appl., vol. 80, no. 16, pp. 24365–24398, Jul. 2021, doi: 10.1007/s11042-021-10707-4.

[4] S. Dreiseitl and L. Ohno-Machado, "Logistic regression and artificial neural network classification models: a methodology review," J. Biomed. Inform., vol. 35, no. 5, pp. 352–359, Oct. 2002, doi:10.101 6/S1532-0464(03)00034-0.

[5] Y. Weng, C. Wu, Q. Jiang, W. Guo, and C. Wang, "Application of support vector machines in medical data," in 2016 4th International Conference on Cloud Computing and Intelligence Systems (CCIS), Beijing, China: IEEE, Aug. 2016, pp. 200–204. doi:10.1109/CCIS.2 016.7790253.

[6] W. Xing and Y. Bei, "Medical Health Big Data Classification Based on KNN Classification Algorithm," IEEE Access, vol. 8, pp. 28808–28819, 2020, doi: 10.1109/ACCESS.2019.2955754.

[7] N. Boyko and K. Boksho, "Application of the Naive Bayesian Classifier in Work on Sentimental Analysis of Medical Data".

[8] M. Khalilia, S. Chakraborty, and M. Popescu, "Predicting disease risks from highly imbalanced data using random forest," BMC Med. Inform. Decis. Mak., vol. 11, no. 1, p. 51, Jul. 2011, doi:10.1186/1472-6947-11 -51.

[9] R. Supriya and S. Kalaiarasi, "Comparing and Improving the Novel Random Forest Algorithm to Logistic Regression Classifier for the Analysis and Accuracy of Fake Notes," J. Surv. Fish. Sci., vol. 10, no. 1S, Art. no. 1S, Mar. 2023, doi: 10.17762/sfs.v10i1S.439.

[10] J. Mrva, Š. Neupauer, L. Hudec, J. Ševcech, and P. Kapec, "Decision Support in Medical Data Using 3D Decision Tree Visualisation," in 2019 E-Health and Bioengineering Conference (EHB), Nov. 2019, pp. 1–4. doi: 10.1109/EHB47216.2019.8969926.

[11] R. Paul and A. S. Md. L. Hoque, "Clustering medical data to predict the likelihood of diseases," in 2010 Fifth International Conference on Digital Information Management (ICDIM), Thunder Bay, ON, Canada: IEEE, Jul. 2010, pp. 44–49. doi: 10.1109/ICDIM.2010.5664638.

[12] H. P. Ng, S. H. Ong, K. W. C. Foong, P. S. Goh, and W. L. Nowinski, "Medical Image Segmentation Using K-Means Clustering and Improved Watershed Algorithm," in 2006 IEEE Southwest Symposium on Image Analysis and Interpretation, Denver, CO: IEEE, 2006, pp. 61–65. doi: 10.1109/SSIAI.2006.1633722.

[13] Yizong Cheng, "Mean shift, mode seeking, and clustering," IEEE Trans. Pattern Anal. Mach. Intell., vol. 17, no. 8, pp. 790–799, Aug. 1995, doi: 10.1109/34.400568.

[14] Y. Zhao, G. Karypis, and U. Fayyad, "Hierarchical Clustering Algorithms for Document Datasets," Data Min. Knowl. Discov., vol. 10, no. 2, pp. 141–168, Mar. 2005, doi:10.1007/s10618-005-0361-3.

5

Optimized Data Retrieval and Data Storage for Healthcare Applications

Pritam Ramesh Ahire[1], Rohini Hanchate[2], and K. Kalaiselvi[3]

[1,2]Assistant Professor, Department of Computer Engineering, Nutan
Maharashtra Institute of Engineering and Technology SPPU,
Pune, Maharashtra
[3]Department of Data Analytics, Saveetha College of Liberal Arts
and Sciences, SIMATS, Chennai, India
E-mail: rohini.shanchate@gmail.com; pritamahire33@gmail.com;
kalaiselvik.sclas@saveetha.com

Abstract

Huge collection of medical datasets from research organisations like hospital
services, institutes, and medical research centres and the use of that data for
subsequent experiments to improve the development of novel treatments for
difficult medical conditions. Such information retrieval systems are designed
to enhance the healthcare system, speed up illness diagnosis, and attempt
to provide patients with better alternatives to traditional medical care. The
internet majorly deals with the entire world being interconnected, making
it incredibly simple for institutions doing medical research to exchange
medical reports and data. They are not obligated to repeat tests that have
previously been conducted in any nation. With the use of gathered medical data from experts in one nation, studies or healthcare institutions can
carry out the next stage of studies. Even nations can collaborate to conduct
medical studies using the recovered data and exchange medical knowledge.
Nonetheless, the goal of this research was to examine the value of medical
information retrieval, its techniques, and the ways in which it might benefit healthcare. In various studies, it is highlighted that the research faces
a number of obstacles because the languages of the various nations vary.

As medical terminology varies from country to country, it can occasionally be challenging to synchronise the information gleaned from various sources. The major challenge is to achieve accuracy in the data.

Although the majority of work in healthcare data analytics focuses on mining and analysing patient data, there is also a massive pool of scientific data and literature that may be used in this process. Today's most popular access methods are those from the information retrieval (IR), sometimes known as search, field. Usually defined as data obtained and structured via observation or experimental study, IR is the discipline concerned with the collection, organisation, and querying of knowledge-based data. Although information retrieval (IR) in biomedical science has traditionally focused on the retrieval of text from the biomedical literature, the scope of content covered has expanded to include newer types of media such as images, video, chemical structures, gene and protein sequences, and a wide range of other digital media relevant to biomedical education, research, and patient care. Even the idea of a library has evolved significantly as a result of the widespread use of IR systems and online information, with the emergence of new digital libraries. The use of IR systems is now practically universal. According to estimates, more than 80% of Americans who use the Internet do so to look for personal health information. Almost all doctors utilise the internet; moreover, access to systems has expanded beyond the standard personal computer and now includes cutting-edge devices like smart devices. Major data retrieval systems for cloud systems, such as AWS, are defined in this chapter to achieve efficient healthcare data access. Addressed the various challenges of these storage systems.

Keywords: Healthcare, cloud, storage system, AWS, information retrieval.

5.1 Introduction

Public healthcare data collection, consumption, collection, and exchange have undergone a significant change. The healthcare business has come a long way in refining its methods for managing data, from traditional storage to digitization of healthcare information.

Healthcare is setting the bar for cloud migration in a sector that has often trailed behind its peers. 35% of the healthcare system firms assessed by West Monroe Partners had more than 50 percent of their infrastructure or data stored on the cloud. So, when compared to other businesses, healthcare showed that it was the most advanced in terms of cloud usage.

More than merely data storage in cloud environments is involved in the broad adoption of cloud computing in the healthcare industry. In order to increase efficiency, streamline processes, save costs involved with providing medical care, and give personalization to treatment plans to enhance results, health practitioners are now utilising this technology.

The goal of this type of data recovery architecture is to enhance the delivery of human services, quickly identify infections, and seek to provide patients with superior replacement medical interventions. The globe is now connected via the internet, making it incredibly simple for therapeutic research organisations to exchange medical information and test results. They are not compelled to conduct the same trials that have recently taken place across the nation. With the aid of therapeutic data obtained from the scientists of one nation, the examining or medicinal services research organisations might carry out all the subsequent levels of trials. It is true that even countries may exchange medical data and work together to conduct therapeutic research using the data they have retrieved. Yet the purpose of this investigation is to consider the value of clinical information, retrieval of healthcare information.

5.1.1 Data retrieval system

There are basically two methods for retrieval. The user has precise control over the objects obtained, thanks to exact-match searching. On the other hand, partial-match searching aims to deliver user material rated by how closely it matches the user's query, despite the imperfection of both indexing and retrieval. After generic descriptions of these techniques, we will present actual systems that access diverse forms of biological material.

5.1.2 Exact-match retrieval

While using accurate searches, the Retrieval system presents the user with all articles that precisely match the search parameters. This kind of finding is sometimes referred to as boolean searching since the Boolean operators AND, OR, and NOT are frequently needed to produce a reasonable group of data. Moreover, this method is also known as set-based searching since the user often creates sets of documents that are controlled with Boolean operators. Even though Salton and McGill were developing the partial-match technique in research systems during that period, the majority of the early operational IR systems from the 1950s through the 1970s employed the exact-match approach. In the present day, retrieval is connected to various databases like bibliographic and annotated databases with exact-match searching, full-text searching, and partial-match searching. In exact-match retrieval, the initial step is to choose words from which to create sets. Additional characteristics, such as the name of the author, the nature of the publication, or the gene identification, may also be chosen to form sets. Using Boolean operators, search term(s) and attribute(s) are merged. A retrieval set is often narrowed to only include documents with two or more ideas using the Boolean AND operator. When a topic may be expressed in more than one form, the Boolean OR operator is typically employed. Boolean NOT operator as a subtraction operator that has to be applied to another set. Some systems more appropriately term this the ANDNOT Some systems more appropriately term this the "ANDNOT operator" [1]. The wild-card character, which adds any words to the search that start with the letters up until the wild-card character, can be used to broaden keywords in searches in some retrieval systems. It is also referred to as truncation. However, employing wild-card characters is not standardised; so the syntax differs from system to system. For instance, PubMed permits a single asterisk to serve as a wild-card character at the end of a term. As a result, adding the phrases cancer and candid to the search as a result of the query word

5.1.3 Partial-match retrieval

Although partial-match searching was envisaged fairly early, it wasn't until the introduction of major search engines in the 1990s that it was extensively used in IR systems. It is most likely due to the fact that "power users" favour exact-match searching, while beginner searchers prefer partial-match searching. Partial-match searching allows a user to enter a few phrases and immediately begin receiving articles, in contrast to exact-match searching, which necessitates knowledge of Boolean operators and (often) the underlying structure of databases (such as the several fields in PubMed). Whoever invented partial-match searching in the 1960s is typically credited with its development.

5.1.4 Retrieval systems

Extraction interfaces come in a wide variety, with a few of their attributes mirroring the structure or content of the underlying database. The NLM's mechanism for searching MEDLINE and other bibliographic databases is PubMed, as mentioned. While providing the user with a straightforward text field, PubMed processes the user's input extensively to recognise MeSH keywords, author names, common phrases, and journal titles. The algorithm tries to match user input to MeSH keywords, journal titles, common phrases, and authors in this automated keyword mapping [2].

PubMed searches text terms to find the remaining text that it cannot map (i.e., words that occur in any of the MEDLINE fields). The technology enables a straightforward search and then gives users access to a wide range of details associated with the results, it can set limits for research type (e.g., randomised controlled trial), species (e.g., human or others), and age group (e.g., age >65 years). Filters for free full-text articles and reviews are available on the right side, along with additional elements like the search's specifics. Users are able to browse PubMed by creating search sets and then combining them using Boolean operators to specifically target their search, as is common practise in most bibliographic systems.

5.2 Data Storage and Managing in Healthcare in Cloud, AI

Data storage options for hospitals. The storage of healthcare data is essential for effective data management. Pharmaceutical businesses may employ cloud, on premise, or a combination of the two. Here are five choices for storing healthcare data to assist you in managing an expanding data set.

5.2.1 Storage network systems (SAN)

Several hosts or devices can connect to a high-performance network of storage devices known as a SAN via specialised fiber channel pipelines. SAN enables the direct transfer of medical data and pictures from storage to workstations without taxing the capacity of already overburdened hospital servers. This helps to:

- Cut down on issues related to latency;
- Reduce issues related to bandwidth;
- Increase the transmission speed of data;
- Expand workflows within hospital departments.

A separate, private network between client and server will enhance SAN performance. It will provide access to the photo archiving and communication systems in practically real-time while keeping file request traffic out of the fibre channel network (PACS).

5.2.2 Nas (network-attached storage) (NAS)

A NAS is a single storage device that gives network access to all the devices, as opposed to a SAN, which is a local network of several devices. It enables hospitals with LAN connections to use an Ethernet connection to get data from a centralised disc storage.

Hospitals get the following benefits with NAS:

Consistently high data sharing; strict access to privacy and security; RAID arrays' provision of data resilience; simple implementation and configuration. Hospital networks with large volumes of corporate data use NAS to support collaboration between their units [3].

5.2.3 External storage devices

According to statistics, 62% of mid- to low-level hospitals store healthcare data, such as radiological pictures, insurance claims, and even electronic medical records, on SSDs, tapes, and discs (EMR). These straightforward, no-setup storage devices are a tempting target for hackers, though. It is imperative to encrypt data if you don't want to become like Cedar Springs Hospital, which lost an unencrypted portable storage device with patient health information in October 2020. Data backups work well with SSDs. Yet, when used as primary storage, they segregate data and render it unavailable for electronic HIE.

5.2.4 Outsourced storage solutions

You'll rack up a sizable expense for hardware and labour if you keep all those amounts of data in on-premise storage facilities. Operating costs can be reduced by transferring to servers run off-site by other businesses. According to statistics, 93% of hospitals plan to outsource their data centres and IT infrastructure in 2021, and 96% will do the same with their database management and analytics.

Healthcare organisations don't solely pick outsourced storage solutions to reduce expenses, though. In order to secure PHI and reduce the danger of healthcare data leaks and fines, several suppliers offer HIPAA, HITECH, and PCI DSS compliance. As a result, hospitals may relieve themselves of this responsibility.

5.2.5 Cloud data storage

To save money on keeping physical data centres on-site, hospitals are migrating their data to the cloud. Also, it gives them greater flexibility in terms of the server space they buy. It's understandable why the healthcare cloud computing industry is anticipated to increase by 14% annually from 2019 to 2026, reaching a value of over $40 billion.

Apart from saving costs, cloud system benefits include:

- Government regulations, compliance, and data security; rapid recovery and backup; faster, safer, and simpler HIE.
- Back-end processes that are automated and simple extension possibilities.

Having said that, moving healthcare data to the cloud is not a rapid resolution for all the issues the industry is having with data storage. The data explosion is forcing healthcare organisations to re-evaluate their infrastructure and storage options. Let's talk about the issues that can make it difficult for them to succeed [4].

The market for healthcare data storage, which was $3.08 billion in 2017, is expected to expand by 10.7% a year through 2027 to reach $6.12 billion. Large amounts of healthcare data needed to be stored and maintained, but the sector was not really ready for that. Here are some of the reasons why managing healthcare data might be difficult for medical professionals.

5.3 Healthcare Provider Data Warehouse Architecture

Understanding the foundational elements of a healthcare data warehouse is essential before constructing one. The following layers make up an enterprise data warehouse architecture that can meet healthcare intelligence and analytics needs.

5.3.1 Layer of data sources

This is made up of data sources that include information important to healthcare professionals. The many sorts of information utilised in healthcare might originate from sources including surveys and EHR reports. CRM systems, prescriptions, radiology reports, and ERP systems are shown in Figure 5.1.

- **Staging Layer:**

A staging area temporarily stores and processes data coming in from disparate sources. Here, ETL (extract, transform, and load) processes are employed to transform, cleanse, and prepare large swathes of data for unified storage and analysis.

- **Data Storage Layer:**

Data storage is a centralised location where ETL/ELT operations' loaded data is kept. For reporting and analytics, it stores and organizes structured

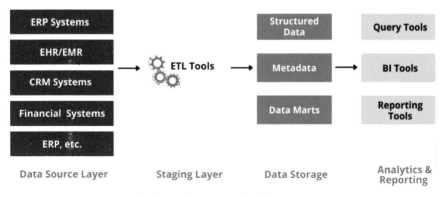

Figure 5.1   Layered architecture.

data. Data marts, which are DWH subsets created for various business domains, can also be carried by the data storage layer.

- **Layer for Analytics and Reporting:**

Data analytics and business intelligence tools are the last layer, which are used to extract useful information from data. With the use of thorough reports, infographics, graphs, charts, and summaries, BI tools may access data from the healthcare data warehouse and communicate analytics and insights.

5.3.2 Key features of a healthcare data warehouse

The adoption of a value-based strategy for healthcare delivery and patient-centred care is made possible by the use of a potent healthcare data warehouse. The healthcare DWH must, however, adhere to specific requirements in order to be successful. Moreover, due to the sensitive nature of health-related data, it must be handled with care and accuracy.

These are a few essential components that any healthcare data warehouse has to consider.

Performance of the Data Warehouse:
Rapid retrieval of data that is ready for analysis and speedy query execution are essential capabilities of trustworthy healthcare data warehouses. The following characteristics demonstrate how well data warehousing techniques work:

- Powerful parallel processing;

- Storage systems may divide labour-intensive querying jobs into manageable, parallel-processable units with the help of parallelization;
- Data Warehouse Automation.

Powerful data warehouse automation technologies, like Astera DW Builder, can automate whole data pipelines inside a DWH design to decrease time-to-market. With automation, data is processed and sent automatically by the data warehouse from the source to the data storage layer. By doing this, healthcare users are guaranteed timely access to essential data without dependent on the time-consuming manual upgrading of the database system [5].

5.3.3 Cloud-based healthcare data storage

Wherever consumers and patients are in contact with one another, including through healthcare management systems and wearable technology, digital health-related data are becoming more prevalent. Nevertheless, the sole source of truth for a person's personal health information is not owned by or under their control.

Now, the providers that submit the data—device makers, hospitals, medical practises, and pharmacies—have control over it since they keep the data for their own specific purposes [6]. An individual can opt to share their health and medical data with providers, allowing them to add or retrieve data as needed. This would be possible with cloud-based solutions for healthcare data storage.

The following are some current restrictions on the collection and utilisation of personally enabled health records:

- Systems are not interconnected, and obtaining integration will probably be the biggest challenge.
- In electronic health record (EHR) systems, data and data models are frequently private and jealously guarded.
- With the possible exception of data taken by smart gadgets, people have very little insight into the data and how it is used.

5.3.4 Data storage using AWS

By 2020, there will be 35 zettabytes of healthcare data, which is anticipated to be created at an ever-increasing rate. For healthcare providers, the ability to handle this data affordably, securely, and for legal, research, or other purposes is becoming increasingly crucial.

Healthcare providers must be able to take in, store, and safeguard large volumes of data, including clinical, genetic, device, financial, supply chain, and claims data. AWS is a good system for managing healthcare data since it has a broad variety of ingestion, backup, and security methods (such as AWS Direct Connect, Amazon Kinesis Streams, Amazon S3, and Amazon Macie) available. In a recent article by Healthcare IT News, a healthcare thought leader noted, "I believe that five years from now, none of us will have data centres." We'll discover more than the cloud system.

Even storing this data is a difficult task. Security is a top priority because healthcare data is becoming more and more alluring to cybercriminals, which makes the problem worse. Individual clinical information is said to have a black market value of hundreds or even thousands of dollars [13].

In addition to the ubiquitous electronic health record (EHR), the sources of this data include:

Genomic sequencers, data from MRIs, X-rays, and ultrasounds, and sensor-enabled wearable gadgets for patients medical equipment like mobile apps, telemetry, human resources, billing management, and finance.

These information sources can provide both organised (such as claims data) and unstructured data (e.g., clinician notes). Some data is transmitted in streams, such as that obtained from patient monitors, while other data are sent in batch format. HL7 messages are one more type of data that arrives in close to real time. Retention guidelines specify how long each piece of data must be kept on file. Due to the lack of a purge mechanism in many current systems, a large portion of this data is kept in storage forever. All of these data types, as well as their access, security, and retention restrictions, may be managed using AWS's services.

5.4 Advantages of Cloud Storage for Clinical Data

How can healthcare businesses use the cloud to boost innovation and ensure continuous operations? With the help of a data fabric that takes advantage of complete data portability, accessibility for any task in any environment, and the advantages that follow:

⇒ Simple Access to Patient Records in Electronic Form:

For proper diagnosis, effective treatment, and continuous care, quick and simple access to critical medical data is crucial. The care team may always act on the most recent information when health records, patient histories, test results, pictures, and other diagnostic data are uploaded into the cloud.

⇒ Role-Based, Gated Availability of Sensitive Health Information:

Providing sensitive data with authorised access is made simpler by cloud technology. For instance, front-line carers might not have access to some patients financial information, such as their payment histories. Similar to how medical and surgical information might be withheld from back-office staff members who don't require it for their jobs.

⇒ Integration with Multiple Applications, Systems, and Third Parties:

Every user or application with a validated need to view and act on the information can access cloud-based medical data. This facilitates the inspection and modification of electronic health records or medical information by upstream and downstream software, systems, and third parties. To check for unintended medication interactions, a pharmacist may, for instance, review a patient's prescriptions. The patient's medical history might also be simply forwarded by a family physician to a specialist for a more accurate diagnosis and course of action [7].

⇒ Easier Collaboration and Handover Between Healthcare Teams and
   Providers:

One of the biggest obstacles to providing quality patient care today is medical error. As data on the cloud is updated in real time, doctors and others always have the most recent information to comprehend and discuss treatment alternatives. Almost everyone has access to the most current patient history for enhanced continuity of treatment, whether there is a handover between healthcare teams during a shift change or a patient is transferred to a new provider.

⇒ Cloud-Based AI and Analysis for Identifying Trends and Improvements:

The healthcare sector as a whole will benefit from improved diagnostics because of machine intelligence and AI. Forecasting, illness modelling, and clinical outcome optimisation may all be done with consolidated and anonymized patient data. Big insights may reveal patterns that can be used in new medication discovery, additional study, or alternate medical diagnostics.

⇒ Continual Backup of Important Healthcare Information:

Healthcare data is backed up in real time by cloud services. Healthcare providers may simply and swiftly recover data in the case of component failure, outages, or data leaks with the least possible impact on patient care. Multiple recovery options, like live restores for instant failover, incremental backups, and data copies.

⇒ Greater Control of Capital and Operational Expenditure through On-Demand Healthcare Storage:

The absence of upfront expenditures to purchase physical servers and other infrastructure is one of the key advantages of the cloud. The majority of providers instead let businesses just pay for the resources they really use. This enables healthcare professionals to pay periodically, depending on the cloud-stored data. For operational cost management and minimising expenditures, this may be quite helpful [8].

For many firms, switching to cloud-based healthcare data storage makes sense. The appropriate patient data can be provided to the correct clinicians at the right time, thanks to appropriate permission, validation, and quick access to the records. The updating of test findings by laboratories and the use of linked systems to help with medical care are both facilitated by healthcare data interfaces. From a business standpoint, larger data sets and more powerful computers aid in research and the advancement of healthcare. Each firm will benefit from improved cost management and the security of backup data.

By putting data to work improving patient outcomes, streamlining and speeding access to critical clinical data, and running any application on-premises or in the cloud, NetApp unleashes the power of the cloud in healthcare. NetApp solutions deliver the performance, reliability, efficiency, and protection that today's demanding healthcare environment requires.

In order to drive digitalization in healthcare, Red8 and NetApp collaborate. Red8 and NetApp made it possible for AltaMed, a renowned healthcare institution serving more than 300,000 Southern Californians, to transition from a dispersed infrastructure to one that is unified, straightforward, and ideally adapted for expansion. Red8 and NetApp worked together to optimise AltaMcd's data management and storage infrastructure with a solution that can expand with the company's growth, from remotely accessing servers to securing data. With the capacity to administer a single, unified environment, IT staff members are now able to focus on high-value strategic projects that will help the company position itself for future development rather than maintaining the day-to-day architecture.

5.5 Healthcare Data Storage and Retrieval Challenge in the Age of Big Data

Healthcare procedures are not an exception to the world becoming more digital and data-driven. In the era of Big Data, keeping up with medical storage costs is challenging but essential to providing outstanding customer service.

According to RBC Capital Markets, the compound annual growth rate of healthcare data will be 36% by 2025. In comparison to many other industries, such as media and entertainment, industrial, or banking sectors, the growth rate of health data is much higher in Big Data [9].

$$A_0 = \frac{\mu_0 \omega_0}{4\pi} = 10^{-7} \omega I_0$$

5.5.1 Challenge 1: Effective data processing

Healthcare facilities use data from patients in a variety of ways, or at least they aspire to. A significant obstacle to the efficient use of Big Data is the many computational phases

Effective Data Capture:

Healthcare companies are involved in constant conflict because, most of the time, Healthcare information is not consistent. There are many different formats for imaging data; for instance, X-rays and MRIs save uniquely. It is difficult to guarantee the data gathered is clean, comprehensive, reliable, and structured appropriately for usage on many platforms, and common hospital photographs will be of a different standard than those of specialty institutions that utilize more sophisticated equipment to obtain more intricate images. Electronic health records (EHR) are not often deployable, inter-operable, or transmittable. In other words, the healthcare sector lacks data consistency [10].

Responsible and Efficient Data Cleaning Appropriate Data Querying:

A procedure that is crucial for efficient analysis and reporting. Yet, rich meta-data and strict stewardship practises are required for efficient data searching (more on this in Challenge 2).

Data governance is not standardised, which restricts the efficient use of data through searching. Disparate and uncommunicative data silos between internal healthcare operations and external data transfers prohibit centralised and systematic querying.

Regular Data Updating:

The repositories need to be updated often and effectively in order for the data to be current and applicable. Medical information can change minute by minute. Consider the information gathered from life support systems or anaesthesia records during the course of a surgery. It's true that some upgrades can be automated, but it's also true that other updates must be done manually. This makes it difficult to figure out how to update swiftly without affecting end users.

5.5.2 Challenge 2: Cyber security

Every company has a cybercrime challenge, but the healthcare sector perhaps faces it more than others due to the very sensitive nature of the data. Organisations must remain attentive at all times to cyber dangers. The three most frequent flaws in healthcare are user authentication, endpoint leakage, and excessive user rights. Data security depends on taking action to enhance these areas [11].

The focus should be on three areas:

- Storage choice.
- The critical storage questions in healthcare are whether you:
    - Stay with on-premises storage;
    - Go to the cloud.

While many health agencies find on-site data storage to be more convenient, they struggle to keep a tight grip on security, access, and availability. On-site storage can be expensive to grow, difficult to manage, and likely to promote the data silos we previously mentioned.

The cloud has several advantages. Examples include near-infinite expansion, cost-effective up-front charges, and rapid catastrophe recovery. Organisations must exercise caution when selecting partners that are knowledgeable about cloud security and healthcare-specific compliance challenges.

Security expertise and tools: Healthcare organisations need to prioritise data security above all else, especially in light of recent high-profile data breaches, hacks, and ransomware demands. Healthcare providers must use enterprise-class data protection and security to secure data and maintain compliance.

They need to:

- Provide secure access to patient care information, such as EMR/EHR, imaging, from any location;
- Maintain privacy and compliance controls;
- Automatically protects data from external threats;
- Integrate with corporate IT security systems;
- Tracking usage by internal users.

Stewardship:

Data governance guarantees that health data is put to useful and beneficial applications and that misuse is avoided.

With the expansion of the availability of electronic health data, health data stewardship has become more urgent:

- A rising understanding of its importance in enhancing public health and healthcare;
- Knowledge of the possible hazards connected to wrong or inappropriate use.

In the UK, the average retention period for medical records is eight years, making continuing data stewardship a major problem. Data must be fit for purpose and reusable for researchers and data analysts; thus, it is crucial to understand when, by whom, and why it was developed.

5.5.3 Challenge 3: Positive patient experiences

Data is useless by itself unless it influences results and enhances the user experience. The urge for organisations to stay on top of cutting-edge healthcare IT developments may be strong, but unless such investments result in better patient experiences, they aren't really worth the money. Let's examine how effectively data may be applied in practise to improve health outcomes [12].

Reporting:

Initially, organisations must make sure that the data they provide is understandable to their target audience and will have a positive downstream effect on the end-user.

Visualisation:

This is crucial because it makes it easier for the physician to understand and use the information. Giving GPs, for instance, detailed and highly technical MRI scan data without any context willn't guarantee that the professional can see what they need to see when they need to. In fact, it could have a detrimental effect on diagnosis and comprehension. It is crucial that the user recognises what's significant and can speed up the clinical procedure. Excellent data visualisation and presentation methods create a more precise image that facilitates patient-record understanding.

Sharing:

External data exchange has become increasingly important when patients contact a variety of organisations for various problems or specialties due to scattered access. Patients find it exhausting to have to repeat the same information to several healthcare experts, especially when data might be shared by avoiding silos.

Differences in system and storage implementation and design may influence clinical judgement and patient follow-up. Contrary to medical specialties, health cannot be neatly divided into categories. Going to the doctor for migraines is not the best course of action since the doctor may not be aware that the patient is taking the combination contraceptive pill if the pharmacy data transfer to the doctor has failed. The patient's general health is a problem when these two pieces of information are taken into consideration, and a proper diagnosis depends significantly on the safe and secure transfer of patient data.

5.6 Challenges

- **Lower costs:**

The foundation of cloud computing is the on-demand availability of computer resources like storing and analysing data. It is no longer necessary for hospitals and other healthcare facilities to buy hardware and servers separately. Cloud data storage doesn't come with any upfront expenses. You just pay for the resources you use, which saves you a lot of money. Also, cloud computing offers the most comfortable scaling environment, which is a desirable quality in the modern world. A cloud-based system is perfect for expanding and undergoing continuous updates while keeping costs down since patient data is pouring in from many sources, including EMRs, healthcare applications, and health wearables [14].

- **Access to Advanced Analytics:**

Both structured and unstructured healthcare data are incredibly valuable resources. Relevant patient data from various sources may be compiled and evaluated in the cloud. Using artificial intelligence and big data analytics on cloud-stored patient data can advance medical research. The increased computing capacity of the cloud makes handling large data collections more practical. The creation of more customised treatment plans for patients can result from the analysis of patient data. It also ensures that nothing is missed while administering drugs and that all pertinent patient data is documented. Cloud-based data analysis can be useful for locating important patient information.

- **Advanced Diagnostic Technology:**

Each sickness or illness may be defeated with an accurate and prompt diagnosis. Diagnostic technology has experienced numerous ground-breaking advancements over the years and established some impressive instances of tech adoption, including ML, AI, IoT, and block chain. Together with automated test report preparation and delivery, laboratory automation has been one of the most important components. Technology adoption is assisting laboratories in managing a large volume of samples, performing precise test processes, and sharing results more quickly in situations like the pandemic. Despite the massive COVID sample load, diagnosis systems may also simplify and handle the other normal tests, ensuring that the research lab operations are flawless and that other patients are equally cared for throughout these COVID examinations.

- **Robotic Process Automation (RPA)/Hospital Automation:**

Automated driving by AI has been implemented across sectors and is considered to be one of the most disruptive elements to bring about efficiency, increase TAT, decrease reliance on human resources, and increase productivity at lower prices. One such technological advancement, known as hospital automation or RPA, may be extremely helpful for managing hospitals and healthcare facilities, especially during situations such as scheduling doctors and nursing staff, assigning beds or rooms, scheduling OR and consulting room assignments, keeping track of patient treatment records, managing outpatient clinics, particularly COVID tests and vaccinations, generating automated reports, and sending reminders and appointments to patients on routine patient visits. In addition to these routine tasks, AI-powered automation is being used to assimilate and analyse patient and treatment-related data that can be important for medical research, assimilate and process the most recent international advancements in oncology, surgery, the COVID pandemic, and other illnesses, and make absolutely sure that the doctors and medical staff are always informed and up-to-date.

Cost reductions, flexibility, and the chance for expert collaboration are just a few advantages of using cloud computing in the healthcare sector. According to the most recent study on the topic, the largest obstacles to using a cloud platform are security worries for medical associations [15].

- **Patient's Ownership of Data:**

Data democratisation and patient ownership over their own health are made possible by cloud computing. By serving as a tool for patient education and engagement, it increases patient involvement in choices relating to their own health and promotes responsible decision-making.

By storing information in the cloud, it is simple to preserve and access patient records and medical photographs. Although cloud security is still an issue, the cloud is unquestionably more reliable for data storage. Data redundancy decreases as system uptime rises. Data recovery is considerably easier since backups are automatic and the data is kept across several touchpoints.

- **Telemedicine Capabilities:**

Cloud storage gives access to data remotely, and a variety of healthcare-related processes, which include telemedicine, post-hospitalization care planning, and virtual medication adherence, might be enhanced by the integration of cloud computing with healthcare. It also makes healthcare services more accessible via telehealth.

Apps for telemedicine improve the patient experience while easing the delivery of healthcare. Cloud-based telehealth systems and applications make it simple to share medical data, increase accessibility, and provide patients with access to care throughout the prevention, treatment, and recovery phases.

5.7 Conclusion

The major analysis on optimised data retrieval analysis for data storage for the health care system in this chapter mainly focuses on various storage systems like cloud systems, AWS, etc., for string medical data in terms of security parameters that need to be focused on as each healthcare data needs to be protected from unauthorised access to give the best results for medical healthcare data retrieval. AWS and cloud systems are the preeminent storage systems, and they give prominent results.

References

[1] D.A. Adjeroh and K.C. Nwosu, "Multimedia Database Management – Requirements and Issues," IEEE Multimedia, pp 24-33, JulySeptember 1997.

[2] Z. Liang, P. Bodorik, and M. Shepherd, "Storage Model for CDA Documents," Proceedings of the 36th Hawaii International Conference on System Sciences (HICSS'03), 2002.

[3] P. Yu and H. Yu, "Lessons Learned from the Practice of Mobile Health Application evelopment," Proceedings of the 28th Annual International Computer Software and Applications Conference (COMPSAC'04), 2004.

[4] H. Chen, "Machine Learning for Information Retrieval: Neural Networks, Symbolic Learning, and Genetic algorithms," Journal of the American Society for Information Science, John Wiley & Sons, Inc., Vol. 46 No. 3, pp. 194-216, 1995.

[5] H. Kammoun, J.C. Lamirel, and M.B. Ahmed, "Neural-Symbolic Machine-Learning for Knowledge Discovery and Adaptive Information Retrieval," Transactions on Engineering, Computing and Technology, World Enformatika Society, Vol. 6, June 2005.

[6] Z. Liang, P. Bodorik, and M. Shepherd, "Storage Model for CDA Documents," Proceedings of the 36th Hawaii International Conference on System Sciences (HICSS'03), 2002.

[7] P. Yu and H. Yu, "Lessons Learned from the Practice of Mobile Health Application evelopment," Proceedings of the 28th Annual International Computer Software and Applications Conference (COMPSAC'04), 2004.

[8] H. Chen, "Machine Learning for Information Retrieval: Neural Networks, Symbolic Learning, and Genetic algorithms," Journal of the American Society for Information Science, John Wiley & Sons, Inc., Vol. 46 No. 3, pp. 194-216, 1995.

[9] H. Kammoun, J.C. Lamirel, and M.B. Ahmed, "Neural-Symbolic Machine-Learning for Knowledge Discovery and Adaptive Information Retrieval," Transactions on Engineering, Computing and Technology, World Enformatika Society, Vol. 6, June 2005.

[10] J. Jiang and C. Zhai. An empirical study of tokenization strategies for biomedical information retrieval. Information Retrieval, 10(4-5):341–363, 2007,

[11] Simpao A.F., Ahumada L.M., Gálvez J.A., Rehman M.A. A review of analytics and clinical informatics in health care. J. Med. Syst. 2014;38:45. doi: 10.1007/s10916-014-0045-x.

[12] Powell, James E. (2014), —Q&A: Advanced data visualization: from atomic data to big data.

[13] Raghupathi W., Raghupathi V. Big data analytics in healthcare: Promise and potential. Health Inf. Sci. Syst. 2014;2:3

[14] Ledbetter, Craig S. & Morgan, Matthew W.(2001), —Toward best practice: leveraging the electronic patient record as a clinical data warehouse‖. Journal of Healthcare Information Management, vol.15, issue.2, pp.119-131.

6

Computational Intelligence System for Healthcare

M. Kiruthiga Devi[1], T. Nalini[2], Kamalakannan Machap[3], and Rajan Kumar[4]

[1,4]Department of Information Technology, Dr. MGR Educational and Research Institute, India
[2]Department of CSE, Saveetha Institute of Medical and Technical Sciences, India
[3]School of Technology, Asia Pacific University, Technology Park Malaysia, Malaysia
E-mail: kiruthigaprofessor89@gmail.com; nalinit.sse@saveetha.com; dr.kamalakannan@apu.edu.my

Abstract

Large-scale technologies like the Internet of Things (IoT) and machine learning (ML) offer improvements and better solutions in a variety of areas that affect our daily lives, including business, healthcare, the space industry, shielding, traffic, agriculture, buildings, and others. The IoT sector has grown in the recent few decades with the ongoing ML development technologies. Medical device innovation is greatly impacted by the integration of IoT and ML techniques. All areas of healthcare, from diagnosis to therapy, can significantly benefit from the combination of ML and IoT. The writers of this chapter provide a summary of current IoT and ML applications for advanced healthcare management, along with all of their advantages and uses. This chapter aids researchers in understanding the development of ML- and IoT-based technologies as well as helping medical professionals diagnose and treat diseases more effectively. The study of digital healthcare (DH) is an interdisciplinary area of study that combines informatics, medical sciences, biology, biochemistry, and neuroscience. Researchers have recently proposed a variety of computational intelligence (CI) tools and methodologies in an effort to create digital knowledge-based systems (DKBS) for a range of medical and healthcare jobs. These systems are built on the ideas and theories of artificial intelligence (AI). There are numerous DKBS kinds in use today, and they are used for various healthcare tasks and areas. The goal of the chapter is to present a thorough and current investigation into DHI, discussing implementations and case studies, determining the optimum design methodologies, and assessing implementation models and practices of AI paradigms, covering a wide variety of CI methodological and intelligent algorithmic challenges.

Keywords: Internet of Things (IoT), digital healthcare (DH), computational intelligence (CI), digital knowledge-based systems (DKBS), artificial intelligence (AI), machine learning (ML).

6.1 Introduction

The Internet of Things' (IoT) expanding amount of health data is used by machine learning (ML) techniques in healthcare to enhance patient outcomes. These techniques provide both positive applications and significant difficulties. IoTs and ML have recently worked together to create a number of things. Using radio frequency identification devices (RFIDs) to incorporate well-known things and their electronic photographs into web frameworks was the initial Internet of Things (IoT) advice. In the end, the healthcare sector's implementation of the Internet of Things included sensors, GPS apps, and cell phones. The global world's constant integration and the supporting tools of these sensors have led to several discovery challenges, ranging from fundamental knowledge to processing and execution. In order to transmit wireless information, many devices have been employed. In the end, the healthcare sector's implementation of the Internet of Things included sensors, GPS apps, and cell phones. The global world's constant integration and the supporting tools of these sensors have led to several discovery challenges, ranging from fundamental knowledge to processing and execution. In order to transmit wireless information, many devices have been employed. Considering this, multiple studies have assessed the use of IoT-ML for data security purposes when screening patients for various medical issues. Research across disciplines on IoT innovation has developed significantly in recent years. In order to address healthcare challenges, multi-objective optimization research is crucial and valuable. As a result, IoT and ML are now being used to develop healthcare from hospitals to homes, as well as for routine medical testing for doctors and patients using medical equipment. Hence, by utilizing this and by transferring some tasks to the home environment, hospitals can also lighten their workload. Patients can avoid paying hospital expenses when they visit the doctor, which is one of the main benefits. The incapacity of the current network infrastructure to handle delicate IoT applications in real time necessitates the need for a network architecture tailored for such applications for software-defined networks, among other limits. AI and IoT are altering healthcare administration in numerous ways. Several fields have utilized ML in various ways. There is a ton of data in hospitals. Patient monitors record vital signs like blood pressure and heart rate, while doctors and specialists provide visual data in the form of MRI and CT scan reports. All of this data has the potential to be extremely valuable but only if the government system has timely access to it and the means to review it in an emergency.

6.1.1 Enhancement of diagnostic accuracy

It can be challenging to assess some prevalent diseases, such as breast and lung cancer. So, in order to diagnose malignancies, physicians must use images of a computer-generated tomography scanner (CTS). False negatives and positives continue to exist frequently even though this method of diagnosis is the most reliable one. Doctors may find this information useful if ML and IoT are combined. As a result, they are changing how hospitals operate where they have been implemented as shown in Figure 6.1. These scans are interpreted by ML, which also enhances their quality. On a number of trials, these ML systems have outperformed radiologists at accurately spotting cancerous lesions in a CT image.

6.1.2 Remote patient observation

IoT sensors are used by remote patient observation systems to offer nurses and doctors information in patient essentials. These sensors enable skilled workers, physicians, and important health indicators to check on a patient's well-being from any location.

6.1.3 Automated follow-up

Other IoT and ML applications can track a patient's health once they have left the hospital, eliminating the requirement of subsequent surveys. For

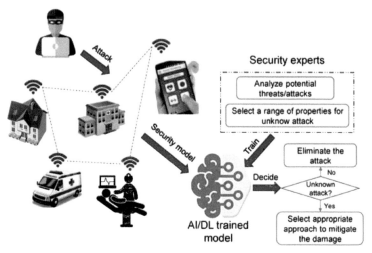

Figure 6.1　DHI Architecture.

instance, IoT devices are used by healthcare professionals to monitor the blood pressure of pregnant adult females who have hyperpiesis. In general, this would need follow-up treatment, even though some people who have the problem note that it usually disappears after birth.

6.1.4 Waiting time minimized

Hospital wait times are also reduced because of ML and IoT technologies. Hospital staff are notified automatically once a bed becomes available, allowing them to quickly admit patients in an emergency.

6.1.5 Critical patient isolation

Finding patients that require immediate attention while hospitals are under pressure and at capacity is essential to giving patients the best care. It is a difficult process. Large volumes of patient data must be analyzed by medical professionals and nurses under a lot of pressure and must make quick decisions. Fortunately, in these circumstances, AI and IoT devices offer assistance. To save their sickest patients, hospitals are turning to new AI-powered virtual assistants. These systems analyze patients' vitals and conditions and notify clinicians when a patient's condition starts to deteriorate. These hospital AI systems have occasionally been able to identify issues that doctors overlooked.

6.1.6 Medical tool tracking

Hospitals may incur enormous costs as a result of lost medical equipment. It is common for hospitals to lose five to six wound pumps used in wound care due to negative pressure each year. Organizations may significantly reduce the danger of losing equipment, cut expenditures, and confirm that pumps are available by using precise tracking systems. Now, if a mobile pump device is sent home with a patient, it can be tracked both inside and outside of the hospital, thanks to RFID and GPS technologies. When a patient's pump is pulled off the shelf, the RFID scanning technology also immediately asks insurance for clearance. If necessary, the patient will get prior approval to bring their device home.

6.2 IoT-ML in Healthcare

6.2.1 Machine learning

Moreover, ML is acknowledged as there are modern-day revolutions. Machine learning is the use of algorithms to analyze data derived from actual events. Simplified, machine learning typically derives from results, recognizes learning objectives that will help you see patterns in the data, and applies those patterns to draw useful conclusions. Math, algebra, data collection, mathematical testing, etc., can all be addressed comprehensively by machine learning. A crucial method for retrieving data from training records is machine learning (ML).

Nowadays, programs for healthcare providers use machine learning extensively. Several medical decision support systems also employ these system learning algorithms to create superior learning habits that enhance human health. The usage of support vector machines (SVMs) in the healthcare sector is a good example of how ML and IoT are applied in this sector. Traditional centralized schooling is depicted in Figure 6.2. There are several techniques to implement pharmaceutical machine learning, including:

- disease identification and analysis;
- customized treatment/behavior options;
- drug discovery/production and clinical test results;
- radiation treatments and radiology machine;
- electronic health records for patients;
- forecasting of epidemic outbreaks.

How the data are collected form variety of sources for analysis and use with IoT−ML tools. A system unit is represented by this data information. To produce training datasets, the system component is being tested. The data point could display patient health data pertaining to a sample of malignant tissue or another item. An outstanding characteristic that has been ascribed to them is visible in the label's details, and it can also be used to refer to things like output or responsiveness. Although most applications can employ both labeled and unlabeled data, in supervised learning, labeled data are often monitored. In unsupervised learning, unlabeled data are present, whereas semi-supervised learning can use both labeled data and unlabeled data.

6.2.2 Supervised learning

Supervised learning is an ML technique employed in real-time uses. One of the supervised learning (SL) model's distinguishing characteristics is the person's innovation in it. Personal involvement is crucial while creating a database in the beginning. In the process of developing the database model, all available inputs and optional outputs are added to and understood from the supplied examples. Then, in order to create outcomes, this model discovers a means to operate independently. The issue appears when a model must independently anticipate the results of a new installation without human aid. Therefore, it is crucial to ensure that the suggested model is accurate.

6.2.3 Usurprised learning

Finding unknown structures within unlabeled data is one of the goals of ML. These challenging-to-study applications are employed in many popular programs because unsupervised ML training knowledge is not being used. As a result, there are not enough indicators of incentive for examining potential future fixes. In this case, the incentive value serves as a distinctive characteristic of the established and unattended. Conversion and integration of databases are included in unsupervised learning. The database's data is altered during the update process to present it in a new, different fashion that will make it simpler for people and computer algorithms to grasp. On the other hand, collections of algorithms separate datasets into significant groupings of connected items.

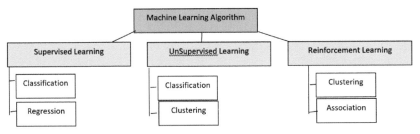

Figure 6.2 Types of machine learning.

6.2.4 Reinforcement learning

Researchers look at how RL can compute ideal values based on prior results without needing any prior biological system knowledge. Since it might be challenging to create the right use for the patient body and have them respond to treatments due to shifting interfaces between treatments and bodies, RL strategies are more sophisticated and straightforward than other ML techniques used in the healthcare sectors.

6.3 Applications of IoT in Healthcare

A physical system called the Internet of Things (IoT) offers remote device administration, analysis, and discovery. The design of computers has been altered to link to edge computers in order to enable mobile sensors and smart devices to communicate effectively. IoT's middleware layer serves as a crucial data processing layer for smart devices. Smart grids, smart cities, smart homes, smart agriculture, smart transportation, and other applications are all examples of IoT applications. The visualization, communication, and device layers are the three main configuration layers for the Internet of Things. Then it enlarges to include the most cutting-edge commercial and construction crust. Healthcare can't be personalized without artificial and portable IoT devices. The following two examples of healthcare applications highlight the key differences between them.

6.3.1 Wearable devices

Metal bracelets, smart watches, pendants, pins, shirts, bracelets, and other mobile systems can be attached to the structure of the human body, such as shoes, exercise equipment, and other medical devices. Direct interaction is feasible with wearable technology that monitors disease, human health, and research center data. The machines have wearable components like screens, computers, and sensors. Its devices are capable of producing data that is naturally collected, such as mobility, heart rate, blood pressure, exercise duration, etc. The client's physical health benefits the most from these devices because they are so powerful and make a significant effect.

Under the human's skin, implantable devices are placed with the intention of repairing the entire or a portion of the organic machine's shape. Implants are undoubtedly commonly employed in many programs, including radiology, neurology, coronary heart attack stents, microchips, etc. Therefore, it is important to provide a comfortable network for these services. Implantable devices may contain any organic compounds, including various metals such as titanium and silicon and carbonates. The composition may also be chosen in accordance with the implant tool's equipment and needs for the various body parts.

6.3.2 Machine learning for disease identification and prediction

The area of ML classification in statistics is broad, and the dataset influences the choice of the classification algorithm. As indicated in Table 6.1, the most well-liked machine learning classification algorithms are listed below.

Table 6.1   ML algorithms and their benefits and limitation.

ML algorithm	Application	Advantage	Disadvantage
Supervised KNN	Classification and regression	Nonparametric method. Easy and no training required	Long calculation. Low performance due to unnecessary datasets. The data might need to use the same features
Naïve Bayes	Probabilistic classification used	Data scan individually	Models that are trained and altered outperform
Decision tree	Prediction and classification	Categorization of attributes	Hard computation for long tree
Random forest	Classification and regression	Increased performance and low correlation value	Need more time for training complexity
SVM	Binary and nonlinear classification	More active in large dimensional space	Hard to select a kernel function and does not work well for noise data
Gradient boosted decision tree	Used for classification and regression	Increase the estimation action iteratively	Does not work for repeated construction of the tree

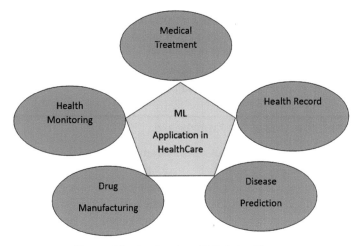

Figure 6.3 Application of ML in healthcare.

Making technologies dependable and effective is the goal of ML−IoT. The machine's role in the healthcare industry is to assist doctors and personnel in providing better care and service. Figure 6.3 depicts ML in use. The application of machine learning in the healthcare industry is thus listed below.

The first stage of machine learning in the healthcare sector is initial therapy. The aim of the analysis is to identify healthcare services. For a specific person utilizing examination methods and personal information additionally, by leveraging the data of specific patients, supervised learning algorithms enable the development of tailored treatments. By combining numerous techniques, such as clinical, pharmacological, and socioeconomic data with ML−IoT, researchers can identify genetic abnormalities that may be treated as well as patterns in individual therapies.

In several applications in the healthcare sector, virtual assistants are becoming more and more common. The development of ML−IoT-based applications, in particular, helps patients throughout all care paths. Because of this, there are virtual nurses on hand to instantly respond to queries from patients' inquiries and give counseling to patients' questions quickly, and there are also virtual nurses on standby to instantly respond to. The purpose of patients' records is to capture both illness and disease histories, as well as disease records for diseases, so that medical professionals can utilize these records for both illnesses and diseases.

These applications also aim to reduce stress associated with medical care and hospital visits. From the initial action of medication to their rate of success, the application of IoT−ML in the early stages of drug development has the potential to provide a variety of services. Additionally, it can provide information and assist with drug safety calculations.

6.3.3 Smart environment for healthcare

Figure 6.4 shows the general layout of a system of smart HLC. The development of a smart HLC system was made possible by a confluence of technologies including cloud computing, wearable technologies, IoT, AI, biosensors, etc. Figure 6.1 illustrates the operation of a straightforward smart HLC system. First, the patient can book appointments for online consultations, create online databases, and make payments using applications and websites. The knowledgeable hospital staff can complete this process. The AI and cloud computing system would suggest to the patient the best doctor who is available based on the type of ailment. This procedure aids in shortening the hospital patient line. Advanced biosensors and wearable technology are used to capture clinical measures like blood pressure, temperature, respiration rate, pulse rate, and others. With the aid of IoT devices, the database is also updated with these measures. Additionally, the doctor or medical professional can communicate with the patient via the cloud network and retrieve the patient's full information, including medical history, vital signs, and current condition, from the cloud database. The cloud network will also make the recommended medications and pathology tests for patients available online.

Additionally, this online information will support home medication delivery services and make pathological test results available for the patient's ongoing care. Cloud networks will also provide supervised AI systems built on machine learning that can help with the management of minor concerns. The smart HLC system's usual architecture clearly demonstrates that it outperforms the drawbacks of the standard HLC setup. Make HLC systems more intelligent and accessible 7 days a week and 24 hours a day, and make them simple. Smart healthcare requirements can be divided into functional and non-functional requirements. The earlier section goes through the numerous conditions that must be met for smart HLC systems to work. Depending on the application and the hardware component employed, different smart HLC systems have different functional requirements. Examining specific qualities, which are typically used to indicate non-functional needs, can help establish the character of an HLC system. Performance criteria and ethical

Typical architectute of smart HLC system

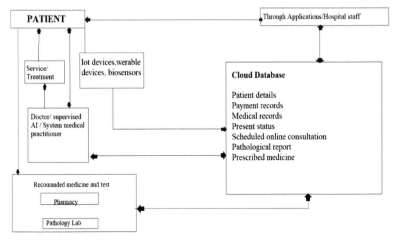

Figure 6.4 Typical architecture of smart HLC system.

requirements are two areas into which these requirements might be split. An HLC system is reliable and effective because of its low power consumption, mobility, and simplicity of use, to name a few qualities. Sensors, actuators, computers, networking, and data storage devices are common categories for the parts of a smart HLC system.

To create a connection or a way for data to travel from sensors to routers and cloud base stations, networking devices are used. Most wireless technologies, including Bluetooth and Wi-Fi, are used as network components. Wi-Fi technology is essential when it comes to transporting information and processed data among the many healthcare network components utilized in an HLC setup. The most crucial component of a smart HLC system is data storage. The basis for all knowledge is provided by these medical facts. A clever HLC mechanism makes it possible to access data and information from chapter files from anywhere via cloud storage, as opposed to a conventional HLC system. Smart healthcare networks comprise a wide variety of smart devices as data storage components, ranging from the sensing device's embedded system memory to a sizable server that can execute big data analytics. People utilize a range of computing devices these days, including smartphones, tablets, laptops, desktop computers, PDAs, servers, and supercomputers. Modern, potent sensors are capable of recognizing biological components and have numerous applications in biomedicine, drug discovery, and illness diagnosis. Sensors or actuators provide support for the monitoring systems. Temperature, motion, EMG, accelerometer, gyroscope, blood sugar level, ECG, blood pressure, SpO2, and other sensors are available for a variety of applications. Things-oriented, semantics-oriented, and app-oriented are the three major subcategories that make up the structure of the intelligent HLC system. The app-oriented architecture ensures a dependable and secure connection between smartphone applications and sensors. Also, it is in charge of building a network just for HLC system users. On-time delivery and real-time monitoring of the new HLC system, increased sensitivity, maintenance of enhanced performance, reduced power consumption, and clever processing are improved with the help of things-oriented designs. The semantically focused designs make sure that user experience is improved by using historical feedback data obtained through shrewd medical care. The user experience is enhanced by these special capabilities.

Patient self-management is given more consideration by the clever HLC system. To keep an eye on patients' conditions, a healthcare professional is not always necessary. It provides real-time advice or comments while continuously monitoring the health of patients utilizing wearable technology like fit bands. Modern sensors, processors, and wireless modules are used by wearable technology to continuously sense and intelligently monitor patient behavior. These comfortable, low-energy devices allow data and health information to be integrated, reducing the risk of illness. It is simpler for medical institutions to track a patient's health, behavior, and disease diagnoses. Smart bands, cell phones, and other devices offer the framework for effective monitoring. People who practice smart health management can keep up a healthy lifestyle, which also saves money and time by reducing the frequency of hospital visits. Managing one's health can benefit from smart homes. Children, the elderly, and those with disabilities can all receive assistance from house assistants in smart homes. Infrastructure-integrated sensors and actuators in smart houses and flats keep an eye on residents' physical signs and surroundings. The smart house also gets better daily life and supports a healthy lifestyle. The home monitoring system helps people who want to improve their quality of life at home and reduce their reliance on HLC specialists by gathering resident health information and providing some basic health services. Smart HLC solutions, whether they come in the form of hardware or software, enable patients to independently manage less serious medical issues.

As a result, the responsibilities of healthcare workers are decreased, and patient care is enhanced by offering more reasonable and suitable medical care. AI assists the HLC personnel with disease diagnosis and treatment. It uses several interactions with training data and algorithms from the medical field to enable the system to make a diagnosis or judgment in the present. Diagnoses using AI are improved people's capacity for thought and judgment in order to create superior diagnoses. Smart diagnostics make recommendations based on patient data. According to reports, especially in pathology and imaging, AI-based systems can sometimes be more accurate than a skilled physician. For instance, when a robotic arm performs surgery instead of a human surgeon, the outcome is more precise. Smart diagnosis lessens the likelihood of missed diagnoses, incorrect diagnoses, and surgical equipment malfunctions while also ensuring that patients receive high-quality care. Medical professionals can precisely create a customized treatment plan for each patient based on their condition and disease state by using the smart diagnosis system. The formulation and execution of surgical plans are simplified by AI applications in the medical field, which also transform medical education, research, communication, and treatment.

A program that interacts with patients is known as a virtual assistant. It is based on technologies like the Internet of Things, deep learning, and speech recognition algorithms that depend on data from consumers. After computations, virtual assistants answer in accordance with the user's preferences or demands (Sharmin et al., 2006). Virtual assistants are essential in the smart HLC for interacting with health institutions and HLC staff. To aid customers with a variety of tasks, from creating reminders to automating their homes, virtual assistants make use of multilingual understanding technologies that have been built by professionals. It greatly simplifies and streamlines communication. Virtual assistants eliminate the language barrier by translating one language into another that is simple to understand. Based on the patient's symptoms and existing medical history in the system, doctors can reply to them automatically. By utilizing virtual assistants, medical institutions and research facilities can save on labor costs and material resources while yet being able to adapt quickly to changing conditions. The virtual assistant can also be utilized to help people with their mental health.

The smart hospital is a component of the smart HLC system constructed using IoT, digital equipment, and smart services. It requires a setting where information and communication technologies are used. In addition to providing services to medical professionals, it also enhances and customizes features for patient care and health tracking. Intelligent buildings and numerous digital systems, including various digital systems, are used in smart hospitals. Using RFID cards, the technology can also be used to identify patients and medical personnel. Individual RFID cards make hospitals safe and ensure that only authorized people can access patient information. The patient can take advantage of numerous advantages in the smart hospital, including a human-free information center that offers accurate information, online appointments, improved doctor—patient relationships, etc. The modern hospital provides quicker and more convenient medical care for its patients. Pharmaceutical companies for the development and study of drug organizations for drug development are also part of smart healthcare. It controls various processes, including manufacturing, circulation, inventory management, and anti-counterfeiting. This enables the circulation of materials in hospitals to be secure, trustworthy, steady, and effective. Smart hospitals can lower medical expenses, help hospitals make development decisions, and make the most use of their medical resources. Smart hospitals also enhance a patient's and doctor's relationship experience and the administration of the hospital's level of service.

Drug development is a drawn-out process that involves numerous clinical studies, target screening, and drug discovery. It takes a long time for traditional drug developments to reach the effective points since they use manual target screening. Nowadays, computerized target screening procedures speed up the process. The selection procedure involves optimized use of a real-time data, which can be acquired at any time using an AI-based system. High throughput screening and synthesis are more expensive and more dangerous and demand more resources. Simulated drug testing based on artificial intelligence is an alternative strategy to decrease the cost and danger. The effectiveness of drug discovery can be increased by using medication discovery using AI to accurately forecast the activities of the drug molecule. Clinical trials also make use of the newest technology, like big data, AI, and IoT. These cutting-edge methods can speed up the screening process and help choose appropriate test volunteers in drug development. With less risk, expense, and time involved in the drug discovery process, these smart technologies can produce efficient and precise results for drug development.

6.4 Case Study

6.4.1 Breast cancer prediction using machine learning

Machine learning phases consist of seven phases, which are described in more detail below.

Data pre-processing:

Gathering the data that we usually have an interest in grouping for pre-processing and using classification and regression algorithms is what we usually do in the first step. Knowledge pre-processing could be a data processing method that entails reorganizing data in an understandable manner. As most knowledge of the world is insufficient, inconsistent, and deficient, it is inevitably flawed. Knowledge pre-processing could be a tried-and-true approach to unraveling these issues. Information is prepared for further processing by knowledge pre-processing. The UCI dataset has been pre-processed using a standardization methodology. This phase is quite important because the caliber and volume of data you obtain can directly confirm how accurate your prognostic model is. In this instance, we tend to gather samples of both benign and malignant cancer. This might be our coaching expertise.

Preparation of data:

The process of converting unprocessed data into an analytically ready format is known as data preparation, often referred to as data pre-processing. Data preparation is crucial in ensuring that the data are correct, complete, consistent, and relevant. The quality of data analysis heavily depends on the quality of the data used.

Data features selection:

The feature selection is the process of selecting a subset of relevant features from a larger set of available features in a dataset for use in machine learning models. The main goal of feature selection is to reduce the dimensionality of the dataset by removing irrelevant, redundant, or noisy features, which can lead to overfitting, increased computational complexity, and decreased model accuracy. There are various methods of feature selection, such as filter methods, wrapper methods, embedded methods, and principal component analysis (PCA). Filter methods use statistical measures to select features, while wrapper methods evaluate model performance on different subsets of features. Embedded methods incorporate feature selection into the model training process, while PCA is a technique for reducing the dimensionality of the dataset. It is essential to choose a proper feature selection method based on the problem domain and the type of data available to improve model performance and computational efficiency. Good feature selection can significantly improve the accuracy and efficiency of a machine learning model while reducing its complexity.

Data feature projection:

Feature projection is a technique used in machine learning to reduce the dimensionality of a dataset by projecting it onto a lower-dimensional space. This can be done by creating new features that are a linear combination of the original features or by selecting a subset of the original features. Feature projection is commonly used to overcome the curse of dimensionality, which refers to the problem of increasing computational complexity and overfitting as the number of features in the dataset increases.

Feature scaling of data:

Machine learning uses feature scaling as a data preparation technique to normalize a dataset's characteristics to a comparable scale. This is required because varying sizes and ranges of features within a dataset may result in some machine learning algorithms performing poorly or converging slowly. By scaling the features, we can make sure that each feature contributes equally to the model, enhancing the algorithm's precision and effectiveness.

Model selection in ML:

The process by which the machine is educated on the data for which the input and output are accurately labeled is known as supervised learning. The model will improve based on coaching expertise and may employ longer-term knowledge to make outcome predictions. These fall under the classification and regression categories. Once the result is a genuine or consecutive price, like "salary" or "weight," there is a regression downside. Once the result is categorized, for as by classifying emails as "spam" or "not spam," there is a classification flaw. Unattended learning: Unattended learning is the practice of freely presenting the computer with the information that has not been classified or marked and then letting an algorithmic software to analyze the information without any guidance. In an algorithmic system for unattended learning, data that has not been tagged or categorized is used to educate the machine to make decisions in the wrong direction. The result variable or variable quantity in our dataset, Y, only has M (Malign) or B as two sets of values (Benign). Hence, the supervised learning program's classification method is implemented there. We have selected three different machine learning classification algorithm types. A simple, low-dimensional, low-linear model is one that we can employ.

Model prediction:

Model prediction in machine learning is the process of utilizing a learned model to generate predictions on fresh, unforeseen data. A machine learning

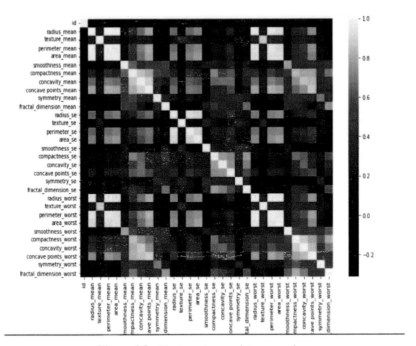

Figure 6.5 Heatmap to correlate promotion.

model's objective is to discover patterns and connections in a training dataset and utilize this understanding to generate precise predictions about incoming data. An illustration of a correlation matrix that shows the relationship between various variables is called a correlation heatmap. Correlation can have any value between −1 and 1. It is not always the case that a correlation between two random variables or bivariate data indicates a causal connection as shown in Figure 6.5.

Proposed methodology:

The work was made to run on an i3 CPU with dual processor. The investigations into the classifiers explained in that chapter were carried out using libraries from the Boa machine learning environment at 30-GHz speed, 2-GB RAM, and 320-GB memory device. In experimental research, we divided 70% for coaching and 30% for testing. Machine learning techniques for categorization, regression, and knowledge pre-processing, bunching, and association rules are included in the JUPYTER software. JUPYTER's machine learning tools are used to address various actual problems. The information analysis's searches are consistent. It usually accesses the 10-fold cross-validation to evaluate. Look at is a method for assessing prophetic models that divide the original set into a coaching sample to guide the model and a look at set to assess it. We frequently attempt to visually assess the information following the use of pre-processing and preparation procedures in order to determine the value distribution according to efficacy and potency. Find out how values are distributed in terms of potency and efficacy.

Dataset information:

The Kaggle Machine Learning Repository hosts the datasets that were utilized in this chapter. Data sets for this dataset were created using digitized fine needle aspirates (FNAs) from breast tumors. The goal feature stores the prognosis (i.e., malignant or benign). The dataset has 286 occurrences and 10 attributes, including 201 no-recurrence events and 85 recurrence events. The attribute (node-caps) status was missing from eight items in the Breast Cancer dataset as shown in Figure 6.6.

The worst concavity and worst concave points represent the highest mean value. The estimated mean value for coastal approximation is represented by fractal_dimension_mean, the standard error of the coastline approximation is represented by fractal_dimension_se, and the highest mean

```
1    diagnosis                    569 non-null    object
2    radius_mean                  569 non-null    float64
3    texture_mean                 569 non-null    float64
4    perimeter_mean               569 non-null    float64
5    area_mean                    569 non-null    float64
6    smoothness_mean              569 non-null    float64
7    compactness_mean             569 non-null    float64
8    concavity_mean               569 non-null    float64
9    concave points_mean          569 non-null    float64
10   symmetry_mean                569 non-null    float64
11   fractal_dimension_mean       569 non-null    float64
12   radius_se                    569 non-null    float64
13   texture_se                   569 non-null    float64
14   perimeter_se                 569 non-null    float64
15   area_se                      569 non-null    float64
16   smoothness_se                569 non-null    float64
17   compactness_se               569 non-null    float64
18   concavity_se                 569 non-null    float64
19   concave points_se            569 non-null    float64
20   symmetry_se                  569 non-null    float64
21   fractal_dimension_se         569 non-null    float64
22   radius_worst                 569 non-null    float64
23   texture_worst                569 non-null    float64
24   perimeter_worst              569 non-null    float64
25   area_worst                   569 non-null    float64
26   smoothness_worst             569 non-null    float64
27   compactness_worst            569 non-null    float64
28   concavity_worst              569 non-null    float64
29   concave points_worst         569 non-null    float64
30   symmetry_worst               569 non-null    float64
31   fractal_dimension_worst      569 non-null    float64
```

Figure 6.6   Data information.

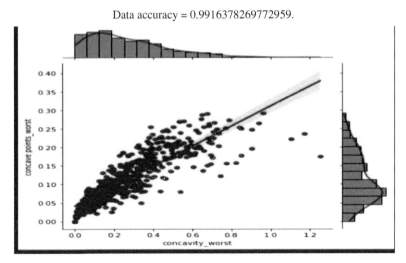

Data accuracy = 0.9916378269772959.

Figure 6.7 Concave point worst.

value is represented by fractal_dimension_worst [17, 18, 30] as shown in Figure 6.7.

6.4.2 Prediction of diabetes using machine learning

Millions of individuals worldwide suffer from the chronic condition of diabetes, and effective treatment depends on early detection and control. Healthcare providers can now provide patients with timely treatments and preventative care, thanks to machine learning algorithms that have demonstrated excellent outcomes in predicting patients' risk of getting diabetes. Data collection and pre-processing are the first phases in the machine learning process for diabetes prediction. Age, weight, blood pressure, and family history are relevant features that are chosen from the dataset, and logistic regression, decision trees, and support vector machines are machine learning algorithms that are trained on the dataset to discover patterns and relationships between the features and the risk of developing diabetes. The model is evaluated on a different set of data once it has been trained to assess its performance in terms of accuracy and generalization. In order to evaluate the performance of the model, several evaluation metrics are utilized, including accuracy, precision, recall, and F1 score. Once the model has been verified, it can be used to forecast the likelihood that new patients will develop diabetes, enabling medical providers to offer individualized care and interventions.

Notwithstanding these difficulties, diabetes prediction using machine learning has the power to transform healthcare by offering individualized and focused interventions to people who are at risk of acquiring diabetes, improving outcomes, and lowering healthcare costs.

Types of diabetes:

Type 1. Immunological dysfunction and poor cell insulin synthesis are two features of diabetes. There are not any efficient prevention treatments as well as no conclusive research that show the causes of type 1 diabetes.

Type 2. Perhaps not enough insulin synthesis by the cells and inappropriate insulin uptake by the body are the characteristics of diabetes. The most prevalent type of diabetes is this one, affecting 90% of those who have it. Its occurrence is influenced by lifestyle choices as well as genetics.

Pregnant women with high blood sugar levels develop gestational diabetes. It will typically recur during subsequent pregnancies in two-thirds of the instances. There is a considerable chance. Following pregnancy, type 1 or type 2 diabetes will develop in which gestational diabetes was present.

Symptoms of diabetes:

- mood swings;
- blurred vision;
- weight loss;
- tired/sleepiness;
- increased thirst;
- frequent infections;
- confusion and difficulty concentrating;
- frequent urination.

Diabetes causes:

High blood sugar levels are the hallmark of the chronic condition known as diabetes, whose causes are multifaceted. The risk of having diabetes can be increased by genetic, environmental, and lifestyle factors such as obesity, inactivity, poor diet, and smoking. In type 1 diabetes, the pancreas is erroneously attacked by the immune system, but in type 2 diabetes, the body develops an insulin resistance. Drugs, other medical disorders, or hormonal abnormalities may be the cause of various forms of diabetes.

Methodology:

In this section, with machine learning, diabetes can be predicted by gathering medical data, pre-processing it, choosing pertinent features, training an appropriate algorithm, validating and optimizing the model, deploying it, monitoring its performance, and updating it as needed. Data collection, pre-processing, feature selection, model selection, training, validation, optimization, and deployment come next in the process. This methodology enables machine learning algorithms to forecast a patient's probability of developing diabetes, improving patient outcomes and lowering healthcare expenditures.

Dataset:

The diabetes dataset is available at the Kaggle website. The collection contains 2000 diabetes cases. Based on the measurements, it should be possible to identify whether the patient has diabetes or not. The dataset was first presented by the National Institute of Diabetes and Digestive and Kidney Diseases, and I was able to get it through Kaggle. The dataset contains outcomes and predictive traits that show if a person has diabetes or not. A patient's classification as having diabetes or not is determined by the dataset, which is a collection of research studies from diverse patients. In order to complete this project, I will test some patient data to see if it falls into the diabetes or non-diabetic categories using the supplied data and a KNN algorithm. This dataset contains 768 investigated lists connected to patients with and without diabetes. To make these data usable, we will modify, scrape, and sanitize them as shown in Table 6.2.

Table 6.2 Diabetes dataset.

Sl. no.	Name of the attribute	Data type	Min. range	Max. range
1	Clump thickness	Integer	1	10
2	Uniformity of cell size	Integer	1	10
3	Uniformity of cell shape	Integer	1	10
4	Marginal adhesion	Integer	1	10
5	Single epithelial cell size	Integer	1	10
6	Bare nuclei	Integer	1	10
7	Bland chromatin	Integer	1	10
8	Normal nucleoli	Integer	1	10
9	Mitoses	Integer	1	10
10	Class	Integer	2	4

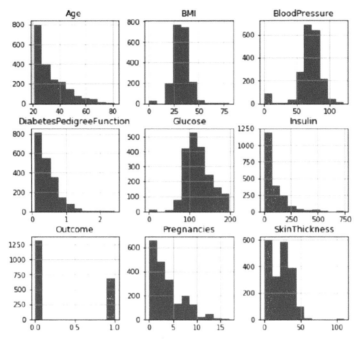

Figure 6.8   Details of each attribute.

Each of the 2000 data points in the collection of diabetes data has nine attributes as shown in Figure 6.8. We are going to forecast a feature called "Outcome," where 0 denotes absence of diabetes and 1 denotes present of diabetes.

This illustrates the need for scaling by showing how every attribute and label is spread across numerous ranges. The presence of distinct bars then essentially indicates that every one of them is a categorical variable. We must manage these category variables before utilizing machine learning. Our result labels come in two categories: 0 for no disease and 1 for disease.

Bar plot for class outcome:

In the plot below, the y-axis represents the neighbors' setting while the x-axis represents the setting of the neighbors as shown in Figure 6.9. Even when just taking into account one nearest neighbor, the prediction on the training set is correct. The training accuracy, however, diminishes when more neighbors are considered, proving that using the one nearest neighbor leads to an excessively complex model. The performance is best in the neighborhood with nine neighbors.

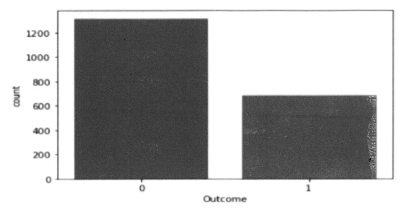

Figure 6.9 Accuracy.

Algorithms:

KNN algorithm:

It is a supervised machine learning technique that emphasizes similarity. The K-nearest neighbor algorithm is a quick way to say this. In essence, it is a classification technique that determines the class of a target variable using a set number of nearest neighbors. You will calculate the distance between each instance in the training dataset and the instance you want to classify. For the library, the default measurement of the separation between two dataset data points or vectors is the Euclidean distance.

Logistic regression:

In binary classification issues, where the objective is to predict the probability of a binary outcome (such as 0 or 1) based on a set of input features, the most popular machine learning approach is logistic regression. A logistic function that maps the input features to a probability between 0 and 1 is fitted to the data in logistic regression. By dividing the exponential of the linear combination of the input features and their corresponding weights by the product of the exponential of the linear combination and 1, the logistic function is defined as the sum of the exponential of the linear combination and 1. A technique known as maximum likelihood estimation is used to learn the weights during the training phase.

By clicking here, you may access the data from Kaggle. The datasets include data on 768 women, a goal variable, and several medical predictor variables. The classification objective is to determine if there is diabetes among the patients in the dataset.

Decision tree:

A machine learning tool for classification or regression is the decision tree. It divides the dataset into sections by using if–else control expressions to the characteristics. Some of the few algorithms that can be used to build decision trees may be ones you are already familiar with. The most popular algorithms are ID3, C4.5, and CART. Nevertheless, the Scikit-learn Python package only supports the classification and regression trees (CART) algorithm. The only basis for this study is the CART algorithm.

SVM:

A well-liked machine learning approach for classification and regression analysis is called support vector machines (SVMs). Finding the ideal hyper-plane with the biggest feasible margin between two classes of data is the aim of SVM. The input data is translated into a higher-dimensional space in SVM so that the classes can be divided using a linear boundary. SVM can handle nonlinearly separable data since it also uses a kernel function to translate the input data to a higher-dimensional space. SVM provides several benefits, such as the capacity to handle high-dimensional data and the ability to perform effectively on small datasets. Although SVM can be sensitive to the choice of hyperparameters and kernel functions, it can be computationally expensive for large datasets.

Random forest:

For predicting diabetes in patients, the well-liked machine learning method random forest classification is extremely helpful. For predicting diabetes, a random forest classifier would use the patient's medical information, including age, BMI, blood pressure, and glucose levels, as input and produce a probability score that would indicate how likely it is that the patient has diabetes. The ability to handle a high number of input features and resistance to overfitting make random forest classifiers particularly well-suited for this task.

They are suitable for processing huge datasets because they are also reasonably quick and effective. Also, because each input feature's significance may be rated according to how much it contributes to the final prediction, random forest classifiers are simple to comprehend. In general, random forest classification is an effective method for predicting diabetes and can give

Table 6.3 Accuracies of the various algorithms.

Algorithms	Accuracy in %
K-nearest neighbors	81
Logistic regression	78
Decision tree	99
Random forest	97
SVM	77

important information about patient risk factors and the development of the condition. Table 6.3 shows the accuracies of various algorithms.

Discussion

One of the most important medical problems that actually exist is detecting diabetes at an early stage. The meticulous efforts of this study are aimed at developing a system that can forecast diabetes. In this chapter, five machine learning classification methods are explored and evaluated using a range of criteria. The John Diabetes Database is the focus of research. Experimental results using the decision tree approach indicate that the suggested system is adequate with a 99% accuracy rate. The created system and machine learning classification methods may be used in the future to predict or identify more diseases. The work can be improved and expanded by incorporating further machine learning techniques for automating the analysis of diabetes methods.

6.4.3 Smart diagnosis during COVID-19

In response to the discovery of the first pandemic case in the world in December 2019, a public health emergency has been proclaimed by the World Health Organization (WHO) (Hosseini Ard et al., 2021). The primary contributor to the current catastrophe is the pandemic's global expansion. The coronavirus known as SARS-CoV-2 is responsible for the severe acute respiratory syndrome, sometimes known as a novel coronavirus (COVID-19). The new coronavirus COVID-19 transmitted swiftly when it was spread from one person to another. To limit the pandemic and stop the coronavirus from spreading, a lockdown has been put in place. COVID-19 weakens billions of people globally, harming their social and economic well-being in addition to their health. Many persons passed away within a short time and suffered health issues resembling COVID-19 symptoms.

The pandemic has made the issue of medical facilities more pressing. Because there were no known therapies or treatments, every country was in a panic over how to restrict and stop the virus's spread as well as how to treat or diagnose the coronavirus. The only services offered by health centers were those linked to emergencies and the coronavirus. In order to stop the coronavirus from spreading, health centers were closed for other medical-related reasons. At the time, smart services helped doctors detect and diagnose patients. Real-time coronavirus detection was the biggest problem; controlling the spread of disease required early diagnosis. The COVID-19's gestation period is exceptionally long, lasting between 2 and 14 days. There are no obvious indications of inflection at this point. From 8 to 16 days after the infection, the symptoms start to appear. The length of the incubation period encourages the virus to propagate and infect people more than once. The following symptoms have been reported as COVID-19 symptoms: fever, cough, tiredness, sore throat, and headache. This appeared to be flu or cold symptoms. As a result, a specific COVID-19 test is necessary. The coronavirus is detected via reverse transcription-polymerase chain reaction (RTPCR), rapid antigen test (RAT), computed tomography scan, and a variety of biosensors. The sensitivity of COVID-19 tests varies depending on the testing procedure, the test's duration, and the testing apparatus. In the present pandemic crisis, medical experts select remote monitoring using mobile computing, AI, and IoT technology for patients' diagnosis and treatment. These sophisticated real-time medical device's data allow for prompt and crucial decisions regarding disease treatment. Modern technology allows for smart healthcare to track the suspicious subject (one with an infection or one without).

6.4.4 Kidney disease prediction using machine learning

We are all aware of the kidney's importance to the human body. Specifically, this oversees excretion and osmoregulation. All toxic and unnecessary substances are gathered and eliminated from the body by the kidney and excretion system. To put it simply, chronic renal disease affects one million people. Chronic kidney diseases (CKD) occur in India each year. A different word for chronic kidney disease is renal failure. Renal function slowly deteriorates as a result of this significant kidney illness. With CKD, the kidneys gradually lose their ability to run for a number of years. A person can develop irreversible renal failure. If CKD is not recognized and treated in its early stages, the following symptoms may manifest in CKD patients: low blood sugar, anemia, poor nutrition, poor health, and nerve damage lowered immune response as a result of the threats of hazardous waste, electrolytes, and fluid accumulation progressive phases in your blood and physique. Early detection of CKD is essential since it has gradual progression and symptoms that are not particular to the illness. Those who have no symptoms at all may benefit from machine learning to determine if they have CKD or not. By using past CKD patient data to create a predictive model, machine learning does this. The glomerular filtration rate (GFR) is the most accurate test to assess kidney health and determine your stage of chronic kidney disease. Using the results, it can be calculated.

Methodology

Dataset:

A dataset for the machine learning technique used to predict chronic renal illness can be downloaded from the Kaggle website. The dataset in question contains 400 patient records. Although they have 25 traits as well, we just use 11 of them to create the model: age, blood pressure, albumin classification, serum creatinine, hemoglobin, white blood cell, anemia, red blood cells, red blood cell counts, pus cells, and pus cells clumping. The model is created using all 11 attributes, including packed cell volume.

Data pre-processing:

Data cleaning: Get online raw data of CKD patients from public sources. We first provided the characteristic names because the names are absent from the data that was retrieved from the Internet. With the WEKA function, missing values from the dataset, such as NAs or blank values, are eliminated. "Replace Missing Values," which replaces NAs with the mean values of that property. Compression of data: Out of the 25 total features, we have identified 14 significant attributes from the dataset, which are crucial for building a predictive model. Table 6.4 shows the chosen properties.

Training and testing dataset:

Each of the two smaller datasets that make up the larger dataset includes 14 attributes. Data for instruction: 300 of the 400 records are present in the training dataset, which was created from the source dataset of CKD records. Data for testing: 100 out of the 400 entries from the primary CKD dataset are included in the testing dataset.

Pre-processing:

Processing before data is the process of changing or encoding corrupted data into a form that a machine can quickly and simply analyze. A dataset can be

Table 6.4   Attribute properties.

Attribute	Value used
Age	Discrete integer values
Blood pressure	Discrete integer values
Albumin	Nominal values
Red blood cells	Nominal values (normal, abnormal)
Pus cell	Nominal values (normal, abnormal)
Pus cell clumps	Nominal values (present, not-present)
Serum creatinine	Numeric values
Hemoglobin	Numeric values
White blood cell count	Discrete integer values
Red blood cell count	Numeric values
Anemia	Nominal values (yes, no)
Classification	Nominal values (CKD, not CKD)
Appetite	Nominal values (good, poor)
Packed cell volume	Discrete integer values

thought of as a grouping of data components. Several criteria that guarantee an object's fundamental properties, such as the physical object's mass or the time at which an event occurred, are used to identify data objects. The dataset's missing values might need to be estimated or eliminated. Filling in the gaps with the mean, median, or mode value of the pertinent, the most typical approach to coping with missing data is the feature. Since object values cannot be used for analysis, the numerical values with type as must be translated. It is necessary to transform the object-typed numerical numbers to float64 values. The categorical attributes' null values are changed to the value currently occurring most frequently in that attribute column. Label By assigning an integer to each distinct attribute value, you can categorize data into numerical traits. The properties are automatically converted to an integer(int) data type as a result. Each missing value in that attribute field is replaced by the mean value, which is calculated beforehand from each column. We are using a function called imputer to figure out the mean value for each column. When the replacement and encoding are finished, it is necessary to train, validate, and test the data. Here, data training is the main concern.

Feature selection:

The procedure called feature selection entails selecting the features that have the biggest influence on our output or prediction variable computationally. In order to find the most important features in the dataset, the ant colony optimization (ACO) was used in this study. It is a technique for discovering effective pathways through graphs to address computational issues. Artificial ants are multi-agent systems that take their cues from actual ant behavior. Pheromone-based communication is often the dominating paradigm among biological ants.

Local search algorithms and artificial ants have been the go-to solution for many optimization problems involving some sort of graph. This approach analyzes pheromone intensities at each iteration, as opposed to aggregating them. The suggested algorithm will modify a modest amount of characteristics in subsets that are picked by the best ants. An algorithm for classification must be used as the wrapper evaluation function to assess the performance of the subgroups.

ACO: To employ an ant colony algorithm, the optimization issue must be the endeavor of discovering the shortest path on a weighted network. Each ant stochastically creates a solution, or the order in which the edges in the graph should be followed, in the first step of each iteration. The second phase compares the different ants' travel paths. At the last stage, the pheromone concentrations on each edge are updated. A solution must be developed for each ant to move across the graph. On selecting, an ant will weigh the length of each edge that is reachable from its current location as well as the constant pheromone level when choosing the next edge in its tour.

The ant colony optimization package is called ACO Pants. We may quickly choose how to visit the associated nodes in order to reduce the path by using pants. Data is represented by nodes, whereas labor is represented by edges that connect nodes. Using a list and a formula that yields the edge length between any two nodes. The precise length of the path might not be provided. In this context, length denotes the effort required to move between nodes. To find the answer, an iterative approach must be used.

In order to find a solution, several ants travel along the path that passes by each and every node in turn. Depending on the length of the solution employed, on each edge, the pheromone concentration is updated. The ant that traveled the shortest distance is thought to represent the local best solution. Every local best solution is documented. The local answer is regarded as the global best solution if it is the closest to the best from any of the preceding iterations. The top ant that was thus detected fortifies the overall best solution path even further by adding its pheromone to it. This procedure is repeated frequently.

In terms of training accuracy, testing accuracy, and cross-validation accuracy, some of the algorithms mentioned above outperformed others. These include the decision tree classifier, the random forest classifier, the boost classifier, and the additional trees classifier, the XGB classifier, and the classifier. The Python Scikit and Kera frameworks were used for the implementations and evaluations. These include the decision tree classifier, boost classifier, extra trees classifier, random forest classifier, XGB classifier, and classifier. Despite the fact that all of the aforementioned models offered 100% accuracy, it is essential to determine the factors that have the biggest impact on each model before choosing one. The relevance of the feature was calculated after calculating the standard deviation of each algorithm's feature importance, which plainly displayed the algorithm's performance.

Almost 14% of people worldwide suffer from the potentially fatal condition, which is referred to as chronic kidney disease (CKD). Pre-processing of the data, handling of missing data, and feature selection are used to determine whether CKD is present or not. This work further emphasizes the significance of adding domain knowledge into feature selection when analyzing clinical data linked to CKD.

6.5 Future Issues and Conclusion

The integration of ML−IoT into all healthcare systems is excessively difficult. Since they feel more comfortable and in control using simple approaches like "pen and paper," senior decision-makers usually choose them. The simplest version is required due to the complexity of ML configurations. Several healthcare organizations are also discouraged from making financial investments in their staff and other ML models. Like how other IoT technologies are developing, there is a lot of ethical debate around ML. We have given up power and control when computers learn to "think and operate for themselves" using our algorithms, and sometimes we are unsure of exactly what the machine has learned, putting patients' lives at risk. Additionally, ML−IoT advancements may cause issues with insurance coverage. One of the fields that are expanding and becoming more expensive is the healthcare industry. Artificial learning and machine learning (ML) technologies offer higher-quality care at cheaper prices. Utilizing IoT technology, medical professionals and patients improve the atmosphere for medical devices. Additionally, ML can assist the healthcare sector better manage operations, control expenses, and help medical professionals diagnose and treat diseases more effectively and precisely. The first step in this ML sector has already been examined by numerous organizations. Additionally, the learning of the scheme was influenced by the vast amounts of data and algorithms that could be used to group data into certain categories using ML−IoT. People occasionally struggle with decision-making and rely on facts while choosing any action, including IoT.

References

[1] Aghdam, Z. N., Rahmani, A. M., Hosseinzadeh, M. J. C. M., & Biomedicine, P. I. (2020). The Role of the Internet of Things in Healthcare: Future Trends and Challenges. Academic Press. Al-Fuqaha, A., Guizani, M., Mohammadi, M., Aledhari, M., & Ayyash, M. (2015).

[2] Internet of things: A survey on enabling technologies, protocols, and applications. IEEE Communications Surveys and Tutorials, 17(4), 2347–2376. doi:10.1109/ COMST.2015.2444095 Athey, S. (2018).

[3] The impact of machine learning on economics. In The economics of artificial intelligence: An agenda (pp. 507–547). University of Chicago Press. Atiqur, R., Liton, A., & Wu, G. (2020).

[4] Content Caching Strategy at Small Base Station in 5G Networks with Mobile Edge Computing. International Journal of Science and Business., 4(4), 104–112. Atrey, K., Singh, B. K., & Bodhey, N. K. (2021).

[5] Feature Selection for Classification of Breast Cancer in Histopathology Images: A Comparative Investigation Using Wavelet-Based Color Features. In A. A. Rizvanov, B. K. Singh, & P. Ganasala (Eds.), Advances in Biomedical Engineering and Technology. Lecture Notes in Bioengineering. Springer. doi:10.1007/978-981-15-6329-4_30 Aziz, M. N., & Islam, A. (2020).

[6] Reviewing Data Mining as an enabling technology for BI. International Journal of Science and Business, 4(7), 46–51. Babar, M., Khan, F., Iqbal, W., Yahya, A., Arif, F., Tan, Z., & Chuma, J. M. (2018).

[7] A secured data management scheme for smart societies in industrial internet of things environment. IEEE Access: Practical Innovations, Open Solutions, 6, 43088–43099. doi:10.1109/ACCESS.2018.2861421 Baker, S. B., Xiang, W., & Atkinson, I. (2017).

[8] Internet of things for smart healthcare: Technologies, challenges, and opportunities. IEEE Access: Practical Innovations, Open Solutions, 5, 26521–26544. doi:10.1109/ACCESS.2017.2775180 Banerjee, N., & Das, S. (2020).

[9] Prediction Lung Cancer. In Machine Learning Perspective. IEEE. Basha, N. (2019). Early Detection of Heart Syndrome Using Machine Learning Technique. 4th International Conference on Electrical, Electronics, Communication, Computer Technologies and Optimization Techniques (ICEECCOT). Birje, M. N., & Hanji, S. S. (2020).

[10] Internet of things based distributed healthcare systems: A review. J. Data Inf. Manag, 2(3), 149–165. doi:10.100742488-020-00027-x

[11] Aljumah, A.A., Ahamad, M.G., Siddiqui, M.K., 2013. Application of data mining: Diabetes health care in young and old patients. Journal of King Saud University - Computer and Information Sciences 25, 127–136. doi:10.1016/j.jksuci.2012.10.003.

[12] Bamnote, M.P., G.R., 2014. Design of Classifier for Detection of Diabetes Mellitus Using Genetic Programming. Advances in Intelligent Systems and Computing 1, 763–770. doi:10.1007/978-3-319-11933-5.

[13] Choubey, D.K., Paul, S., Kumar, S., Kumar, S., 2017. Classification of Pima indian diabetes dataset using naive bayes with genetic algorithm as an attribute selection, in: Communication and Computing Systems: Proceedings of the International Conference on Communication and Computing System (ICCCS 2016), pp. 451–455.

[14] Dhomse Kanchan B., M.K.M., 2016. Study of Machine Learning Algorithms for Special Disease Prediction using Principal of Component Analysis, in: 2016 International Conference on Global Trends in Signal Processing, Information Computing and Communication, IEEE. pp. 5–10.

[15] "Global Facts: About Kidney Disease," [Online]. Available: https://www.kidney.org/kidneydisease/global-facts-about-kidney-disease/. [Accessed: 20-Feb-2020].

[16] F. E. Murtagh, J. Addington-Hall, P. Edmonds, P. Donohoe, I. Carey,K. Jenkins, and I. J. Higginson, "Symptoms in the month before death for stage 5 chronic kidney disease patients managed without dialysis, "Journal of pain and symptom management, vol. 40, no. 3, pp. 342–352,2010.

[17] J. Xiao, R. Ding, X. Xu, H. Guan, X. Feng, T. Sun, S. Zhu, and. Ye, "Comparison and development of machine learning tools in the prediction of chronic kidney disease progression," Journal of translational medicine, vol. 17, no. 1, p. 119, 2019.

[18] W. Gunaratna, K. Pedrera, and K. Kahandawaarachchi, "Performancee-valuation on machine learning classification techniques for disease-classification and forecasting through data analytics for chronic kid-neydisease (ckd)," in 2017 IEEE 17th International Conference on Bioin-formatics and Bioengineering (BIBE). IEEE, 2017, pp. 291–296.

[19] A. J. Aljaaf, D. Al-Jumeily, H. M. Haglan, M. Alloghani, T. Baker,A. J. Hussain, and J. Mustafina, "Early prediction of chronic kidneydisease using machine learning supported by predictive analytics," in2018 IEEE Congress on Evolutionary Computation (CEC). IEEE,2018, pp. 1–9.

7

High-performance Intelligent Systems for Real-time Medical Imaging

V. Kanchana Devi[1], E. Umamaheswari[1], A. Karmel[1], Nebojsa Bacanin[2], David A. Maxim Gururaj[1], and R. Sreenivas[1]

[1]Vellore Institute of Technology, India
[2]Singidunum University, Serbia
E-mail: kanchanadevi@vit.ac.in

Abstract

Health is always the first thing to be taken care of particularly when a human being is taken into consideration. Most of the people are unaware of hidden diseases inside their bodies. Medical imaging can be pitched in as a solution for this. Generally, medical imaging is used to detect diseases inside the body, and visuals of organs, tissues, and other body parts can be drawn out. The incorporation of artificial intelligence (AI)/machine learning (ML) with high-performance computers pave way for high-performance intelligent systems. Some high-performance intelligent systems can be used in the field of medical imaging to identify the hidden diseases. High-performance intelligent systems use artificial intelligence (AI)/machine learning (ML), and deep learning (DL) technologies. The latter is used to reduce the lesions caused during a surgery. It also automates time-consuming processes in the field of medicine. Deep learning is used mainly for the quick diagnosis and analysis of diseases and lesions. Such high-performance intelligent systems help people in the medical field in various ways and can be used in a variety of applications.

Keywords: Medical imaging, artificial intelligence, deep learning, high performance computers, health.

7.1 Introduction

Human beings toil hard to fill their stomach. They consume food to stay healthy and fit. There are many unknown diseases inside a human body. This can lead to chronic ailments, or even fatalities, if not treated. To make the diagnosis of a disease easier, medical image processing is used. Medical image processing [8] makes use of high-performance intelligent systems. These systems play a major role in supporting the doctors, by automating humongous tasks. Deep learning (DL) is widely used in real-time medical imaging [9]. Convolutional neural network (CNN), which is a subset class of deep learning (DL), can be used, which would be of high help in diagnosing diseases using real-time medical imaging. There are other deep learning algorithms that can be used, which are convolutional neural network (CNN), multi-layer perceptron (MLP), residual network (ResNet), and generative adversarial networks (GANs). These deep learning concepts can enhance medical image processing. A gist of these algorithms is listed below.

- Convolutional neural network (CNN):
  CNN is used in medical image processing for its strong nature of feature extraction. The regional features of segmentation function are analyzed [8]. The architecture of CNN is shown in Figure 7.1.
- Multi-layer perceptron (MLP):
  MLP is a subclass of artificial neural network (ANN). This MLP has fully connected layers. It is capable of mapping input dataset into a set of desired outputs. Utilizing MLP in medical image analysis has been the focus of research efforts over the past few decades. The layered architecture of multi-layer perceptron is shown in Figure 7.2.
- Residual network (ResNet):
  ResNet is a deep learning architecture, which falls under convolutional neural network (CNN). Usually, the number that is followed by the

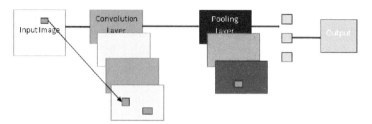

Figure 7.1 Architecture of CNN.

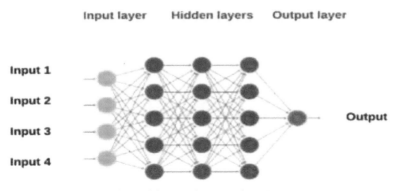

Figure 7.2   Architecture of an MLP.

ResNet depicts the number of layers. The more the number of layers in ResNet, the greater is the accuracy. For example, ResNet-101 depicts that the model is 101 layers deep. To overcome the challenge of training deep CNNs and prevent model performance degradation, ResNet is presented. ResNet's elemental concept is residual learning, which is predicated on the idea that it is simpler to optimize the residual mapping than the original, unreferenced mapping. The efficacy of residual learning has led to extensive application of ResNet in the restoration of real-time medical images.

- Generative model (GAN):
  GAN is the well-known generative models in deep learning. GAN has gained increasing attention for its exceptional performance in a variety of computer vision applications, including the reconstruction of medical images. The real-time medical images are captured and reconstructed with GAN, which will help in precise decision-making.
  With the help of the above-mentioned deep learning (DL) algorithms, an image from a medical dataset can be classified, segmented, and the features can be extracted. These algorithms can also be used in the reconstruction of real-time medical images.

7.2 Background Study

An overview of deep learning in medical imaging (2021) [1]:

This chapter has introduced the concept of deep learning techniques such as artificial neural networks (ANNs), recurrent neural networks (RNNs), and convolutional neural network (CNN) algorithms, such as, EfficientNet, U-Net, ResNet, DenseNet, etc., in the field of medical image processing. This paper introduces methods that fit in for the best optimization technique with a meager amount of data that is required for training. A detailed parameter of each architecture and algorithm is also listed in this paper.

Intelligent systems and computational methods in medical and health-care solutions with their challenges during the COVID-19 pandemic (2021) [2]:

This paper discusses the use of intelligent systems and computational methods in medical and healthcare solutions when COVID-19 was at its peak. This is basically a journal and particularly dives deep into the improvements in healthcare industry incorporated by intelligent systems and their computational methods. This journal also focuses on signal processing and machine learning (ML) algorithms, which play a vital role in diagnosing diseases through medical imaging.

A review of the application of deep learning in medical image classification and segmentation (2020) [3]:

This paper focuses on applying the technique of Big Data analysis incorporated along with the concepts of intelligent imaging and deep learning (DL), which is helpful in early diagnosis of chronic diseases and ailments. This study first describes how deep learning algorithms are used in medical image analysis, then it elaborates on deep learning classification and segmentation techniques, and last it introduces the more traditional and contemporary mainstream network models. The classification and segmentation of medical images, including fundus, CT/MRI tomography, ultrasound, and digital pathology based on various imaging modalities, was then covered in detail. Finally, it examines potential issues and foresees how deep learning medical imaging analysis will grow.

The role of artificial intelligence in medical imaging research (2019) [4]:

This is a review article paper. This paper discusses the challenges that need to be resolved before incorporating artificial intelligence (AI) in the field of medicine. This paper also discusses the use of AI in radiology and radiation oncology explicitly, along with the algorithms used. Some of the algorithms used in the latter are U-Net-GAN, fully convolutional networks (FCN), and so on. Principal component analysis (PCA), support vector machine (SVM), and so on are used in the former. These algorithms are highly effective in medical imaging.

Review and prospect: Artificial intelligence in advanced medical imaging (2021) [5]:

This is a review paper. This review paper discusses on how deep learning (DL) is tactically used to reconstruct the images obtained by MRIs, CTs, and PETs. Steps to reconstruct the images depends on technical developments of deep learning. These steps consist of (i) data preparation, (ii) network architecture design, (iii) loss function, and (iv) settings required for training the model.

Deep learning in medical imaging (2019) [6]:

The development, history, and applications of deep learning (DL) in medical Imaging. This is a review article. This article gives the pin-point definition of machine learning (ML). This article also highlights and dives deep into the three categories of artificial intelligence (AI). The different types of neural networks, i.e., deep neural networks (DNN) and artificial neural networks (ANN), are also focused on in this paper.

Preparing medical imaging data for machine learning (2019) [7]:

This paper focuses on the preparation of medical imaging data incorporated with artificial intelligence (AI). This paper also discusses the different steps involved in the preparation of medical imaging dataset.

Convolutional neural networks in medical image understanding: A survey (2021) [8]:

This paper discusses the applications of convolutional neural networks (CNN) in medical imaging. The ultimate motto of this paper is to motivate researchers to apply the concept of CNN in medical imaging. Apart from these, a brief introduction on CNN is given along with its architectures. Concepts relating to understanding of medical imaging such as image classification, segmentation, localization, and detection have also been discussed.

Deep-learning-enabled medical computer vision (2021) [9]:

This paper discusses the key algorithms involved in medical imaging with the use of computer vision (CV). This paper also surveys the methodologies used by computer vision (CV), incorporated along with medicine. This also focuses on research into various applications of medicine, such as medical imaging, medical videos, and clinical deployments in real time.

Designing clinically translatable artificial intelligence systems for high-dimensional medical imaging (2021) [10]:

An overview of high-dimensional medical imaging's machine learning's unique architectural requirements and dataset curation quirks, as well as a discussion of explainability, uncertainty, and bias in these systems are discussed. In the process, we offer a guide for researchers who are interested in overcoming some of the problems and difficulties associated with developing clinically applicable AI systems.

Application of *K*-nearest neighbor classification in medical data mining (2014) [11]:

In retrospect, the KNN classifier's performance is highly dependent on the distance metric used to identify the query points' *K*-nearest neighbors. The standard Euclidean distance is commonly used in practice. In order to make diagnoses based on historical data, this study makes extensive use of data storage. It uses a proprietary algorithm to calculate the likelihood of occurrence of a specific ailment. This KNN algorithm boosts diagnostic precision. The algorithm can be used to improve automated diagnoses, such as distinguishing between multiple diseases with similar symptoms.

Random forest algorithm-based ultrasonic image in the diagnosis of patients with dry eye syndrome and its relationship with tear osmotic pressure (2022) [12]:

The study's goal was to investigate the diagnostic utility of ultrasound for dry eye disease using the random forest segmentation algorithm, as well as the relationship between dry eye degree and tear osmotic pressure. For the study, 100 patients with dry eye syndrome were divided into two groups, with 50 patients in each: group A (conventional ultrasonic detection) and group B (ultrasonic detection based on the random forest segmentation algorithm). An ultrasonic measurement was the gold standard for assessing the effectiveness of ultrasonic diagnosis. To assess the severity of dry eye, the Ocular Surface Disease Index (OSDI) Questionnaire and the DR-1 tear film lipid layer (TFLL) test were used. Tear osmotic pressure can be used to determine the severity of dry eyes quickly. The ultrasound-based random forest segmentation algorithm has a high clinical application value in the diagnosis of dry eye syndrome.

Assessing the role of random forests in medical image segmentation (2021) [13]:

In the field of medical image segmentation using a GPU, neural networks are a field of study that can produce very good results very quickly. Random forests are one method for producing good results without the use of GPUs. For this purpose, two random forest approaches were compared to a cutting-edge deep convolutional neural network. For the comparison, the PhC-C2DH-U373 and retinal imaging datasets were used. According to the evaluation, the deep convolutional neutral network produced the best results. However, one of the random forest approaches outperformed the others. The results show that random forest approaches are a good alternative to deep convolutional neural networks for medical image segmentation, allowing the use of a GPU to be avoided.

Application of support vector machine modeling for prediction of common diseases: The case of diabetes and pre-diabetes (2010) [14]:

Based on support vector machine (SVM) techniques, this paper presents a potentially useful alternative approach to classifying people with and without common diseases. This paper also demonstrates how diabetes and pre-diabetes can be detected in a cross-sectional representative sample of the US population.

An improved SVM classifier for medical image classification (2007) [15]:

The support vector machine (SVM) has a high classification accuracy as well as good fault tolerance and generalization abilities. The rough set theory (RST) method is useful for dealing with large amounts of data and eliminating redundant information. In this paper, the authors have combined SVM and RST to create the improved support vector machine (ISVM) for digital mammography classification. The experimental results show that this ISVM classifier can achieve 96.56% accuracy, which is approximately 3.42% higher than the SVM classifier's 92.94% accuracy, and error recognition rates are close to 100% on average.

A random-forest-based predictor for medical data classification using feature ranking (2019) [16]:

In the field of medical informatics, medical data classification is regarded as a difficult task. Despite the fact that many works have been published, there is still room for improvement. A feature ranking-based approach for medical data classification is developed and implemented in this paper. A dataset's features are ranked using appropriate ranker algorithms, and the random forest classifier is then used to build the predictor only on highly ranked features. Authors conducted extensive experiments on ten benchmark datasets, and the results are encouraging. As a result, highly accurate predictors for ten different diseases as well as a methodology that is general enough to perform well for other diseases with comparable datasets are presented.

Image classification based on ResNet (2020) [17]:

This paper proposes the concept of ResNet (residual network), as a solution to train deeper network. ResNet solves the problem of gradient descent, and many other parameters. In particular, the weight matrix product operation must be performed in each step of back propagation from the last layer to the first layer in the gradient descent process, so that the gradient drops exponentially to 0. (In rare cases, there is the issue of gradient explosion, which occurs when the gradient grows exponentially to the point of overflow during the propagation process.) As a result, during the training process, it will be discovered that as the number of layers increases, so does the rate of gradient. As a result, while deepening the network allows it to express any complex function, training the network becomes increasingly difficult as network layers increase.

A holistic overview of deep learning approach in medical imaging (2022) [18]:

This paper is an overview of various deep learning algorithms and methods used in medical imaging. This paper has explained the different types of medical imaging. Deep learning frameworks are brought under limelight in this paper. The deep learning methodologies such as convolutional neural network (CNN) and recurrent neural network (RNN) have been discussed, which fall under the supervised learning category. The complete concepts of unsupervised learning, i.e., autoencoders, generative adversarial networks, and restricted Boltzmann machines, have been summarized. Semi-supervised learning, reinforcement learning, and self-supervised learning have also been discussed. This paper has also presented a perspective of the best deep learning algorithms that can be used in medical imaging along with methodologies. In a nutshell, this paper is an overview of the different deep learning algorithm used in medical imaging.

Multi-layered deep learning perceptron approach for health risk prediction (2020) [19]:

This paper aims at the health risk prediction using a supervised learning approach. As a solution, multi-layer perceptron algorithm is proposed for this investigation. In this proposed solution, for the need of accurate classification, and analysis of risk, MLP, which is based on data classification, is used. An algorithm has been proposed for the prediction of health risk. The process of feature extraction and classification has also been imposed. The dataset that has been used is discussed in this paper. As a result, this paper primarily relies on the deep learning framework to predict the risk of health.

Medical image segmentation model based on triple gate multi-layer perceptron (2022) [20]:

The triple gate multi-layer perceptron U-net (TGMLP U-Net) is an MLP-based medical image segmentation model in which authors designed the triple gate multi-layer perceptron (TGMLP), which is composed of three parts. The authors propose the triple MLP module based on multi-layer perceptron for encoding feature position information in this model. It uses linear projection methodology to encode features from the high, wide, and channel dimensions, allowing the model to capture the long-distance dependence of features along the spatial dimension as well as the precise position information of features in three dimensions with less computational overhead. The global perceptron partitions the feature map and performs correlation modeling for each partition to determine the global dependency between partitions. To investigate the relationship of context feature information within the structure, the local priors employ multi-scale convolution with high local feature extraction ability. Finally, a gate-controlled mechanism to effectively solve the problem of learning the dependence of position embeddings between patches and within patches in medical images due to the relatively small number of samples in medical image segmentation data has been proposed.

A multi-layer perceptron-based medical decision support system for heart disease diagnosis (2006) [21]:

A multiplayer perceptron-based decision support system is developed in this paper to aid in the diagnosis of heart diseases. The system's input layer contains 40 input variables that are classified into four groups and then encoded using the proposed coding schemes. A cascade learning process determines the number of nodes in the hidden layer. Each of the five nodes in the output layer represents a different heart disease of interest. The substituting mean method is used in the system to handle a patient's missing data. In addition, the system is trained using an improved back propagation algorithm. A total of 352 medical records from patients with five different heart diseases were used to train and test the system. Three assessment methods are used to evaluate the system's generalization: cross-validation, holdout, and bootstrapping. The findings show that the proposed MLP-based decision support system has very high diagnosis accuracy ($>90\%$) and relatively small intervals (5%), demonstrating its utility in assisting clinic decision-making for heart diseases.

7.3 Explanation of Algorithms

7.3.1 Convolutional neural networks (CNNs)

Now thinking about the patterns and the connections of biological neurons in the human nervous system, machine learning can be incorporated with these biological neurons. Neural networks are one of the widely used frameworks in real-time medical imaging. Neural networks have the tendency to make predictions obtained from a medical image or a dataset. For this reason, this particular framework is used in most of the video recognition tasks and activity recognition tasks. The imitation of biological neural network models by machine learning is known as artificial neural networks (ANN). As a solution to propel the performance of the ANNs, the deep learning (DL) frameworks were introduced. These layers are interconnected. The input data are weighted and summarized at each node in the network before being sent to an activation function. During training, weights are dynamically optimized. There are three types of layers associated with this concept. They are input layers, hidden layers, and the output layers. There are various types of ANN DL architecture. One such architecture that is used in real-time medical imaging is convolutional neural networks (CNNs). Convolutional neural networks (CNNs) are a widely used concept in image classification and in medical imaging. This algorithm is used to detect patterns in images and predict the output based on the same. This DL framework is used to treat spatial data. It has the following layers: pooling, convolution, and fully connected.

(i) Pooling layer: The input image is down-sized, which plays an important factor in the reduction of the number of parameters involved, the computational memory involved, and the memory load involved. The neurons

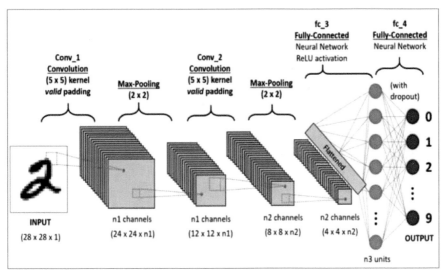

Figure 7.3 Visual architecture of CNN.

involved in the pooling layer are connected to its neighboring neurons. The average of the input is taken.

(ii) Convolution layer: Only the pixels in their receptive fields are connected to the neurons in the first convolutional layer. Only the neurons in the first layer that are situated inside a tiny rectangle are connected to each neuron in the second convolutional layer. Figure 7.3 depicts the visual architecture of CNN.

Convolution:

A convolution method using learnable filters, also known as kernels or weights, is applied to the input image. The output of the convolution operation is a set of feature maps that represent the learned features at each location in the image.

Formula for convolution layer is shown in eqn (11.1):

$$z(i, j, k) = \text{sum\_}\{m = -k\} \wedge (\{k\}\text{sum\_}\{n = -k\}$$
$$\wedge \{k\} x(i + m, j + n, l) \ ) * w(m, n, l, k) + b(k) \quad (7.1)$$

where x is the input image, b is the bias term, k is the size of the filter, z is the output feature, and w is the learnable feature.

ReLU:

In order to induce nonlinearity and enable the network to learn complex patterns, the output feature map is element-by-element treated to a nonlinear activation function.

Formula for the ReLU layer is given in eqn (11.2):

$$ReLU(x) = max(0, x) \tag{7.2}$$

where x is the input to the activation function.

Pooling:

The output of the activation function is subjected to a pooling operation in order to reduce the spatial resolution of the feature maps and increase the network's receptive field.

Eqn (7.3) shows the formula for pooling layer:

$$y(i, j, k) = \max\_\{m = 0\} \wedge \{p - 1\} \, [\max]\_\{n = 0\} \wedge \{p - 1\}$$
$$z(sp * i + m, \; sp * j + n, \; k) \tag{7.3}$$

where p is the pooling window and sp is the stride.

Fully connected layers:

Using the output of the convolutional layers, which has been flattened into a vector, a sequence of fully connected layers performs the final classification or regression process.

The formula for fully connected layers is given in eqn (7.4):

$$y = f(Wx + b)s. \tag{7.4}$$

7.3.1.1 Advantages and disadvantages of CNN

Human supervision is not required for the identification of important features in CNN. The accuracy produced in the recognition of images and classification of images is high and is hence used in image recognition. When compared with other neural networks, the computational memory is lesser. Object orientation and position are not encoded. They find it difficult to classify photos with different positions. A substantial amount of training data is necessary for the CNN to function well. CNNs frequently function much more slowly due to techniques like max-pool. If the computer's GPU is not up to par, training a convolutional neural network with several layers could take a very long time. The image will be recognized by convolutional neural networks as distinct patterns made up of pixel clusters. They do not understand them as components of the image.

7.3.1.2 Why is CNN used in medical imaging?

The classification of real-time medical images is crucial to both clinical care and academic tasks. The conventional approach's performance has reached its apex, though. Furthermore, it takes a lot of time and effort to identify and extract the categorization criteria from them. The deep neural network is a cutting-edge machine learning method that has proven effective for a number of categorization issues. Convolutional neural networks excel at classifying images across a range of tasks, with the best performance. The labeling of such real-time medical images, however, necessitates a high level of specialized knowledge, making real-time medical image collections difficult to compile. Hence, CNN is used for medical imaging. Convolutional neural networks (CNNs) are a popular option in medical imaging due to their ability to automatically learn and extract pertinent properties from images. The use of CNNs in medical imaging has the following benefits: CNNs can be used to organize medical images into a variety of categories, such as healthy and diseased tissues and organs. Also, they can be used to group medical images into different stages of illness progression, which aids in diagnosis and therapy planning. In real-time medical images, such as those showing organs or lesions, CNNs can be utilized to distinguish different areas of interest. To aid in diagnosis and treatment planning, abnormalities' size, shape, and location can be quantified. The registration of medical pictures from many modalities or points in time can be done using CNNs. This can be useful for determining how well a drug is working, tracking the progression of an illness, and merging complementary data from several imaging modalities. It can be used in transfer learning, i.e., it can be used on large datasets.

7.3.1.3 Applications of CNN

Convolutional neural networks (CNNs) are widely used in ADAS (self-driving cars), and so on, due to its capability of object detection, which helps in facial recognition. Convolutional neural networks are used in the annotation of images, making it simpler for persons who are blind to comprehend the messages that are being sent [2], thus acting as a useful algorithm for image captioning. It also acts as a powerful algorithm for natural language processing (NLP) applications, such as feedback systems and voice synthesis. The simple neural network depicts that the number of hidden layers is limited. In contrast, deep neural network depicts that there are "*n*" number of hidden layers, and these depend on the number of input layers. In a nutshell, the number of hidden layers plays an important role in the complexity of the neural network.

7.3.2 Multi-layer perceptron (MLP)

The most basic sort of artificial neural network is the multilayer perceptron, sometimes known as a fully linked network. An input layer, an output layer, and one or more hidden layers combine to form a network's layered structure. Each layer consists of a number of units that are connected to surrounding layers (both input and output) but not to the units of the same layer. Perceptron is otherwise known as artificial neural networks (ANNs).

　　The perceptron adds up the input values after multiplying them by weights that correspond to the synaptic connections among living neurons. The weights, often referred to as training parameters, are modified after the network has been trained. The activation function (nonlinear function), which simulates the activation or generates the output of each perceptron, is then inserted with the weighted sum. As there is no restriction on the number of perceptron per layer and layers per network, the multilayer perceptron structure can be created with an endless number of configurations despite its small number of constituent parts. In proportion to the number of layers and perceptron per layer, a simple perceptron model can be added to a solid and complicated mathematical model. For instance, using eqn (7.5), the output y_1 of the first perceptron can be written as, given the vector of inputs $x = [x_1, x_2, x_3, ..., x_n]$ x_i R.

$$Y_1(x, w_1, b_1) = f\left(b_1 + \sum_{i=1}^{4} w_i x_i\right) \tag{7.5}$$

where the training parameters are w and b.
The activation function is depicted by f.
Eqn (6) shows the hidden layer

$$y(l) = f(l)(W(l)y(l-1)) \tag{7.6}$$

where W denotes the weight, f denotes the activation function, and $y(l)$ represents the output of the hidden layer.

7.3.2.1 Why is MLP used in medical imaging?

An image needs to be extracted numerically and classified in order to be processed further. This holds the same for dataset that includes real-time medical images. With the help of multi-layer perceptron, a medical image can be segmented. MLP analyzes the risk of a medical dataset and is also used for a precise classification of the dataset. The major usage of MLP in medical imaging is because it niches to provide a single output, when several input images are fed into the model. The concepts of backpropagation and hidden layers play a major role in MLPs.

(i) The backpropagation algorithm is based on the weights of the input. This, when adjusted, reduces the difference between the actual output and the desired output. This reduction in the difference improves the accuracy of the model. Backpropagation is calculated by the root mean squared error (RMSE) method. There are two types of passes in this algorithm, i.e., forward pass and the backward pass.

    (a) Forward pass: In this, the output layer's decision is compared to the ground truth labels as the signal flows from the input layer via the hidden layers to the output layer during the forward pass.

    (b) Backward pass: Using backpropagation and the chain rule of calculus, partial derivatives of the error function pertaining to various weights and biases are backpropagated through the MLP during the backward pass. The parameters may be altered along a gradient or error landscape produced by the differentiation process in order to move the MLP nearer to the error minimum. Any gradient-based

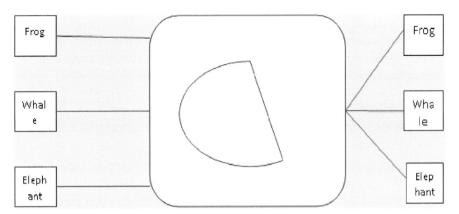

Figure 7.4 Learning through examples.

Figure 7.5   Trained model.

optimization algorithm, such as stochastic gradient descent, can be used to do this.
(ii) The hidden layers, on the other hand, are the nodes of the neurons stacked in the midst of the input and the output, which facilitates in the learning of complicated features.

7.3.2.2 Advantages and disadvantages of multi-layer perceptron

MLPs, or multilayer perceptrons, are the standard among neural networks. This is made of single-layer neurons or several layers. Usually, the input layer receives data; one or more hidden layers may offer several levels of abstraction, and the output layer is called the visible layer, which helps in predictions. They are extremely adaptable and are utilized to learn input-to-output mapping. They can be used with other kinds of data because of their adaptability. For example, it is possible to feed an MLP with an image's pixels condensed to a single long row of data. An MLP can be given words from a document that has been condensed into one long row of data. It is possible to condense even the lag observations for a time series prediction issue into a long row of data that can be fed into an MLP. This MLP is completely integrated, and its limitations are of too many parameters; some of the number parameters are width, depth, and height. In a particularly dense web, every node is connected to every other node, which causes duplication and inefficiency.

7.3.2.3 Applications of MLP

There is a wide range of applications where multi-layer perceptron is used. They are listed as follows:

(i) They are used in data compression (PCA), given the fact that redundant data are removed.
(ii) Used in hand-written character recognition, given the fact that the error loss is less than 1%.

(iii) Also used in the autonomous driving system. This helps in reducing the fatality rates due to road mishaps.
(iv) Used in medical imaging. MLP recognizes the images of a medical dataset and helps in identifying the related diseases corresponding to the medical image.

7.3.3 ResNet

CNN has different types of architecture, amongst which ResNet is a sub-division. Residual network (ResNet) is an architecture that has many layers and lesser number of parameters. This is used to train the model with a skip connection. A skip connection is used to skip some layers. In the case of a ResNet model, multiple skip connections are used. These skip connections consist of ReLU and batch normalization. Batch normalization is an important factor as it allows each layer in a network to learn in an independent and efficient manner. A model is trained in order to make it a target function. ResNet stands for residual network. To overcome the challenge of training very deep CNNs and prevent model performance degradation, ResNet is presented. ResNet's fundamental concept is residual learning, which is predicated on the idea that it is simpler to optimize the residual mapping than the original, unreferenced mapping. The efficacy of residual learning has led to an extensive application of ResNet in the restoration of real-time medical images. Gradient descent is used in the backpropagation technique used to train neural networks, which lowers the loss function and identifies the weights that minimize it. If there are too many layers, performance saturates or declines with each additional layer, and repeated multiplications will eventually cause the gradient to "disappear." The ResNet "skip connections" function presents a fresh approach to the vanishing gradient problem. Convolutional layers that are initially inactive (such as those in ResNet) are stacked, skipped, and the activations from the previous layer are used again. Skipping speeds up the initial training process by reducing the number of layers in the network. After the network has been retrained with all layers expanded, the remaining parts, also known as the residual parts, are free to explore more of the feature space of the input image. With batch normalization and nonlinearity in between, the majority of ResNet models skip two or three layers at once. HighwayNets, a kind of more complex ResNet architecture, have the ability to learn "skip weights," which determine how many layers to skip on the fly.

Below is the figure of a skip connection.

The formula for skip connection is shown in eqn (7.7):

$$x\left(l+1\right)=\ f\left(x\left(l\right),\ W\left(l\right)\right)+\ x\left(l\right) \tag{7.7}$$

where f represents the residual mapping, $x(l)$ is the output of the lth layer, and $W(l)$ is the weight of the lth layer.

The ResNet design can be implemented in practice using a variety of layers and skip connection configurations, including "ResNet-18," "ResNet-34," "ResNet-50," "ResNet-101," and "ResNet-152," which differ in the number of layers and the skip connection patterns used.

There are two major components in a skip connection.

 (i) Identity block
(ii) The convolution block

The convolution block aids in modifying and reorganizing the incoming data so that the first layer's output matches the third layer's dimensions and may be appended. The accuracy of a deep learning model depends on the above two components, i.e., the identity block and the convolution block. This also helps in the optimization of the model.

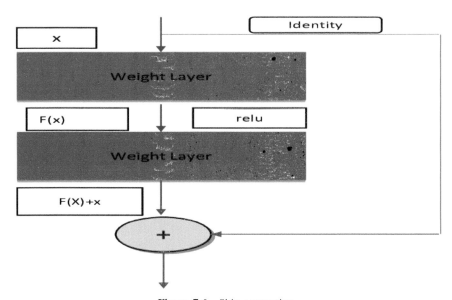

Figure 7.6   Skip connection.

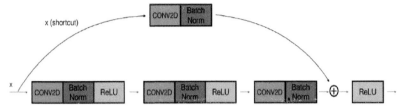

Figure 7.7 Convolutional block.

7.3.3.1 Why is ResNet used in real-time medical imaging?

Real-time medical image classification falls under the concept of computer vision (CV). A suitable algorithm for this concept would be the architecture of ResNet, taking into consideration many parameters. The fundamental aim of the ResNet architecture is to solve the vanishing gradient problem. There are many types of ResNet architecture, such as ResNet-50, ResNet-101, and so on. The numbers that are indicated after ResNet are the number of layers involved in the architecture. In ResNet, the greater the number of layers, the better is the accuracy, and the lesser is the complexity. When a real-time medical image dataset is taken into account, it all depends on the image and the image classification, i.e., a medical image can be classified accordingly, and the corresponding disease can also be identified. There is a degradation concern when considering how deeper networks will eventually converge throughout the deep learning process, which means that accuracy will initially rise before being saturated. As depth is raised, accuracy will decrease. As the accuracy decreases in both the training set and the test set, it is clear that the influence is not the result of overfitting. A cross-layer feature fusion enhances ResNet's ability to extract network features, and as networks go deeper, performance gradually increases. ResNet fares well in terms of accuracy and classification performance, when compared with other models. It is used in real-time medical imaging as a powerful tool. It is used to perform tasks such as image classification, detection, segmentation, and registration.

7.3.3.2 Advantages and disadvantages of ResNet

The ResNet architecture is always considered for image recognition because of the residual structure that is used, which makes the model easily learnable. It solves the vanishing gradient problem caused by the network depth when the process of reverse propagation is going on. ResNet has a good accuracy and performance when compared to other models. The classification accuracy is higher as the hierarchy is dense. The fundamental limitation of ResNets is that error detection gets difficult with deeper networks. Moreover, learning could be inefficient if the network is too shallow.

7.3.3.3 Applications of ResNet

(i) Image classification ResNet has attained cutting-edge performance in image classification tasks like the ImageNet challenge, which involves classifying images into one of the 1000 categories.

(ii) Object detection ResNet has also been applied to object detection tasks, which aim to locate and categorize things in images. Modern results have been attained using ResNet-based models on well-known benchmarks like COCO and PASCAL VOC.

(iii) Semantic segmentation: The objective of semantic segmentation is to provide a class name to each pixel in an image. Modern results have been attained using ResNet-based models on well-known benchmarks like Cityscapes and PASCAL VOC.

(iv) Face recognition: ResNet has been applied to challenges where the objective is to recognize a person from a database of faces in face recognition tasks. Using well-known benchmarks like LFW and MegaFace, models based on ResNet have produced cutting-edge performances.

(v) Real-time medical image analysis: ResNet has been used for a variety of medical image analysis tasks, including the detection and classification of lung nodules, the detection of breast cancer, and the detection of diabetic retinopathy.

7.3.4 Generative model (GAN)

It is a combination of basically the discriminator model and the first CNN network, called the generative model. Scientists compare the two networks to two players in a game of rivalry in order to better understand how GANs operate, where the generator network tries to trick the discriminator network by producing data that is nearly authentic (such as artificial images), while the discriminator network tries to tell the difference between the generator output and the real data. The network's name is derived from the generator's goal of defeating the discriminator. The generator's goal is to beat the discriminator. Both the generator and discriminator networks improve after training, with the first producing more real data and the second learning to differentiate between the two types of data more effectively until, at the end of the process, the discriminator network is unable to distinguish between real and artificial data (images).

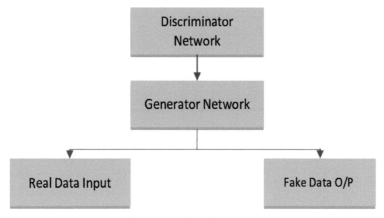

Figure 7.8 GAN flowchart.

In actuality, backpropagation for both Markov chains and dropout are also used as criteria by which the two networks learn from one another. GANs have been used for image synthesis to create realistic images of a range of subjects, including people, animals, scenery, and objects. GAN-based models have shown exceptional results in terms of visual quality, diversity, and originality. The conversion of low-resolution photos into high-resolution photos, the transformation of sketches into lifelike images, and the transformation of daylight photos into night time photos have all been accomplished using GANs. In a number of image-to-image translation issues, GAN-based models have achieved contemporary performance. Video synthesis: GANs have been used to produce lifelike films of human behaviors, traffic scenes, and natural phenomena by extending image synthesis techniques to the temporal domain. GAN-based models have shown promising results in terms of video quality, continuity, and diversity. Text-to-image synthesis, which turns textual descriptions like "a yellow bird with a red beak sitting on a tree limb" into images, has been done using GANs. GAN-based models have shown the ability to interpret and generate complex visual concepts from spoken language inputs.

The generating network and the discriminator network are the two neural networks that are simultaneously trained in a GAN. The generator network creates fictitious data samples using random noise as input. The discriminator network attempts to discriminate between inputs of authentic and bogus data samples. The generator's objective is to create data samples that are identical to the real data; the discriminator's objective is to discriminate between the two types of samples. Fake data samples are created by the generator network during training and sent into the discriminator alongside actual data samples. The discriminator is taught to distinguish between genuine and false data samples. The generator is taught to create data samples that the discriminator can mistake for real ones. This procedure is repeated until the generator can create samples of realistic data that are identical to the genuine data. The equation for generator network is given in eqn (7.8).

$$G : z \rightarrow G(z) \tag{7.8}$$

where Z is the input noise vector and $G(z)$ is the fake output data.

The equation for discriminator network is shown in eqn (7.9):

$$D : x-> D(x) \tag{7.9}$$

where x is the input data sample and $D(x)$ is the probability.

Eqn (7.10) shows the loss function:

$$\min\_\{\theta\_g\} \max\_\{\theta\_d\} V(D, G) = E\_\{x \, p\_data(x)\} [\log(D(x))]$$
$$+ E\_\{z \, p\_z(z)\} [\log(1 -- D(G(z)))] \tag{7.10}$$

where $p\_data(x)$ is the distribution of the real data and $p\_z(z)$ is the distribution of the noise vector.

7.3.4.1 Why is GAN used in real-time medical imaging?

Because of its capacity to produce high-quality images that closely mimic genuine medical images, generative adversarial networks (GANs) have demonstrated promising outcomes in medical imaging applications. The following are some justifications for using GANs in medical imaging:

(i) Data augmentation: Due to the high cost of data gathering and the requirement for professional annotation, medical imaging datasets are frequently constrained in size. GANs can produce artificial images that can be used to supplement the training data, enhancing deep learning model performance and lowering overfitting.

(ii) Domain adaptation: Images can be converted across various domains using GANs. For example, they can be used to turn CT scans into MRI scans or to create precise images of organs or tissues that are difficult to capture with conventional imaging techniques.

(iii) Medical images routinely deteriorate due to artifacts, noise, and other sorts of contamination. GANs can be used to restore damaged photos by producing high-quality, artifact-free images.

(iv) Disease diagnosis: Using synthetic images of healthy and diseased tissues or organs produced by GANs, machine learning models can be trained to automatically detect and diagnose diseases.

GANs have the potential to totally alter the area of medical imaging by assisting scientists and medical professionals in the creation of synthetic images that may be utilized to improve diagnosis, therapy planning, and sickness comprehension.

7.3.4.2 Advantages and disadvantages of GAN

GANs are able to generate data that is extremely close to real data in terms of realism and quality. This is especially useful in fields like image and video generation, where GANs may create visuals and cinematic works that resemble those created by individuals. Because GANs are unsupervised learning algorithms, they can draw conclusions about the outside world without the need for labels or annotations. They are therefore especially helpful for tasks where obtaining tagged data is challenging or expensive. The ability of GANs to identify complex distributions and patterns in the data allows them to generate novel and creative new data. GAN training can be difficult and computationally intensive. As a result of the training process's potential reliability issues, it can take multiple cycles to get respectable results. Mode collapse is a condition in which GANs only produce a subset of the data distribution rather than the complete distribution. The generated data may not be as diverse as it may be as a result. The choice of hyperparameters may affect how GANs function and provide a range of outcomes. This can make it difficult to compare different models or duplicate results.

7.3.4.3 Applications of GAN

With the aid of GANs, it has been possible to produce realistic images and movies that match the training dataset exactly. They can be used to enhance low-resolution photographs, create brand-new images, or create artificial images for training computer vision models.

(i) Data augmentation: GANs can be used to generate new data samples that can be added to the training dataset in order to improve the performance of machine learning models. This is especially useful when there are not enough tagged data available.

(ii) GANs can be used to transfer the esthetic of one image while maintaining its content. This technique allows for the creation of artistic images or movies.

(iii) The technique of converting text descriptions into realistic images is known as text-to-image synthesis and can be accomplished using GANs. This can be useful when developing product pictures from product descriptions.

(iv) Data anomaly detection: GANs can be used to locate data anomalies by comparing new data samples with the distribution of the training dataset. The detection of fake goods or fraud may be accomplished with this technique.

 (v) Drug development: Novel chemicals that can be used in drug research can be created utilizing GANs. They can be used to produce entirely new compounds or novel molecules that are connected to currently available medications.

The above-mentioned are some of the applications of GAN used in the medical industry.

7.4 Use-cases

A family of computing systems known as high-performance intelligent systems (HPIS) combines powerful processing with cutting-edge artificial intelligence capabilities. Table 7.1 shows some typical HPIS use-cases.

Table 7.1   Use-cases.

Applications	Results
Autonomous vehicles	HPIS can be used to build self-driving cars that can perceive their environment, make snap judgments, and adapt to changing conditions. These systems need a lot of computing power to process and analyze the data from various sensors, and the AI algorithms must be able to make decisions quickly and accurately.
Financial trading	HPIS can be used to build intelligent trading systems that analyze a large amount of financial data, predict market patterns, and carry out trades automatically. These systems require quick data processing and sophisticated AI algorithms in order to make accurate forecasts and take advantage of market possibilities.
Healthcare	HPIS enables the development of intelligent healthcare systems that can analyze patient data, offer diagnoses, and make treatment recommendations. These systems must quickly process enormous volumes of data while maintaining a high standard of reliability and accuracy.
Natural language processing (NLP)	Intelligent chatbots, virtual assistants, and other applications for natural language processing can be made with HPIS. These systems require highly developed AI algorithms with quick data processing capabilities and the ability to understand and interpret human language.

7.5 Conclusion

This chapter focuses on the deep learning techniques used for real-time medical imaging for high performance intelligent systems. There are various deep learning techniques and algorithms used to detect medical images and the corresponding diseases. The algorithms discussed in this chapter are convolution neural network (CNN), multi-layer perceptron (MLP), residual network (ResNet), and generative adversarial network (GAN). Computer vision (CV) paves way for these algorithms since classification, segmentation, and other parameters relating to images cannot be excluded. These models prove to be effective in terms of accuracy and classification performance. This chapter has also brought the different steps and methodology involved in the above-mentioned algorithms to light. The equations and diagrams have also been brought under the light, for easier understanding of the basic concepts, which paves the foundation for core concepts. The use-cases for high performance intelligent systems (HPIS) have also been discussed.

7.6 Acknowledgement

This chapter focuses on real-time medical imaging for high performance intelligent systems using deep learning techniques. We have taken references from the papers listed in the References section.

Conflicts of Interest

The authors declare no conflict of interest.

References

[1] Anaya-Isaza, A., Mera-Jiménez, L. and Zequera-Diaz, M., 2021. An overview of deep learning in medical imaging. *Informatics in Medicine Unlocked*, 26, p.100723.
[2] Mohammed, M.A., Maashi, M.S., Arif, M., Nallapaneni, M.K. and Geman, O., 2021. Intelligent systems and computational methods in medical and healthcare solutions with their challenges during COVID-19 pandemic. *Journal of Intelligent Systems*, 30(1), pp.976-979.
[3] Cai, L., Gao, J. and Zhao, D., 2020. A review of the application of deep learning in medical image classification and segmentation. *Annals of translational medicine*, 8 (11).

[4] Tang, X., 2019. The role of artificial intelligence in medical imaging research. *BJR| Open*, *2*(1), p.20190031.

[5] Wang, S., Cao, G., Wang, Y., Liao, S., Wang, Q., Shi, J., Li, C. and Shen, D., 2021. Review and prospect: artificial intelligence in advanced medical imaging. *Frontiers in Radiology*, *1*, p.781868.

[6] Lee, J.G., Jun, S., Cho, Y.W., Lee, H., Kim, G.B., Seo, J.B. and Kim, N., 2017. Deep learning in medical imaging: general overview. *Korean journal of radiology*, *18*(4), pp.570-584.

[7] Willemink, M.J., Koszek, W.A., Hardell, C., Wu, J., Fleischmann, D., Harvey, H., Folio, L.R., Summers, R.M., Rubin, D.L. and Lungren, M.P., 2020. Preparing medical imaging data for machine learning. *Radiology*, *295*(1), pp.4-15.

[8] Sarvamangala, D.R. and Kulkarni, R.V., 2022. Convolutional neural networks in medical image understanding: a survey. *Evolutionary intelligence*, *15*(1), pp.1-22.

[9] Esteva, A., Chou, K., Yeung, S., Naik, N., Madani, A., Mottaghi, A., Liu, Y., Topol, E., Dean, J. and Socher, R., 2021. Deep learning-enabled medical computer vision. *NPJ digital medicine*, *4*(1), pp.1-9.

[10] Shad, R., Cunningham, J.P., Ashley, E.A., Langlotz, C.P. and Hiesinger, W., 2021. Designing clinically translatable artificial intelligence systems for high-dimensional medical imaging. *Nature Machine Intelligence*, *3*(11), pp.929-935.

[11] Khamis, H.S., Cheruiyot, K.W. and Kimani, S., 2014. Application of k-nearest neighbour classification in medical data mining. *International Journal of Information and Communication Technology Research*, *4*(4).

[12] Jiang, L., Sun, S., Chen, J. and Sun, Z., 2022. Random Forest Algorithm-Based Ultrasonic Image in the Diagnosis of Patients with Dry Eye Syndrome and Its Relationship with Tear Osmotic Pressure. *Computational and Mathematical Methods in Medicine*, *2022*.

[13] Hartmann, D., Müller, D., Soto-Rey, I. and Kramer, F., 2021. Assessing the Role of Random Forests in Medical Image Segmentation. *arXiv preprint arXiv:2103.16492*.

[14] Yu, W., Liu, T., Valdez, R., Gwinn, M. and Khoury, M.J., 2010. Application of support vector machine modeling for prediction of common diseases: the case of diabetes and pre-diabetes. *BMC medical informatics and decision making*, *10*(1), pp.1-7.

[15] Jiang, Y., Li, Z., Zhang, L. and Sun, P., 2007, June. An improved svm classifier for medical image classification. In *International Conference on Rough Sets and Intelligent Systems Paradigms* (pp. 764-773). Springer, Berlin, Heidelberg.

[16] Alam, M.Z., Rahman, M.S. and Rahman, M.S., 2019. A Random Forest based predictor for medical data classification using feature ranking. *Informatics in Medicine Unlocked*, *15*, p.100180.

[17] Liang, J., 2020, September. Image classification based on RESNET. In *Journal of Physics: Conference Series* (Vol. 1634, No. 1, p. 012110). IOP Publishing.

[18] Yousef, R., Gupta, G., Yousef, N. and Khari, M., 2022. A holistic overview of deep learning approach in medical imaging. *Multimedia Systems*, *28*(3), pp.881-914.

[19] Bikku, T., 2020. Multi-layered deep learning perceptron approach for health risk prediction. *Journal of Big Data*, *7*(1), pp.1-14.

[20] Yan, J., Wang, X., Cai, J., Qin, Q., Yang, H., Wang, Q., Cheng, Y., Gan, T., Jiang, H., Deng, J. and Chen, B., 2022. Medical image segmentation model based on triple gate MultiLayer perceptron. *Scientific Reports*, *12*(1), pp.1-14.

[21] Yan, H., Jiang, Y., Zheng, J., Peng, C. and Li, Q., 2006. A multilayer perceptron-based medical decision support system for heart disease diagnosis. *Expert Systems with Applications*, *30*(2), pp.272-281.

8

A Real-time Patient Health Monitoring System

P. C. Khanzode, Anamika P. Mohod and Prajal P. Raut.

Department of Computer Science & Engineering,
Sipna College of Engineering & Technology, India
E-mail: prachi.khanzode@gmail.com; anamikamohod23@gmail.com;
praju2252002@gmail.com

Abstract

The proposed system is a real-time patient health monitoring system that aims to provide timely and efficient healthcare services through the use of wearable and remote monitoring devices. These devices are used to measure various health parameters such as temperature, pulse, ECG, blood pressure, etc., which are used to evaluate the patient's health condition. The collected information is then communicated to the doctor through an interface, enabling two-way communication between the doctor and patient. The system's objective is to collect the required parameters and evaluate the data obtained from the sensor devices, providing the patient with possible precautionary measures to be practiced by them. The system also suggests medical care and next steps to be followed in case of critical situations. The system's main advantage is that it allows remote patients to receive the latest healthcare services, which might not be possible otherwise due to low doctor-to-patient ratio. Overall, the proposed system is reliable and efficient, providing a rapid response to the patient's health condition. By utilizing technology to enable remote monitoring and communication between doctors and patients, this system can improve the quality of healthcare services and provide patients with timely medical attention, potentially saving lives in critical situations. The benefits of this system are numerous, as it allows for timely and efficient healthcare services to be provided to remote patients who may not have access to medical facilities due to low doctor-to-patient ratios. It also ensures rapid response in critical situations and helps to prevent severe health conditions by providing precautionary measures to be practiced by the patient. Overall, the IoT-based real-time patient health monitoring system is an innovative solution that holds great promise for the future of healthcare, especially in the realm of remote patient care.

Keywords: Internet of Things, real-time patient health monitoring system, current procedural terminology code.

8.1 Introduction

The growing population and increasing life expectancy have significant implications for healthcare services worldwide. With an aging population, the demand for healthcare services increases, as older people tend to require more healthcare than their younger counterparts. The rise in chronic diseases such as heart disease, cancer, stroke, diabetes, chronic liver disease and cirrhosis, and kidney disease has also increased the cost of healthcare provision. The increase in life expectancy should be viewed as an opportunity for people to live longer and better, but it requires substantial improvements in both healthcare services and living standards. To address the challenges posed by an aging population, healthcare services need to be more efficient and effective. This can be achieved through the use of technology, improved infrastructure, and better access to healthcare services.

In addition, it is essential to encourage healthy living to prevent chronic diseases and promote overall health and wellbeing. Governments, healthcare providers, and individuals must work together to create a healthy living environment and promote healthy habits. This can include initiatives such as public education campaigns, promoting healthy eating habits, encouraging regular exercise, and reducing stress levels. We can say that the growing population and increasing life expectancy pose significant challenges for healthcare services worldwide. However, by focusing on preventative measures, improving healthcare infrastructure, and promoting healthy living, we can create a healthier and happier world for all.

Recent advancements in technology have made it possible to provide efficient and effective healthcare services to patients with chronic diseases and elderly people. One of the key advancements is the integration of mobile communication with wireless sensors and wearable devices, which enables a shift from clinic-centric to patient-centric healthcare services.

Internet of Things (IoT) is another technological advancement that has revolutionized the healthcare sector. IoT is a network of interconnected devices, including sensors, smart devices, and cyber sensors, that gather and share data about their usage and environment. IoT applied to the care and monitoring of patients is increasingly common in the health sector, seeking to improve the quality of life of people. There is a wide variety of sensors available that can read vital signs such as blood pressure, glucose levels, and heart rate. These sensors, including electrocardiograms, allow patients to take their vital signs daily, which are then sent to their doctors. Based on the readings, doctors can recommend medications and workout routines that allow patients to improve their quality of life and overcome chronic diseases.

Overall, the integration of mobile communication with wireless sensors and wearable devices, combined with the power of IoT, is transforming the healthcare sector by making healthcare services more accessible, efficient, and effective, particularly for those with chronic diseases and elderly patients.

The real-time patient health monitoring system can be very beneficial for patients with chronic illnesses, as it allows for constant monitoring of their health parameters through wireless sensor systems. This type of system can be adopted to monitor various health conditions such as cardiac diseases, diabetes, hypertension, and hypothermia.

The system can be implemented in two ways: live communication type, which requires the presence of a doctor and patient and high bandwidth and good data speed, and store and forward type, which acquires medical parameters and transmits them to a specialist in a hospital.

The RPHMS is particularly useful for patients who are located far from medical facilities, as it allows for real-time monitoring of their health conditions. The system is also portable, which means patients can carry it with them while traveling, ensuring they receive the necessary medical attention if any emergency occurs. The system has various sensors embedded in it, such as temperature, blood pressure, ECG, and respiration sensors, which monitor patients' health parameters in real time. The data from these sensors is transmitted wirelessly to medical personnel, who can provide appropriate treatment to patients on time. Overall, the RPHMS has the potential to improve healthcare services and provide better healthcare to patients with chronic illnesses.

The mobile application on the smartphone will allow the patient to view their health status, get suggestions and reminders on medication, and schedule appointments with their doctor. The web interface allows the doctor to monitor multiple patients simultaneously, view the patient's medical history, and track their progress. The system can be further enhanced by incorporating machine learning algorithms to analyze the patient's data and predict any potential health issues in advance. Overall, the real-time patient health monitoring system provides an efficient and effective way to monitor and manage chronic diseases, while also improving the quality of life for patients.

8.2 Literature Review

Nowadays, the term remote health monitoring is in vogue, but it is since ages. It was started in the 1800s, when two physicians consulted over a telephone using smoke signals. In 1876 a doctor named Alexander Graham Bell gave his first patient treatment through telephone. With the course of time, radio signals were used for such consultation in 1924. The use of telemedicine continued to expand throughout the 1990s and 2000s. In 1995, the American Telemedicine Association was formed, further advancing the field. With the increasing availability of the Internet, telemedicine became even more accessible and widespread. In the early 2000s, remote monitoring systems became increasingly popular for patients with chronic illnesses such as diabetes, heart disease, and hypertension. Wearable devices such as glucose monitors, blood pressure cuffs, and heart rate monitors could transmit data wirelessly to healthcare providers, allowing for real-time monitoring and intervention [1].

Today, telemedicine and remote monitoring systems continue to evolve with advancements in technology. Mobile apps, virtual consultations, and artificial intelligence are all being integrated into telemedicine practices. As healthcare providers continue to seek more efficient and cost-effective ways to deliver care, telemedicine is expected to play an increasingly important role in the future of healthcare.

With the evolution of the Internet, telemedicine has been transforming to continually monitor the health parameters and providing medical assistance to patients rather than just consulting over telephone or just sending X-ray reports. With this internet facility, an IoT-based patient health monitoring system was proposed by 2016, which is capable of capturing health parameters such as blood pressure and heart rate and giving healthy assistance. In 2019, changes to the CPT codes were done, which makes remote patient monitoring systems most profitable and cost-effective, but its adaption is not as expected. But in 2020 with the surge of COVID-19 pandemic, there was a need to encourage the adoption of telehealth, and as a result, there was rapid usage of remote health monitoring systems. This adoption was more in western countries. But this adoption is not as high as compared to traditional techniques of medical science. If demand for this is increased, they are taken for this adoption, and then there are a lot of opportunities in this field.

Patients receive quality healthcare by just wearing a belt and clicking a button. One can even get blood reports remotely by a technique called micro-sampling. With technological advancements, it is possible to get treatment overseas.

8.3 Architecture

A real-time patient health monitoring system is becoming more advanced and capable of detecting underlying health conditions in real time. The use of wearable sensors to extract multiple parameters such as heart rate, blood pressure, and body temperature simultaneously is a major improvement in healthcare technology. It is also promising to see that these systems have two interfaces, one for patients and one for doctors, making it easier for both parties to access and interpret the collected data. The use of Bluetooth low energy technology to transmit the collected data to an Android-based listening port is also a smart choice, as it is a reliable and widely used wireless communication protocol. The ability to show reports on the doctor interface is also important as it makes it easier for doctors to interpret the collected data and make informed decisions about the patient's health. Overall, it is exciting to see how technology is advancing to make healthcare more efficient and effective. Figure 8.1 shows architectural overview for real-time health monitoring system, which shows flow of patients data.

IoT-enabled healthcare systems have the potential to revolutionize health-care delivery by providing personalized and proactive healthcare services [2]. By utilizing a variety of interconnected medical sensors, IoT-enabled healthcare systems can continuously monitor and collect real-time data on patients' health conditions. This data can then be analyzed and processed

Figure 8.1   Architectural overview for real-time health monitoring system [1].

to extract valuable insights into patients' health status, enabling healthcare professionals to make informed decisions and provide timely interventions.

The sensing layer of the IoT-enabled healthcare architecture is responsible for collecting the biomedical parameters from patients. Wearable sensors such as ECG and blood pressure monitors, temperature sensors, heart rate sensors, GPS sensors, and RFID tags can be used to monitor patients' physical, mental, and emotional health conditions. Smart homes equipped with sensors can also be used to collect information on patients' immediate surroundings.

The network layer of the architecture is responsible for ensuring efficient and secure transmission of the collected data to the data processing module. Short-range communication protocols such as ZigBee, LowPAN, NB-IOT, and LoRa can be used for this purpose.

The data processing module is responsible for analyzing and processing the collected data to extract valuable insights into patients' health conditions. Learning-based approaches such as machine learning and deep learning can be used to mine the data and extract insights.

Finally, based on the insights extracted from the data processing module, intelligent services and applications can be delivered. These include disease diagnosis, behavior recognition, and smart assistance, among others. The IoT-enabled healthcare architecture has the potential to provide smart, accurate, and cost-effective personalized healthcare services that can significantly improve patients' health outcomes [3].

It is important to note that while wearable sensors like Zephyr BT and Omron Wireless Upper Arm Blood Pressure Monitor can provide accurate readings for heart rate and blood pressure, respectively, they should not be solely relied upon for diagnosis or treatment decisions. These sensors are useful for monitoring trends and providing alerts for abnormal readings but should always be interpreted in the context of a patient's overall health and medical history by a qualified healthcare professional.

Additionally, it is crucial to ensure that the data collected by these sensors is transmitted securely to prevent unauthorized access or data breaches. Encryption and authentication protocols should be implemented to protect patient privacy and confidentiality.

Overall, the use of multiple sensors in a real-time monitoring system can provide valuable insights into a patient's health and assist in early detection and management of potential health issues. However, it is important to carefully select and evaluate the accuracy and reliability of the sensors used and ensure that appropriate measures are taken to protect patient data privacy and security. Figure 8.2 shows layered architecture for monitoring.

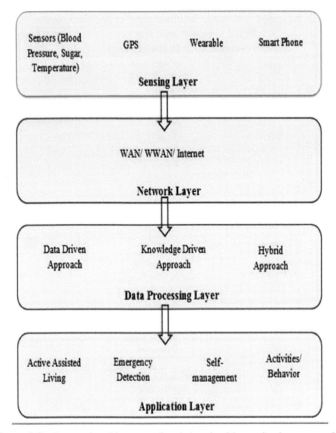

Figure 8.2   Layered architecture of real-time health monitoring system [3].

Table 8.1 shows the normal range of value for blood pressure and heart rate for all age groups. According to this value, the doctor gets notification if any patient's value for this parameter is above or below this range.

Figure 8.3 shows the flow of the overall system, which is started by initiating sensors. It then discovers the device; if any device is found, then it will get connected and if not, then restart the Bluetooth of your phone. If connection between the sensors and phone is established successfully, then the system is ready to extract data from sensors. Once the data is extracted, the data gets transmitted to the web application, which is the center of control for further activities; this data is also stored for further reference. The values that are continuously received by web applications are checked against normal values according to the patient's age and health conditions [4].

Table 8.1   Age-wise range for blood pressure and heart rate.

Age (Years)	Blood pressure (mm Hg)		Heart rate (bpm)
	Systolic range	Diastolic range	
0.1	45–80	35–55	120–160
0.1–1	65–100	35–65	80–140
1–5	80–115	55–80	80–130
6–13	80–120	45–80	75–110
14–18	90–120	50–80	60–100
19–40	95–135	60–80	72–75
41–60	110–145	70–90	76–79
60 Above	95–145	70–90	70–73

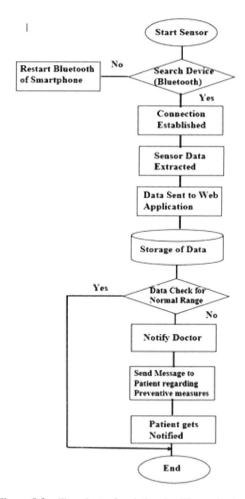

Figure 8.3   Flowchart of real-time health monitoring system.

If these values are above or below the normal range, then the respective doctor gets notified and also patients get an alert. Then the doctor suggests the appropriate measures that should be taken by the patient and the patient gets notified about this.

8.3.1 Web interface

Web interface is used to interact with the system, the users of RPHMS, i.e., doctors, medical personnel, medical centers, and patients, make use of this interface for the system to be used. The data is only accessible by authorized users, as this portal requires a user ID and password. The data from the sensor is presented to both doctors and patients, while both these users are participating in the communication process.

As shown in the Figure 8.4, the user first needs to be registered to the web portal to access the system. If the user is registered, then, and only then, he will be able to log in to the system. Patients are able to see only their own health parameters and can appoint any doctor they want. On other hand, doctors are able to see health related data of those patients who are under doctors' observation. Once the patient is logged in to the system, he will get a screen as shown in Figure 8.5. He can appoint a doctor, who will give him treatment [5]. Under "View Health Data," he will be able to see all the values of health parameters along with a comparison of his current real-time health data and normal range of those health parameters according to his health conditions and age. Under "History," he will be able to see previous records. In the "Messages" menu, he will send a message to the doctor and also receive messages from doctor; on receiving the message, he will be notified. An "Edit Profile" menu is provided to edit personal details of patients.

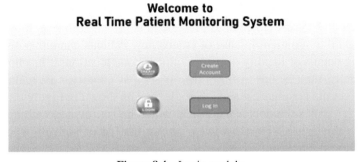

Welcome to
Real Time Patient Monitoring System

Figure 8.4 Login module.

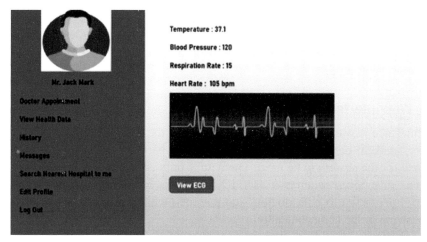

Figure 8.5 Patient module.

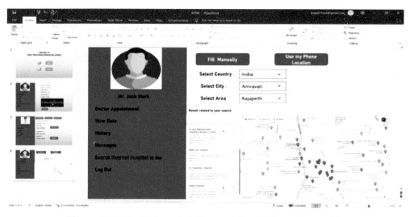

Figure 8.6 Patient module (nearest hospital search result).

The "Search Nearest Hospital to Me" menu is provided to search for the nearest hospital to a patient in case of emergency. Patients can either search by providing details of locality or by providing phone location. If he chooses to fill manually, then he has to fill in details such as country, city, and area, and he will get the hospital list and a Google map as shown in Figure 8.6.

Figure 8.7 shows the doctor module in which he is provided with menus as shown in the figure. "Patient's Data" shows the list of patients who are treated by this doctor.

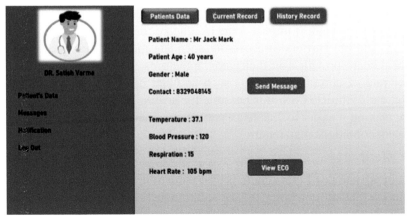

Figure 8.7 Doctor module.

By clicking on one particular patient, the doctor will be able to see a screen as shown in the right pane, in which he is able to see the personal details of patients along with their health data, which is separated by current record and history record. Under the "Messages" menu, he will be able to send and receive messages to and from patients [6]. If any patient's health parameters are below or above their normal ranges, then the doctor gets notified under the notification menu.

8.4 Benefits

• Remote monitoring:

Remote monitoring using IoT devices can provide real-time data about a patient's health condition, allowing healthcare providers to diagnose and treat illnesses quickly and effectively. This can be particularly important in emergency situations where time is critical. By empowering patients to take an active role in monitoring their own health, remote monitoring can also promote greater accountability and autonomy, leading to better outcomes. Overall, the use of IoT devices in remote monitoring has the potential to revolutionize healthcare and improve patient care [7].

• Improved healthcare and treatment management:

Using IoT devices, healthcare authorities can get valuable information about equipment and it will be more effective to the staff and it seems like an innovation. With the help of IoT devices, it reduces the medical error to treatment management. It improves the healthcare for rural residents as they deal with multiple barriers to accessing adequate medical care because of fewer healthcare providers in their geographic area. As a result, they have a higher rate of chronic conditions such as heart disease, diabetes, blood pressure, etc. With RPHMS, it is possible for healthcare providers to bridge the gap, making it easier to enable all patients to receive the continuous care their health conditions may require.

- Cost effective:

The major advantage of this system is cost reduction, and, in addition, it can also improve patient outcomes [8]. By continuously monitoring patients in real time, healthcare providers can identify and treat potential health problems before they become serious. This can lead to better disease management and prevention of hospital readmissions. Patients who are actively involved in their own care and have access to their health data can also make better decisions about their health and lifestyle, leading to improved overall health outcomes. Furthermore, remote patient monitoring can provide greater convenience for patients, as they can receive care from the comfort of their own homes. This can result in greater patient satisfaction and compliance with treatment plans.

8.5 Current Challenges

- Risk of failure:

Failure or bugs in hardware, as well as power failure, can affect the performance of sensors and connected equipment, which can potentially impact the quality of care and patient safety. Moreover, skipping a scheduled software update can leave healthcare systems vulnerable to cybersecurity risks, which can result in data breaches or other serious consequences. Therefore, it is crucial to ensure that hardware and software components are regularly maintained and updated to minimize the risk of failures and ensure the safe and effective use of remote patient monitoring systems [9].

- Integration:

Ensuring compatibility and seamless integration between different components is crucial for the successful development of RPHMS. Utilizing cloud services for data transmission and storage can help to minimize onboard memory usage and simplify development. However, it is important to ensure data security and privacy when using cloud services. Additionally, careful management of patient records and system migration is necessary to avoid any issues or data loss. Compatibility testing and thorough quality assurance processes can help to minimize bugs and ensure the system functions as intended [10].

8.6 Future Scope

The aim of implementation of this system is to provide effective and efficient healthcare services to remote patients at the comfort of their home, but there are also concerns related to the security and privacy of the patient data. As the data is transmitted wirelessly and stored in the cloud, there is a risk of unauthorized access or data breach. Measures such as encryption, authentication, and access control need to be implemented to ensure the security of the data. Moreover, there is a need for regulations and standards to ensure the privacy of the patient data and to establish guidelines for data sharing and usage.

Another challenge is the interoperability of different devices and systems used for remote patient monitoring. Different devices may use different protocols and standards for communication, which can create compatibility issues. The lack of standardization can hinder the integration and sharing of data across different systems, leading to incomplete or inaccurate patient information. Therefore, there is a need for standardized protocols and interfaces to ensure seamless interoperability and data exchange among different systems.

In summary, while IoT technology has the potential to revolutionize personalized healthcare through remote patient monitoring, there are still several challenges that need to be addressed. These include the development of intelligent sensor data-filtering mechanisms, ensuring the security and privacy of patient data, and standardization of protocols and interfaces for interoperability. Dynamic service discovery and mapping refer to the process of discovering and mapping services based on their availability, capabilities, and preferences. In the context of remote patient monitoring, this means that the system should be able to detect the availability of various services such as sensors, communication channels, and data analysis tools, and map them to the appropriate patients based on their needs and preferences.

To achieve this, the system must be able to gather and process data from multiple sources, including wearable sensors, health records, and patient feedback. It must also be able to analyze this data in real-time to identify patterns, trends, and anomalies, and generate personalized recommendations for patients and their caregivers.

Furthermore, the system should be able to adapt to changing patient needs and preferences over time and provide personalized services that are tailored to each individual. This requires the use of advanced machine learning and artificial intelligence algorithms that can learn from patient data and adapt to changing circumstances.

Overall, the development of adaptive, personalized, and user-friendly services for remote patient monitoring is a complex and challenging task that requires a multidisciplinary approach involving healthcare professionals, software developers, and data scientists. However, the potential benefits of such a system in terms of improving patient outcomes and reducing healthcare costs make it a worthwhile investment.

This system further can be enhanced by incorporating the power of artificial intelligence (AI) into it. With this technology, the system is itself able to provide notifications, preventive measures, and even the treatment to the patients without any intervention by medical personnel.

8.7 Conclusion

The rate of chronic disease is increasing day by day. The increasing ratio of these cases with population and age is becoming a serious concern. There are several reasons for this such as insufficient medical facilities, lack of medical personnel, high cost of treatment, or even disregard of health. The cases like this are more often seen in localities that are far away from medical facilities such as rural areas, tribal locality, etc. The only solution to such a problem is the timely diagnosis and treatment with wireless technology. With this it is possible to reach remote areas with appropriate medical facilities. The real-time patient health monitoring system provides this undue advantage of timely treatment. This system consists of wearable sensors that are connected with phones by either Bluetooth or Wi-Fi. Once connected, the system starts by sending the values measured by this sensor wirelessly to the web server, thereby transmitting to the web application where further processing takes place. According to values received, the web application generates alerts if these values are below or above the normal range.

This study presents an overview of existing approaches for health and behavior monitoring using wearable IoT technologies and proposes a novel health monitoring system framework. The system aims to enable real-time monitoring of patients or elderly users and allows access to information over the web. This can help provide timely diagnosis and treatment to patients while reducing the cost of medical care.

Wearable IoT technologies have revolutionized the field of healthcare by providing continuous monitoring of vital signs and activity levels. This data can be used to identify health issues before they become serious, thereby preventing hospitalization and reducing the overall cost of healthcare. The proposed health monitoring system framework leverages wearable IoT technologies to provide real-time monitoring of patients or elderly users.

By monitoring patients in real time, healthcare providers can provide timely diagnosis and treatment, thereby improving patient outcomes. Additionally, this system can reduce the need for patients to travel to hospitals or clinics, reducing the cost of medical care. The information collected from wearable IoT technologies can also be accessed over the web, making it easier for healthcare providers to monitor patients remotely. The implementation of wireless remote patient monitoring systems has faced several challenges in the past, but with the advancements in technology and high-speed data communication and transmission capabilities, these challenges can be minimized. This can ultimately lead to a more powerful and useful system, providing various advantages over traditional medical care.

In conclusion, the proposed health monitoring system framework presents a promising solution for real-time health and behavior monitoring using wearable IoT technologies. It has the potential to revolutionize the healthcare industry by providing timely diagnosis and treatment, reducing hospitalization rates and lowering the overall cost of medical care.

Acknowledgement

A moment of pause to express a deep gratitude to several individuals without whom this chapter could not have been completed.

We express our sincere thanks to Dr. V. K. Shandilya, Head of Department, Computer Science & Engineering, and the other staff members of the department for their kind cooperation.

We express our sincere thanks to Dr. S. M. Kherde, Principal, Sipna College of Engineering & Technology for his valuable guidance.

We also express our sincere thanks to the library staff members of the college.

Last but not the least, we are thankful to our friends and parents whose best wishes are always with us.

References

[1] hindawi.com/journals/ijta/2015/373474/

[2] https://blog.prevounce.com/history-of-remote-patient-monitoring-how-it-began-and-where-its-going

[3] https://jwcneurasipjournals.springeropen.com/articles/10.1186/s13638-018-1308-x

[4] https://www.objectivity.co.uk/blog/remote-patient-monitoring/

[5] https://link.springer.com/chapter/10.1007/978-3-030-33846-6_14

[6] https://iopscience.iop.org/article/10.1088/1742-6596/1818/1/012044/pdf

[7] https://www.neoteryx.com/microsampling-blog/a-brief-history-of-remote-patient-monitoring#:~:text=In%201967%20physicians%20started%20transmitting,were%20Kaiser%20Foundation%20and%20Lockheed

[8] S. Meystre, "The current state of telemonitoring: a comment on the literature," *Telemedicine Journal & e-Health*, vol. 11, no. 1, pp. 63–69, 2005.

[9] World Health Organization, *Health Statistics and Health Information Systems*, World Health Organization, 2012.

[10] W. H. Organization, *Global Status Report on Noncommunicable Diseases 2010*, World Health Organization, Geneva, Switzerland, 2011.

9

Ensembled Convolutional Neural Network for Multi-class Skin Cancer Detection

R. V. Siva Balan, T. Senthilnathan, J. Jayapriya, and C. Balakrishnan

Department of Computer Science, Christ (Deemed to be University), India
E-mail: sivabalan.rv@christuniversity.in; senthilnathan.t@christuniversity.in; jayapriya.j@christuniversity.in; balakrishnan.c@christuniversity.in

Abstract

A skin cancer diagnosis is critically important in medical image processing. The role of dermoscopy and dermatologists is inevitable in skin cancer diagnosis. But, considering the time constraints on diagnosing patients on time, even medical experts need computer-assisted methods to automate the diagnosis process with a higher accuracy rate and with good performance. Such computer-assisted methods with induced artificial intelligence (AI) algorithms are gaining significance. The challenging task of medical image processing is finding benign/malignant pigmented skin lesions after the input image of patients. To identify this difference, AI-based classification algorithms shall be deployed. During the implementation of such algorithms, several performance aspects are evaluated. Once the best such algorithm is identified and evaluated for its performance attributes, it shall be deployed to assist dermatologists. This book chapter explains such a novel multi-class skin cancer classification algorithm. The proposed algorithm uses the best of the attributes and parameters of a deep convolutional neural network (CNN) to give the best-ever enactment among similar existing algorithms. The result achievement of the developed deep CNN based multi-class skin cancer classification algorithm (DCNN-MSCCA) is demonstrated using the HAM10000 dataset. To establish the significance of the developed algorithm, the performance parameters of the DCNN-MSCCA are compared with a few existing significant algorithms. The maximum accuracy of DCNN-MSCCA in predicting the exact multi-class skin cancer is 95.1%. This book chapter explains the implementation details of DCNN-MSCCA using python and libraries supporting CNN.

Keywords: Multi-class skin cancer, artificial intelligence, medical image processing, HAM10000 dataset, classification.

9.1 Introduction

Digital processing happens in all domains for the betterment of the information gathered for analysis. Among them, the medical field is considered to be important where many analyses are done for many applications. Internal organs must be seen with medical imaging in order to identify abnormalities in their anatomy or function. The function of the inside organs is captured and presented in different forms like images or videos by health image-capturing devices like X-ray, CT, MRI, PET, and ultrasound scanners. For an accurate diagnosis of functional abnormalities or the detection of anomalies, the images and videos need to be understood. If an anomaly is found, its precise location, dimension, and form must be determined. Conventionally, trained medical professionals rely on their expertise and judgment to carry out these responsibilities. Using intelligent medical image understanding, these tasks will be carried out by intelligent healthcare systems. Understanding medical images rely heavily on the classification, segmentation, detection, and localization of images. Figure 9.1 depicts the major steps involved in image processing analysis.

A dermatologist is a medical professional who diagnoses skin conditions. Skin diseases, also known as cutaneous diseases, affect nearly two out of every three people. However, records from various healthcare agents indicate that 50% of the realm's people do not have access to important

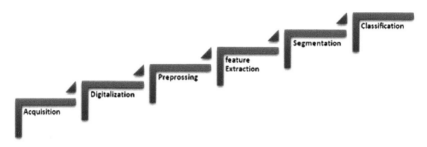

Figure 9.1   Image processing analysis.

healthcare. Alternative strategies for achieving universal skincare coverage are required due to the widespread misdiagnosis of skin diseases and the lack of readily available skin care. Technology has the probability to shorten the gap between what patients want and the quality of healthcare they receive. Teledermatoscopy and image-based decision mechanisms have been the only areas of dermatology technology research in the past. Effective treatment and the prevention of the socioeconomic burden associated with skin diseases necessitate prompt diagnosis.

Two methods are used by a dermatologist to diagnose a skin condition. Pattern recognition from a visual examination of the lesion is the first method. A lot of this usually happens subconsciously. A person's ability to subconsciously recognize patterns improves with experience; so the ability to visually analyze skin diseases improves with experience. A methodological investigation of the ill person's record, indications, and investigative test results is the second method.

Figure 9.2 represents the different branches of intelligent systems. Artificial intelligence is a process in which the computer is able to function like the human brain. Machine learning is considered a method in which machines are trained to enhance a task performance. Deep learning uses multiple layers of algorithms that are interconnected with each other.

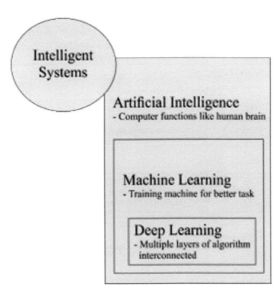

Figure 9.2   Branches in intelligent systems.

DL procedures are a type of ML algorithm, which practices artificial neural networks with multiple layers to learn and model complex patterns in data. They are commonly used in an extensive variety of uses such as voice and video identification, natural language processing, self-driving cars, etc. Some popular deep learning algorithms include recurrent neural networks (RNNs) and CNNs. These algorithms are employed to accomplish state-of-the-art outcomes in a number of tasks and continue to be an active area of research. Figure 9.3 depicts the different forms of deep learning algorithms

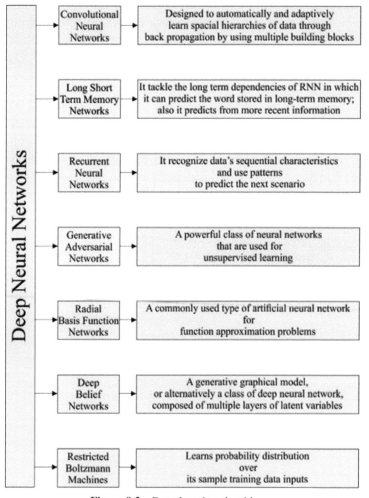

Figure 9.3   Deep learning algorithms.

and their purpose. Each algorithm and methods have its own merits and demerits.

CNNs are highly efficient at image classification tasks. They can mechanically and adaptively acquire spatial hierarchies of attributes from input images. This allows them to effectively detect and recognize objects and patterns in images with high accuracy. One of the key factors that contribute to the efficiency of CNNs is their usage of convolutional layers, which inevitably study spatial hierarchies of features from the input images. This allows them to effectively detect and recognize objects and patterns in images with high accuracy. Additionally, CNNs are designed to be highly parallelizable, allowing them to be implemented on high-performance GPUs and specialized hardware such as TPUs, which enables them to process enormous amounts of information quickly.

In contemporary centuries, researchers have developed various architectures such as ResNet, DenseNet, and EfficientNet, which have accomplished state-of-the-art enactment on numerous image grouping benchmarks. These architectures have also enabled CNNs to be applied to new and increasingly challenging problem domains such as self-driving four wheelers, medical image analysis, and natural language processing with significant success.

Ensemble algorithms are methods that associate the predictions of various individual models to increase the altogether enactment of the system. This is done in order to address issues such as overfitting, improve generalization, and increase the robustness of the predictions. Ensemble algorithms are particularly useful in machine learning and statistics where they are used to advance the accurateness of predictive models and make them more stable. Some popular ensemble algorithms include random forests, gradient boosting, and bagging.

An ensemble CNN for multi-class skin cancer identification is a machine learning model that uses a combination of multiple CNNs to categorize images of skin lesions as one of several types of skin cancer like melanoma, basal cell carcinoma, etc., or as benign. This method can raise the accuracy of skin cancer recognition associated with using a single CNN model. The multiple CNNs are trained on the same dataset but with different architectures or hyperparameters and their outputs are combined to make the final prediction. Ensemble methods are commonly employed to develop the enactment of machine learning models, by reducing overfitting and increasing generalization.

The objectives of an ensemble of CNNs for multi-class skin cancer detection are:

(1) To upsurge the overall accuracy of the skin cancer detection system by combining the predictions of multiple CNNs.
(2) To increase the robustness of the system by training multiple CNNs on dissimilar subsets of the data and coalescing their predictions.
(3) To reduce overfitting by training multiple CNNs with different architectures and combining their predictions.
(4) To increase the generalization ability of the system by training multiple CNNs on different data augmentation techniques and combining their predictions.
(5) To identify the most important features for skin cancer identification by analyzing the output of the different CNNs in the ensemble.

9.2 Literature Review

In this section, the models that have been used by researchers are shown in two forms: one is prior work and the other one is derivative work in classifying skin diseases using various algorithms.

In Figure 9.4, the way different years of academic paper relate to each other is shown. Similarity-based papers are arranged. The number of citations is denoted by the node size where small size represents fewer citations and

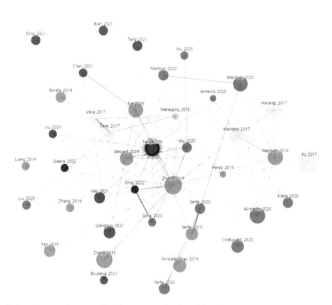

Figure 9.4   Research contribution towards the skin diseases classification using AI.

node color is the publishing year where dark colors denote recent one and lighter colors denote older one. Similar papers are represented by strong connecting lines and cluster together. From Figure 9.4, it is observed that many researchers have instigated many models and algorithms for classifying skin diseases using artificial intelligence concepts. Following are some of the researcher contributions given in this section.

To simplify the preparation of systems that are knowingly profounder than those that have been utilized in the past, this chapter presents a residual learning framework. It explicitly reformulates the layers as learning residual functions with reference to the layer inputs as an alternative to learning unreferenced functions. It affords wide-ranging observed evidence indicating that these enduring networks can improve the accuracy after the significantly increased depth and are simpler to optimize. It evaluates residual nets with up to 152 layers on the ImageNet dataset, 8 layers deeper than VGG nets [40] but still with lower complexity. On the ImageNet test set, an ensemble of these remaining nets has an error of 3.57%.

The latest dermoscopic image analysis benchmark challenge's design, implementation, and outcomes are discussed in this chapter. The objective is to provide funding for algorithms for automated melanoma diagnosis, the deadliest skin cancer. The challenge consisted of three tasks: disease classification, feature recognition, and lesion segmentation. With 593 registrations, 81 pre-submissions, 46 final submissions, and around 50 attendees, this is relatively the largest standardized study up-to-date in this field. Even though the formal provisional duration for trails is completed and participant status has been finalized, snapshots of the dataset can still be used for additional research and development.

S2 TL;DR: Studies establish a simulated aptitude accomplished of classifying skin cancer with a level of capability similar to that of dermatologists using only pixels and disease labels as inputs. This research focuses on the relationship between a convolutional link's deepness and its correctness in large-scale image identification. It provides a comprehensive evaluation of networks with increasing depth as its main contribution by employing an architecture with very small (3 × 3) convolution filters. This demonstrates that expanding the depth to 16−19 weight layers has the potential to significantly improve the configurations that are currently in use. The strategy and estimation efforts of the combined team of Casio & Shinshu University won the ISBI Challenge 2017 − Skin Lesion Analysis to Melanoma Detection: The challenge of the grouping of lesions is hosted by ISIC. The online authentication score was 0.958, by the melanoma classifier having an AUC of 0.924 and the seborrheic keratosis classifier having an AUC of 0.993, respectively.

Our method for diagnosing skin lesions automatically is described in this report. It aims to incorporate dermatologists' expertise into the well-known CNN framework, which has demonstrated impressive performance in numerous visual recognition tasks. Particularly, it has developed a number of networks that enable the final diagnosis of clinical cases, lesion area finding, and lesion subdivision into organizational patterns. Additionally, new CNN block designs have been developed to incorporate this data into the diagnosis processing pipeline. In this ISIC 2017 skin lesion study trial, deep ResNets are suggested for robust visual feature learning and representation.

"Skin Lesion Analysis Towards Melanoma Detection" is described in this extended abstract (ISBI 2017). Even though our team has worked with melanoma classification for a long time, this was our first time working with skin lesion segmentation at the ISIC Challenge 2017. Our final submission utilized four of our models for segmentation in part 1: two were trained for 250 and 500 epochs, respectively, with all 2000 samples and no validation split; and the remaining two were trained and validated over 220 epochs using two distinct 1600/400 splits. Each of these four models received an official validation score between 0.780 and 0.783.

The original cutting edge for gathering and finding in the ImageNet Huge Scope Visual Acknowledgment Challenge 2014 (ILSVRC14) is accomplished by this chapter's plan of a profound convolutional brain network engineering codenamed Commencement. The superior usage of the organization's processing assets is this engineering's essential component. Through carefully crafted design, it maintains a constant computational budget while simultaneously expanding the network's deepness and width. The architectural choices are made based on the intuition of multi-scale processing and Hebbian principle in order to improve the prediction quality. GoogLeNet, a 22-layer profound organization whose characterization and identification quality is assessed, is one specific manifestation utilized in our ILSVRC14 accommodation.

The objective of that paper is to conduct a thorough work review of cutting-edge CAD methods that will be available between 2011 and 2020. There were a total of 365 distributions recognized involving the Favored Revealing Things for Precise Surveys and Meta Analyses (PRISMA) technique, 221 of which managed skin injury division and 144 with skin sore grouping. Using a variety of methods, these articles are analyzed and briefed to provide crucial information about the CAD system development procedures. S2 TL;DR: This study looked at the significance of image segmentation and its impact on the classification efficiency and performance of dermatoscopic skin lesion classification. That work emphasizes on the usage of a baseline classifier as the reference model with no segmentation masks. S2 TL;DR: For collaborative learning of segmentation on skin lesion and recognition of melanoma, two crucial melanoma diagnosis tasks, an original data alert deep structure, are proposed.

The anticipated hybrid-CNN classifier will produce deeper feature maps of the same lesion by combining three separate feature identifiers with the same set of images. These attached feature maps are categorized by means of the various completely associated layers, and then an ensemble is used to acquire a final calculation probability. The preprocessing makes use of lesion division, amplification, and class rebalancing. Class rebalancing, which penalizes the learning process on the loss of the class with majority data and adds more images with significant features to the classes with less data, has also been used to improve lesion recognition. To demonstrate its ability on transfer learning, it also uses a small dataset to build a generic classifier from information from a pre-trained model.

This study examines the effectiveness of eight current CNN models' deep features. Also, it explores what limit restriction and standardization techniques mean for melanoma location. S2 TL;DR: A channel modulation scheme is used to explicitly integrate dermoscopic feature segmentations into a diagnosis network in this study's melanoma diagnosis system. The diagnosis's interpretability is enhanced, and clinicians are provided with intuitive and useful clues as a result. Since 2016, 45 studies have utilized deep learning technology to identify skin diseases. It takes a gander at these examinations according to the point of view of the sickness type, informational collection, innovation for handling information, innovation for upgrading information, a model for picture acknowledgment of skin illnesses, a profound learning system, assessment markers, and model execution. Additionally, it provides a synopsis of both conventional and device learning-based approaches to skin disease diagnosis and usage. It likewise looks at the growth that has been made in this area up to this point and suggests four potential areas for future research.

This training suggests a new ensemble deep learning system built on the dual path system with confidence preservation and residual network with next dimension to improve the prediction performance skin lesions classification algorithm. Skin lesions shall be classified more quickly, thanks to the proposed algorithm, which uses the distributed computing paradigm to accelerate the inference process by 0.25. Experiments showed that the algorithm could differentiate between 12 ensemble deep learning algorithms and 16 deep learning algorithms. The investigational evaluation was carried out using the images taken from the International Skin Imaging Collaboration's public databases. There are several challenges in the classification of skin diseases, including:

- Variability in presentation: Skin diseases can present in a wide variety of ways, making it difficult to accurately classify them based on visual characteristics alone.
- Overlapping symptoms: Many skin diseases share similar symptoms, making it difficult to differentiate between them.
- Limited data: There is a lack of high-quality, annotated data for skin diseases, which can make it difficult to train accurate classifiers.
- Manual annotation: The process of manually annotating images of skin diseases can be time-consuming and subjective, leading to potential errors in the data.
- Variability in skin type: The visual appearance of skin diseases can vary greatly depending on the individual's skin type, such as pigmentation, texture, and hair growth.
- Privacy concerns: Privacy concerns about sharing the personal images for research or clinical use.
- Limited generalizability: Classifiers trained on one population may not perform well on other populations due to differences in skin type and disease prevalence.

There are several research gaps in the classification of skin diseases, including:

(1) Lack of standardization in diagnostic criteria and terminology, which can lead to confusion and inconsistent reporting of cases.
(2) Limited availability of high-quality, diverse datasets for training and evaluating machine learning models, which can lead to poor generalizability and bias.
(3) Insufficient attention to rare and under-studied skin conditions, which can lead to a lack of understanding and effective treatments for these conditions.
(4) Limited understanding of the underlying causes and pathophysiology of many skin diseases, which can make it difficult to develop targeted therapies.

(5) Lack of integration of patient-reported outcomes and quality of life measures in the classification and management of skin diseases, which can lead to a lack of understanding of the impact of the disease on patients' lives.

(6) Inadequate attention to the intersection of skin diseases with other chronic conditions and risk factors, such as diabetes and obesity.

(7) Limited use of modern technologies and techniques, such as artificial intelligence and digital imaging, in the ordering and management of skin diseases.

9.3 Tools and Methods

The input pictures from the HAM10000 dataset are of high resolution; to be trained and tested on any ordinary personal computer or laptop, it is nearly not possible. Indeed, it requires a high-configuration computer to train a model with this dataset. Actually, a laptop with just 8-GB RAM and 2-GB GPU was initially used to train the custom-built deep learning model. It took 23.43 hours on average to execute each epoch of the training process.

The high-resolution images (Figures 9.8 and 9.9) are preprocessed (Figure 9.5) to a size of $256 \times 256 \times 3$, so that they shall be used to train the custom-built model with 1,979,919 parameters. Out of all the 1,979,919 available parameters, 1,978,911 parameters are trainable and 1008 parameters are non-trainable. Before finalizing this model to train and predict with HAM10000, eight existing models were used to predict using HAM10000. But none of the models gave an accuracy of more than 65%. In order to do this, the output layer of these models was scrapped and new dense layers were added to accommodate seven (corresponding to the number of classes of skin lesions) output neurons, which are activated using the softmax function. The existing models used in this study are ResNet50, ResNet152, Xception, VGG16, EfficientNetB4, InceptionV3, DenseNet201, and MobileNet.

Dataset: HAM10000 (Human Against Machine with 10,000 training images) is one of the best datasets accessible to train machine learning and deep learning algorithms to detect benign/malignant pigmented skin lesions. Dermatoscopic images are collected from different sources to represent significant classifications of pigmented skin lesions. With promising results and pathologically confirmed 53% of lesions, HAM10000 is the best dataset to train machine learning and deep learning algorithms. The quality of dermatoscopic training images relies on the accuracy of annotations associated with such

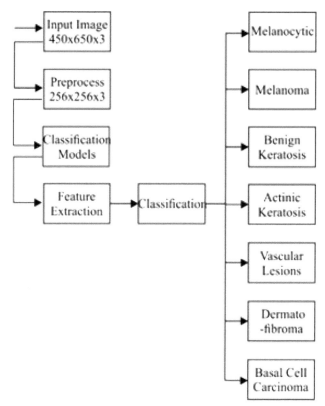

Figure 9.5 Proposed classification process.

images. The hand-labeled images of the HAM10000 training dataset inherit such quality due to the preprocessing performed on the collected images.

9.3.1 Dataset analysis

The strip plot shown in Figure 9.6 is used to represent the ratio in the number of male and female candidates (from the population) diagnosed with the classes of cancer. The strip plot represents the complete population of the dataset. The python code representation for the strip plot is given below for reference.

```
plt.figure(figsize=(15,4))
sns.stripplot(x='lesion',y='age',data=df, jitter=True, hue='sex', dodge=True)
plt.savefig('HAM10000 Dataset/Graphs/strip_plot.png', dpi = 300)
```

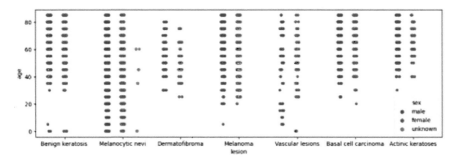

Figure 9.6   Multi-class diagnosis based on gender.

The count plot given shown in Figure 9.7 is used to represent the bifurcation in the number of candidates, from the population (based on their age group), diagnosed with the classes of cancer. The count plot also represents the complete population of the dataset. The python code representation for the strip plot is given below for reference.

```
fig, ax1 = plt.subplots(1, 1, figsize = (10, 5))
sns.countplot(y='lesion',data=df, hue="age",ax=ax1)
plt.savefig('HAM10000 Dataset/Graphs/countplot.png', dpi = 300)
```

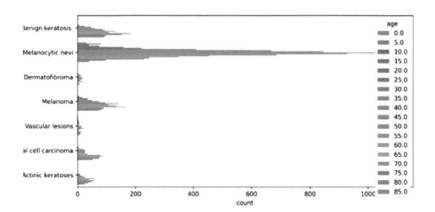

Figure 9.7   Multi-class diagnosis based on age.

From the results of the count plot, it is evident that the class of "Melanocytic nevi" is prevalent among the age group of 45−60, within the sample of a diagnosed population. Also, this count plot represents that the ratio of people diagnosed with "Melanocytic nevi" is very much higher than any other classes of the lesion under consideration. "Dermatofibroma" and "Melanoma" are found to be available with a very low distribution of samples within the population. The class of "Actinic keratoses" is prominently found only in old age people. "Basal cell carcinoma" is found almost in people aged greater than 45.

The classes of diseases under study (with the corresponding label usages for the ML model) are listed as follows: actinic keratoses and intraepithelial carcinoma/Bowen's disease (akiec), basal cell carcinoma (bcc), benign keratosis-like lesions (solar lentigines/seborrheic keratoses and lichen-planus like keratoses, bkl), dermatofibroma (df), melanoma (mel), melanocytic nevi (nv), and vascular lesions (angiomas, angiokeratomas, pyogenic granulomas, and hemorrhage, vasc). Part 1 of the (Figure 9.8) dataset has 5000 Jpeg files and Part 2 of the same dataset (Figure 9.9) has 5015 Jpeg files in it.

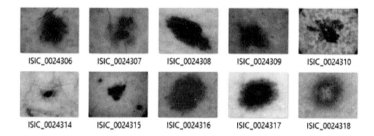

Figure 9.8   HAM10000 dataset\HAM10000_images_part_1.

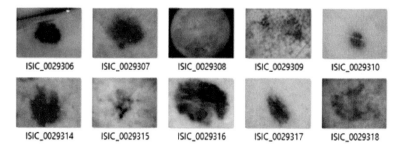

Figure 9.9   HAM10000 dataset\HAM10000_images_part_1.

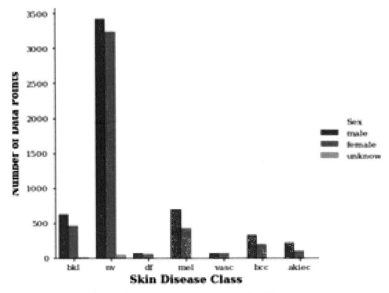

Figure 9.10　Benign/malignant classification.

Few CSV files are associated with the dataset. Those CSV files are used to describe (Figure 9.10) the dataset with the metadata (Table 9.1) organized within. HAM10000_metadata is the file that shall be used to retrieve the information on the classes of images (Figure 9.11).

A feature named "dx" is used to describe the class labels associated with each image. These CSV files are used to extract additional latent features on the HAM10000 dataset. During the training process, the feature "dx" is used as the target for the predictor attributes (feature matrix).

Melanocytic lesions: Melanocytic lesions are pigmented skin lesions that may be benign, moles, or malignant lesions growing on the skin. Melanocytic

Table 9.1　Count of classified lesions in the HAM10000 dataset.

S. no.	Lesion	Total in dataset
1.	Melanocytic nevi	6705
2.	Melanoma	1113
3.	Benign keratosis	1099
4.	Basal cell carcinoma	514
5.	Actinic keratoses	327
6.	Vascular lesions	142
7.	Dermatofibroma	115

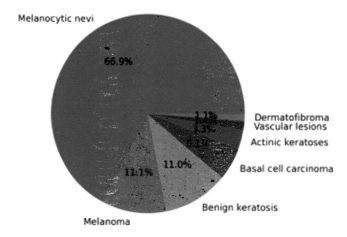

Figure 9.11   Distribution of classified lesions in the HAM10000 dataset.

lesions are formed due to the exponential growth of neural crest-derived melanocytic cells. Percentage of classified lesions in the HAM10000 dataset is 66.9%, which is very high in data quantity when compared with other classified labels.

Melanoma lesions: Diagnosis of melanoma lesions is challenging, and if it is wrongly diagnosed, then it may lead to a life-threatening dangerous medical situation. Melanoma lesions look like irregular larger brownish-black spots with speckles. Melanoma lesions will spread to the skin cells nearby and damage more skin cells.

Benign keratosis: Waxy/scaly benign is common in old age people; it may grow colored as a tan/brown/black. It grows slowly in old age people as patches and scales and shall be treated by dermatologists to freeze/scrap/burn to get normal skin, sometimes the treatment results in getting black patchy scars.

Actinic keratosis: Scaly benign is developed on the skin due to higher exposure to sunlight. Even though they are not seriously harmful, they may sometimes develop into malignant. Cryotherapy is a suitable treatment done to mitigate further growth of actinic keratosis.

Vascular lesions: Vascular lesions may appear at the birth of a child. It is the damage created on the skin or on the tissue underneath the skin. So, these vascular lesions are a few times considered birthmarks, according to their location and significance.

Dermatofibroma: Researchers are still working on identifying the reasons for the creation of dermatofibroma on skin cells. It is the result of the excessive growth of a mixture of human cells underneath the skin. In a few cases, external damage caused to the skin is also a reason for dermatofibroma.

Basal cell carcinoma: Glossy bumps with a rolled border in black/brown color are the symptom of basal cell carcinoma. This skin cancer is developed due to high exposure to sunlight. Surgical excision shall be a good solution for this kind of skin cancer.

The input images: High-quality images are required to train a neural-network-based diagnosis algorithm. And it is mandatory that the images should be of high quality to serve the purpose. These trainable images should be of high quality to serve the purpose. These trainable images should be clearly annotated, precisely. These images are initially clustered and then labeled to classes before training a selected model. Images of size $450 \times 560 \times 3$ are chosen as trainable images. All images considered to train the model are downsized to the size of $256 \times 256 \times 3$ to maintain uniformity.

Preprocessing the images: The training images should be preprocessed before they are applied to the tools and methods. Suitable preprocessing methods should be selected before inferring details from the data (image). Manyfold preprocessing methods are available. Selecting a suitable pre-processing method itself is a complete process that needs more effort and concentration. The process of preprocessing starts with the task of downsizing all input images to a uniform size of $256 \times 256 \times 3$. The first two values (256) of this product represent the height and width of the image in pixels and the third value (3) represents the three true-color values.

The classification models: Medical image processing algorithms are available in plenty in a few base algorithms (Table 9.2) and their newer versions are also available for medical usage. But, significant ML-based medical image processing algorithms (Table 9.3) with a practical approach are a handful. Still, the issue with such algorithms is that they are application specific; even if there is a possibility to generalize these algorithms, it shall be done to an extent, but again it will be specific to a domain. This implicitly means that the algorithm for multi-class skin cancer detection should be an algorithm that is specialized in the domain of dermatoscopy. However, such significant ML-based algorithms are application-specific; in cancer detection, there should be a few dedicated algorithms that are generalized for the domain of dermatoscopy.

Table 9.2 Metadata on the classification algorithms under study.

S. no.	AI model	Class labels	Dataset	Model type	References
1.	Custom-made shallow CNN	2	Dermoscopy	Conv2D	[19]
2.	ResNet-50	6	Dermoscopy		[20]
3.	Ensemble InceptionV3/ResNet-50	7	Dermoscopy/clinical photographs		[21]
4.	Enhanced ResNet-50	6	Dermoscopy/clinical pho-tographs/clinical data		[22]
5.	InceptionV4	26	Clinical pho-tographs/clinical data		[23]
6.	Enhanced EfficientNetV2	4	clinical photographs		[24]
7.	ResNet-152	12	Clinical photographs		[25]
8.	GoogleLeNet	14	Clinical photographs		[26]
9.	Ensemble SENet-154/SEResNeXt-50	178	Clinical photographs		[27]
10.	Pruned ResNet18	2	297 FF-OCT images		[28]
11.	DenseNet201	1000	HAM10000 and PH2 dataset		[29, 30]

Image dataset generator: The image dataset is initially converted into a batch of images, then these images are converted into augmented objects, and then before using these images for training/testing, they are randomly transformed into batches of images (image dataset; original batch of images; image augmentation object; randomly transformed batch of images; train CNN on batch).

Glob: Read large number of files from folder and sub-folders (CSV, images, text files, etc.).

Image data generator: Batches of tensor data for the input images are processed for augmentation and taken into the model for training purpose. While creating the tensor data of images, selected preprocessing algorithms shall be used for augmenting the images.

Table 9.3 Number of layers, trainable parameters. and total parameters.

S. no	AI model	Class labels	No. of layers	Trainable parameters	Total no. of parameters
1.	ResNet50	1000	177	25,583,592	25,636,712
2.	ResNet152	1000	517	60,268,520	60,419,944
3.	Xception	1000	134	22,855,952	22,910,480
4.	VGG16	1000	23	138,357,544	138,357,544
5.	EfficientNetB4	1000	477	19,341,616	19,466,823
6.	InceptionV3	1000	313	23,817,352	23,851,784
7.	DenseNet201	1000	709	20,013,928	20,242,984
8.	MobileNet	1000	92	4,231,976	4,253,864

Early stopping: During the process of training the model with a selected number of augmented images, the training process shall be iterated for a fixed number of epochs. But still, even if the global maximum is arrived, the training process will undergo till the specified number of epochs are in running. This issue shall be sorted out by using the EarlyStopping module from the tensorflow.keras.callbacks package. EarlyStopping shall be done by passing any metrics (like loss with a patience value) of the training|validation process.

Transfer learning models: All eight existing architectures support 1000 class-labels; so in order to classify the samples into seven class-labels of images, the input of the selected base model is reconstructed to accept an input with the shape of (256 × 256 × 3), then a 2D-global average pooling is added to the base model, and then six dense layers with respectively 512, 128, 64, 32, 16, and 8 neuron units are added one after another in the mentioned sequence with "relu" activation functions for each such layers. Then to the architecture, a final dense layer with seven neurons (to represent seven classes) is added. The softmax functions are used to activate the final dense layer to get the maximum likelihood on the output probability. The new model supporting "7" output class-label is constructed. The base models are not trainable. The models are compiled with the "Adam" optimizer, and the categorical cross-entropy is used as the loss function and "accuracy" is the quantifying metric.

   The first custom-built model is constructed with a total of 1,190,207 parameters; out of that, trainable parameters are 1,189,183 and non-trainable parameters are 1024. This model comes with 30 layers, out of which 12 layers are convolutional 2D layers and 6 max pooling layers are included after each couple of convolutional 2D layers. Each max pooling layer is followed by a batch normalization layer. After the fifth max pooling layer, the image feature tensors are flattened, so that the immediate interconnected dense layers (with eight neurons) will work with a total of 1032 parameters. Just before the last layer (with SoftMax activation function), a dense layer with eight activated neurons are regularized with L1L2 kernel regularizer with L1 = 1e − 5 and L2 = 1e − 4. The "relu" activation function is used for all convolutional 2D and dense layers (except the output layer with "Softmax" and seven activated neuron units).

An initial custom-built model: An initial custom-built thin model was constructed to demonstrate the process. It had a total of 1,190,207 parameters out of which 1,189,183 parameters are trainable and 1024 are non-trainable parameters. Still, this thin model performed almost equal to the pre-built models explained in Table 9.3. This model (initial) shall be executed in computers with the least configuration (with a GPU).

The architecture model 1 — "An initial" tied two-stacked layer model:
Layer (type) Output shape Param #
```
=====================================================
input_1 (InputLayer) [(None, 256, 256, 3)] 0
conv2d (Conv2D) (None, 256, 256, 256) 7168
conv2d_1 (Conv2D) (None, 256, 256, 256) 590080
max_pooling2d (MaxPooling2D) (None, 128, 128, 256) 0
batch_normalization (BatchNo) (None, 128, 128, 256) 1024
max_pooling2d (MaxPooling2D) (None, 128, 128, 256) 0
. . . .
flatten (Flatten) (None, 128) 0
dense (Dense) (None, 8) 1032
batch_normalization_5 (Batch) (None, 8) 32
dense_1 (Dense) (None, 8) 72
batch_normalization_6 (Batch) (None, 8) 32
dense_2 (Dense) (None, 7) 63
=====================================================
Total parameters: 1,190,207
Trainable parameters: 1,189,183
Non-trainable parameters: 1024
```

The final custom-built model (DCNN-MSCCA): A final custom-built model was constructed to get an accurate prediction. It has a total of 1,979,919 parameters out of which 1,189,183 parameters are trainable. Still, this model performed better than any of the pre-built models explained in Table 9.3. This model (DCNN-MSCCA) shall be executed in computers with the least configuration (with a GPU) but will take an excessive estimated time of arrival (ETA).

The final architecture model – "Tied three-stacked layer model":
Model: "model"
Layer (type) Output shape Param #
===
input_1 (InputLayer) [(None, 256, 256, 3)] 0
conv2d (Conv2D) (None, 256, 256, 256) 7168
conv2d_1 (Conv2D) (None, 256, 256, 256) 590,080
conv2d_2 (Conv2D) (None, 256, 256, 256) 590,080
. . .
. . .
max_pooling2d_4 (MaxPooling2) (None, 8, 8, 8) 0
flatten (Flatten) (None, 512) 0
dense (Dense) (None, 8) 4104
batch_normalization_5 (Batch) (None, 8) 32
dense_1 (Dense) (None, 7) 63
===
Total parameters: 1,979,919
Trainable parameters: 1,978,911
Non-trainable parameters: 1008

9.3.2 Analysis of results

The initial model with the architecture in Table 9.4 has converged to its maximum after the 14th iteration (Figure 9.12) and has given 60.05% validation accuracy, even though the training accuracy was 83.5%; still, 1.0665 is a very high unit metric value of the loss. In the initial model, the convergence was good for the fifth class (mel). But, for other class labels, the model was not converging enough – not up to the mark, as expected. In the case of the final model (DCNN-MSCCA), except for the last class (vasc), precisions for other classes were greater than 85%; exception is the fourth class (df) with 60% precision.

Table 9.4 Performance of the initial model versus the final model (DCNN-MSCCA).

Results	The initial model			DCNN-MSCCA		
	Precision	**Recall**	***F*1-score**	**Precision**	**Recall**	***F*1-score**
akiec	0.00	0.00	0.00	0.88	0.73	0.80
bcc	0.00	0.00	0.00	0.86	0.88	0.87
bkl	0.08	0.01	0.02	0.91	0.97	0.94
df	0.00	0.00	0.00	0.60	0.11	0.18
mel	0.08	0.00	0.00	0.96	1.00	0.98
nv	0.61	0.98	0.75	0.97	1.00	0.98
vasc	0.00	0.00	0.00	0.00	0.00	0.00
Accuracy			0.60			0.95
Macro Avg.	0.11	0.14	0.11	0.74	0.67	0.68
Weighted Avg.	0.40	0.60	0.46	0.93	0.95	0.94

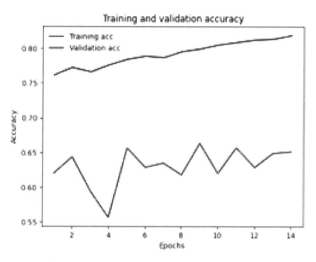

Figure 9.12 Result of the initial "Tied two-stacked layer model" (loss: 1.0665; accuracy: 0.6005).

The overall performance of the DCNN-MSCCA model is highly accept-able for its accuracy with the consideration that this model could be trained and tested in any computer with a basic graphical processing unit. Because of the lightweight configuration of the architecture of DCNN-MSCCA, the robustness of the system may struggle against high configuration tensors or for a heavy-weight dataset bigger than HAM10000 (with unevenly distributed classes in a large dataset).

The stacked layers of the DCNN-MSCCA play an important role in enhancing the performance of the algorithm. The number of parameters in the DCCN-MSCCA algorithm helps in improving the accuracy of diagnosing multi-class-pigmented skin lesions. The uneven distribution of samples of multiple classes plays a significant role in reducing the performance of models used for the experiment.

9.4 Conclusion

Diagnosing the skin lesions from the input images is a challenging task in medical image processing. The proposed algorithm, DCNN-MSCCA, uses the stacked layers from the most significant algorithms. These ensembled layers are stacked in between a custom-made input layer and a multi-class-supported output layer. Comparatively, DCNN-MSCCA is constructed with a smaller number of parameters. Because of this smaller number of parameters, the training process will take much less time to train the model. Still, DCNN-MSCCA provides good accuracy in diagnosing multi-class skin cancer from the input images of pigmented skin lesions. This algorithm uses an optimal number of parameters for a deep convolution neural network and gives an optimal performance, which is considered as best among similar existing algorithms. The performance of this deep-CNN-based multi-class skin cancer classification algorithm, DCNN-MSCCA, is demonstrated using the HAM10000 dataset. A maximum of 95.1% of accuracy is provided by the DCNN-MSCCA algorithm in predicting the exact cancer type among the multi-class skin cancers listed in this work.

References

[1] He, Kaiming, et al. "Deep residual learning for image recognition." *Proceedings of the IEEE conference on computer vision and pattern recognition*. 2016.
[2] Codella, Noel CF, et al. "Skin lesion analysis toward melanoma detection: A challenge at the 2017 international symposium on biomedical imaging (isbi), hosted by the international skin imaging collaboration (isic)." *2018 IEEE 15th international symposium on biomedical imaging (ISBI 2018)*. IEEE, 2018.
[3] Esteva, Andre, et al. "Dermatologist-level classification of skin cancer with deep neural networks." *nature* 542.7639 (2017): 115-118.

[4] Simonyan, Karen, and Andrew Zisserman. "Very deep convolutional networks for large-scale image recognition." *arXiv preprint arXiv:1409.1556* (2014).

[5] Matsunaga, Kazuhisa, et al. "Image classification of melanoma, nevus and seborrheic keratosis by deep neural network ensemble." *arXiv preprint arXiv:1703.03108* (2017).

[6] Díaz, Iván González. "Incorporating the knowledge of dermatologists to convolutional neural networks for the diagnosis of skin lesions." *arXiv preprint arXiv:1703.01976* (2017).

[7] Bi, Lei, et al. "Automatic skin lesion analysis using large-scale dermoscopy images and deep residual networks." *arXiv preprint arXiv:1703.04197* (2017).

[8] Menegola, Afonso, et al. "RECOD titans at ISIC challenge 2017." *arXiv preprint arXiv:1703.04819* (2017).

[9] Szegedy, Christian, et al. "Going deeper with convolutions." *Proceedings of the IEEE conference on computer vision and pattern recognition.* 2015.

[10] Hasan, Md, et al. "Skin Lesion Analysis: A State-of-the-Art Survey, Systematic Review, and Future Trends." *arXiv preprint arXiv:2208.12232* (2022).

[11] Mahbod, Amirreza, et al. "The effects of skin lesion segmentation on the performance of dermatoscopic image classification." *Computer Methods and Programs in Biomedicine* 197 (2020): 105725.

[12] Wang, Xiaohong, et al. "Knowledge-aware deep framework for collaborative skin lesion segmentation and melanoma recognition." *Pattern Recognition* 120 (2021): 108075.

[13] Hasan, Md Kamrul, et al. "DermoExpert: Skin lesion classification using a hybrid convolutional neural network through segmentation, transfer learning, and augmentation." *Informatics in Medicine Unlocked* 28 (2022): 100819.

[14] Gajera, Himanshu K., Deepak Ranjan Nayak, and Mukesh A. Zaveri. "A comprehensive analysis of dermoscopy images for melanoma detection via deep CNN features." *Biomedical Signal Processing and Control* 79 (2023): 104186.

[15] López-Labraca, Javier, et al. "An interpretable CNN-based CAD system for skin lesion diagnosis." *Artificial Intelligence in Medicine* 132 (2022): 102370.

[16] Hasan, Md Kamrul, et al. "Dermo-DOCTOR: A framework for concurrent skin lesion detection and recognition using a deep convolutional

neural network with end-to-end dual encoders." *Biomedical Signal Processing and Control* 68 (2021): 102661.

[17] Li, Ling-Fang, et al. "Deep learning in skin disease image recognition: A review." *Ieee Access* 8 (2020): 208264-208280.

[18] Okuboyejo, Damilola A., and Oludayo O. Olugbara. "Classification of Skin Lesions Using Weighted Majority Voting Ensemble Deep Learning." *Algorithms* 15.12 (2022): 443.

[19] L. Wang, A. Chen, Y. Zhang, X. Wang, Y. Zhang, Q. Shen, Y. Xue, AK-DL: A shallow neural network model for diagnosing actinic keratosis with better performance than deep neural networks, Diagnostics. 10 (2020), https://doi.org/10.3390/diagnostics10040217.

[20] R.C. Maron, et. al., "Systematic outperformance of 112 dermatologists in multiclass skin cancer image classification by convolutional neural networks", Eur. J. Cancer. 119 (2019) 57–65. 10.1016/j.ejca.2019.06.013.

[21] P. Tschandl, et. al., Expert-Level Diagnosis of Nonpigmented Skin Cancer by Combined Convolutional Neural Networks, JAMA Dermatol. 155 (2019) 58–65, https://doi.org/10.1001/jamadermatol.2018.4378.

[22] A.G.C. Pacheco, R.A. Krohling, The impact of patient clinical information on automated skin cancer detection, Comput. Biol. Med. 116 (2020), 103545, https://doi.org/10.1016/j.compbiomed.2019.103545.

[23] Y. Liu, et. al., A deep learning system for differential diagnosis of skin diseases, Nat. Med. 2020 266. 26 (2020) 900–908. 10.1038/s41591-020-0842-3.

[24] R. Karthik, et. al., Eff2Net: An efficient channel attention-based convolutional neural network for skin disease classification, Biomed. Signal Process. Control. 73 (2022), 103406, https://doi.org/10.1016/j.bspc.2021.103406.

[25] S.S. Han, et. al., Classification of the Clinical Images for Benign and Malignant Cutaneous Tumors Using a Deep Learning Algorithm, J. Invest. Dermatol. 138 (2018) 1529–1538, https://doi.org/10.1016/j.jid.2018.01.028.

[26] Y. Fujisawa, et. al., Deep-learning-based, computer-aided classifier developed with a small dataset of clinical images surpasses boardcertified dermatologists in skin tumour diagnosis, Br. J. Dermatol. 180 (2019) 373–381, https://doi.org/10.1111/BJD.16924.

[27] S.S. Han, et. al., Keratinocytic Skin Cancer Detection on the Face Using Region-Based Convolutional Neural Network, JAMA Dermatol. 156 (2020) 29–37, https://doi.org/10.1001/jamadermatol.2019.3807

[28] Ho, C. J., Calderon-Delgado, M., Chan, C. C., Lin, M. Y., Tjiu, J. W., Huang, S. L., & Chen, H. H. (2021). Detecting mouse squamous cell carcinoma from submicron full-field optical coherence tomography images by deep learning. Journal of Biophotonics, 14(1), e202000271.

[29] Khan, M. A., Sharif, M., Akram, T., Damaševičius, R., & Maskeliūnas, R. (2021). Skin lesion segmentation and multiclass classification using deep learning features and improved moth flame optimization. Diagnostics, 11(5), 811.

[30] Huang, G., Liu, Z., Van Der Maaten, L., & Weinberger, K. Q. (2017). Densely connected convolutional networks. In Proceedings of the IEEE conference on computer vision and pattern recognition (pp. 4700-4708).

10

Similarity Index Retrieval for School Kids' Sitting Posture Identification

Munish Gupta[1], Sachin Sharma[1], Madhulika Bhatia[1], and Nikhil Gupta[2]

[1]Department of Computer Science and Engineering, Amity School of Engineering and Technology, India
[2]Department of Computer Electrical Engineering, GNIOT Engineering College, India
E-mail: munish.gupta1@s.amity.edu; sachina3010@gmail.com; mbhadauria@amity.edu; Nikhil.ee@gniot.net.in

Abstract

A good sitting posture is very important in one's individual life. Since the past time, it has been said that a person who sit in a good posture is more able to focus on their studies. In today's world, a lot of students and adults are suffering from this problem of poor sitting posture due to which the number of people at a physiotherapist's center is increasing. These physiotherapists help them to correct their posture. The main objective of developing the sitting posture is that it will help the students to correct their posture since school time, which can help them in future to sit in a good posture. A good sitting posture enhances blood flow and safeguards the health of the nerves and blood vessels. This paper describes the standing upright and in the proper alignment of a person. Therefore, it is highly useful to accurately monitor students' sitting posture in the classroom and alert them of poor posture. This chapter suggests a sitting posture for students during class by using a variety of student images as raw data for a model that will scan the images and determine whether the student is seated correctly. The model will use OpenPose, which provides the posture feature, to determine whether the student is hunched over, folding their hands, kneeling, and sitting straight. Convolutional neural networks are built using Keras datasets to identify student the sitting posture.

This model will ultimately state the percentage error of a speciïïňÄc image that it will scan in a speciïïňÄc amount of time. The accuracy of the model that we built getting is 98% at the time when there is nothing behind the object.

Keywords: Machine learning, tensorflow, keras, convolution neural network, openpose.

10.1 Introduction

10.1.1 Problem statement

According to survey, up to 80% of people in the modern world suffer from back pain and another 70% from neck pain and ïňĆattened back muscles. As a result, they are unable to carry out their daily tasks, making it difficult for students and adults to focus on their work and learn new things, causing disturbance to their sleep, etc. Sitting posture recognition is a model that takes us a step closer to break these barriers with the help of ML and DL techniques. It can unite millions of people who have poor posture or are unaffected by it, which will help us create a world that is more equitable and welcoming [1].

10.1.2 Motivation

The goal is to create a model used to address the issue, which people and children are having due to poor posture in daily life. After analyzing the present scenario, it was decided that it would be a fantastic idea to create a model that would notify people whether they are sitting in the right position or not and assist them in doing so, such that they will not experience back or neck pain and can concentrate on their work and can bring change in this world with their innovative minds [2].

10.1.3 Types of posture

In our daily lives, posture is something that is significant. A person with good posture can have huge energy levels and more confidence, while a person with poor posture will always deal with negativity, lack of confidence, etc. [4].

There are five different types of posture problems as shown in Figure 10.1.

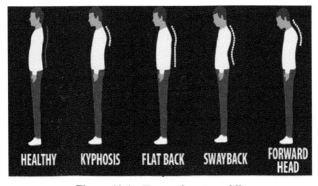

Figure 10.1 Types of postures [6].

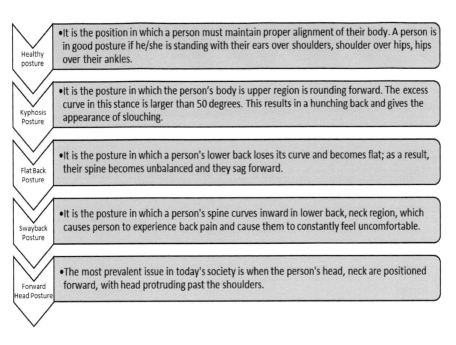

Healthy posture
- It is the position in which a person must maintain proper alignment of their body. A person is in good posture if he/she is standing with their ears over shoulders, shoulder over hips, hips over their ankles.

Kyphosis Posture
- It is the posture in which the person's body is upper region is rounding forward. The excess curve in this stance is larger than 50 degrees. This results in a hunching back and gives the appearance of slouching.

Flat Back Posture
- It is the posture in which a person's lower back loses its curve and becomes flat; as a result, their spine becomes unbalanced and they sag forward.

Swayback Posture
- It is the posture in which a person's spine curves inward in lower back, neck region, which causes person to experience back pain and cause them to constantly feel uncomfortable.

Forward Head Posture
- The most prevalent issue in today's society is when the person's head, neck are positioned forward, with head protruding past the shoulders.

10.1.4 Goals and objective

People will learn about their sitting posture via this role-model project, and it will also help them in adopting a proper sitting posture. The goal is to make it freely available to all schools so that teachers there can utilize this model to instill a positive sitting habit in students from an early age. Deep learning (DL) model is the model that tells about a person's or a student's posture [5].

10.1.5 Advantages of sitting in a good posture

A good body posture has a lot of benefits on a person's body. Some of them are listed in the figure below [7].

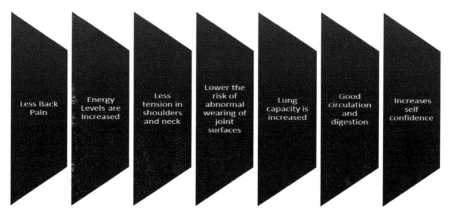

Figure 10.2   Advantages of Sitting in Good Posture

10.1.6 Disadvantages of sitting in a bad posture

Some of the disadvantages are mentioned in the figure below.

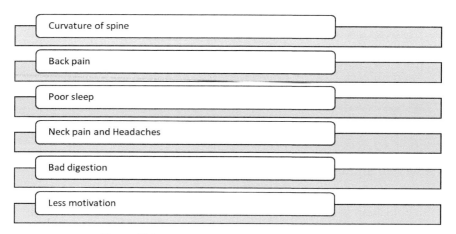

Figure 10.3   Disadvantages of Sitting in Bad Posture.

10.1.7 Tools, platform, and language

Following are the conditions for the successful implementation of the model developed in this initiative:

- Operating system: Cross-platform (Windows, Linux, and macOS).
- Programming Language: Python
- Python packages: numpy, OpenCV, Tensorflow, Keras, Pandas, Scikit-learn, Keras-and preprocessing.

10.2 Main Text

10.2.1 Literature review

Nowadays, body posture plays a very important role in a person's day-to-day life. If a person's body posture is correct, he will feel confident, energetic, attractive, etc. He can do his work on his own, and he will not rely on others for help. A subset of human posture recognizing system is the sitting posture recognition system. It was a heated topic when the first human body position recognition technology was created. As the people tell them about their body posture, but the limitation of this model is that it only tells about joints but does not tell them about the proper form of sitting. Later, this model was modified, and it was given the label "literature model" since it employs the CPM approach and gives information about incorrect posture in the form of images or text [8].

Broadly, sitting posture recognition is done in two ways:

- Sensor based
- Image based

Sensor based: It is the method in which sensors are used to detect the sitting posture a person needs to sit on a special type of chair. The chair has a lot of sensors on its surface, which will tell the person's posture with the help of those sensors.

Image based: It is the way in which the raw data (different sample of images) is provided to the machine which it would process and apply image classification algorithm to detect posture of person.

There is another way to detect the sitting posture by not providing the pre-determined images to the model using a real camera, which will detect the posture on the spot. It will use openCV to get the posture feature and will tell about the posture of the person [9].

Figure 10.4   Good and bad sitting postures in school [7].

As shown in Figure 10.4, there is one good and one bad sitting posture. Since COVID-19, for the past two years, many people and students have been compelled to sit for extended periods of time in front of a computer screen, which has a negative impact on their health and posture. However, sitting incorrectly, they have forgotten the benefits of having a good posture, which has a positive impact on their health. A benefit from this model is to learn about their posture, and students who are of school age will have their posture corrected [10].

10.3 Methodology

10.3.1 Machine learning

Machine learning (ML) is a subset of AI that improves the accuracy of software, models, and applications without being explicitly programmed. Machine learning algorithms use historical data as input to predict the values of outputs [11].

They have the ability to learn by themselves before which they must be trained. We can employ the following learning strategies as shown in below figure:

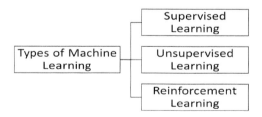

Figure 10.5   Types of Machine Learning.

For recognition of the human posture, we have used the convolution neural network (CNN) algorithm.

10.3.2 Convolution neural network

It is a kind of artificial neural network used to process and recognize images. Contrary to other types of neural networks, CNN layers have neurons arranged in three dimensions: width, height, and depth. Instead of all the neurons being fully connected, the neurons in one layer will only be connected to a small portion of the layer before it. The CNN model can work on any model and improve its attractiveness because it performs parameter sharing, special convolution, and pooling operations [12].

• **Convolution layer:** A convolutional layer is a key building block of convolutional neural networks (CNNs) used in deep learning. It performs the mathematical operation of convolution on the input data to produce a feature map, which represents the presence or absence of specific features or patterns in the input.

As shown in Figure 10.6, in a convolutional layer, a set of learnable filters, also known as kernels or weights, is applied to the input data. Each filter slides over the input data and performs a dot product operation between the filter weights and the local input data at each position. The result of this operation is a single value that represents the activation of that filter at that position. The

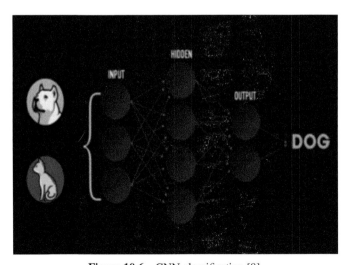

Figure 10.6 CNN classification [8].

output of this process is a set of activation maps, also known as feature maps, which highlight the presence of specific patterns or features in the input.

The size of the output feature maps depends on the size of the input, the size of the filters, the stride (the step size of the filter movement), and the padding (the number of zeros added to the input to preserve its spatial dimensions). By stacking multiple convolutional layers with non-linear activation functions, such as ReLU or sigmoid, CNNs can learn increasingly complex and abstract features from the input data.

Convolutional layers are widely used in image recognition and computer vision tasks, where they are effective in detecting patterns in visual data. They have also been applied to other types of data, such as audio and text, with some modifications to the convolution operation.

• **Pooling layer:** A pooling layer is a type of layer in a convolutional neural network (CNN) that is typically used after one or more convolutional layers. The purpose of a pooling layer is to reduce the spatial dimensions of the feature maps produced by the convolutional layers, while retaining the most important features.

The most common type of pooling layer is the max pooling layer. In a max pooling layer, the feature map is divided into non-overlapping rectangular regions, called pooling windows or filters. For each pooling window, the maximum value of the corresponding features is retained, and the other values are discarded. This process reduces the size of the feature map by a factor determined by the size of the pooling window and the stride, which is the step size between adjacent pooling windows.

Max pooling has several advantages. It reduces the amount of computation required in the network, which can speed up training and reduce overfitting. It also introduces a level of translation invariance, meaning that the output of the pooling operation is insensitive to small translations in the input. This can be useful in tasks such as object recognition, where the position of the object in the image may vary.

Other types of pooling layers include average pooling, which computes the average value of the features in each pooling window, and L2 pooling, which computes the square root of the sum of the squares of the features in each pooling window. These pooling methods are less commonly used than max pooling but can be useful in some applications.

Overall, pooling layers are an important component of convolutional neural networks, as they help to reduce the size of the feature maps and extract the most important features, while introducing a level of translation invariance.

10.3.3 TensorFlow

TensorFlow is an open-source software library for dataflow and differentiable programming across a range of tasks. It is developed by Google and was first released in 2015. TensorFlow is designed to be a flexible, scalable, and efficient platform for building and training machine learning models.

TensorFlow is based on a graph-based computation model where nodes in the graph represent mathematical operations and edges represent the flow of data between them. This makes it easy to parallelize computations and optimize performance, especially for large-scale machine learning tasks.

TensorFlow provides a wide range of tools and APIs for building and training various types of machine learning models, including neural networks, decision trees, and regression models. It also includes pre-built libraries and tools for common deep learning tasks, such as data preparation, feature extraction, and model evaluation.

In addition to its core functionality, TensorFlow also supports a range of other tools and libraries for data analysis, visualization, and deployment. For example, TensorBoard is a powerful visualization tool for monitoring and debugging machine learning models, while TensorFlow serving is a scalable platform for serving machine learning models in production.

Overall, TensorFlow is a powerful and flexible machine learning framework that is widely used in industry and academia for a wide range of applications, including computer vision, natural language processing, and speech recognition [13].

10.3.4 Keras

Keras is an open-source neural network library written in Python. It is designed to be a user-friendly, modular, and extensible deep learning framework that allows developers to build and train machine learning models quickly and easily. Keras was developed by François Chollet and was first released in March 2015.

Keras provides a high-level API that allows developers to easily build and train neural networks without having to worry too much about the low-level implementation details. It also supports various backends, such as TensorFlow, Theano, and Microsoft Cognitive Toolkit, which allow users to run their models on different hardware and software platforms.

Keras supports various types of neural networks, including feedforward, convolutional, recurrent, and combination models. It also includes a wide range of pre-built layers and utilities for common deep learning tasks, such as data preparation, regularization, and optimization.

Figure 10.7   Data used in this model.

Overall, Keras is a popular deep learning framework that is easy to use, flexible, and powerful, making it a popular choice for both beginners and experienced developers.

10.3.5 Dataset

The term "dataset" refers to a group of graphs, facts, images, etc., used in a specific model at a specific time.

Only a collection of images is used in the dataset for this model (sitting posture recognition). These photos were randomly gathered, where students are enrolled in classes. Students within this dataset are seated with a variety of positions, some with good posture and some with poor posture [14].

As shown in Figure 10.7, the dataset has been created manually by collecting images of the students of different age groups sitting in a classroom.

10.3.6 Working of the model

We have first trained our model for a simple posture (good posture) by giving the coordinates of good posture to that model. When the model is trained, we then pass any image for which we want to check the posture. In this model, we have set good posture by default, which will compare with every image and then tell us about the posture of the image for which we want to check. When an image is passed, it will pass through the CNN algorithm and then it will be matched with the trained data [15]. The model will find the image and then match the coordinate of it with the coordinates that are already provided to it. If the coordinates match accurately, then it will print the result as straight, but if the image coordinates are coming as negative (−ve) as compared to the pre-defined coordinates, then it will show that the person is leaning forward and vice versa.

Giving information about the posture, it will tell the user about the percentage error which is found out after calculating the distance of all images, and by that distance, it will be compared with the actual distance, which is already entered in the model. This is how the percentage error is given by the model [16].

10.4 Results

I was able to accomplish to get pretty good results from my model. It is working perfectly and told about the posture of school students. I have built this model in a manner that it can run on any system and can tell about the posture of any image provided to it. It just needs some libraries to be installed before running it on any system.

Example 1:

In Figure 10.8, we can see that the student's hands are not folded, but his back is hunched; so now check the result with the model.

Figure 10.8 Input image for the model.

In Figure 10.9, the image has the key points that are made by the model.

Figure 10.9 Output image with key points.

In Figure 10.10, the result of our prediction and the result of the model are the same.

```
processing time1 is 7.31966
processing time2 is 8.29688

Not kneeling
Not Folding Hands
Hunchback, percentage error is : 28 %

Process finished with exit code 0
```

Figure 10.10 Output 1 of the model.

Example 2:

As shown in Figure 10.11, the student is sitting in a good posture with his back straight, hands not folded, and legs not kneeling.

Figure 10.11 Input image 2 for the model.

So now check with the model once.

In Figure 10.12, the image has the key points that are made by the model.

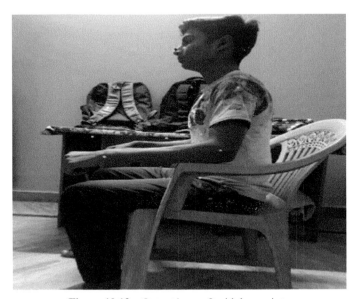

Figure 10.12 Output image 2 with key points.

```
processing time1 is 6.50381
processing time2 is 7.37501

Not Kneeling
Not Folding Hands
Straight, percentage error is : 0 %

Process finished with exit code 0
```

Figure 10.13   Output 2 of the model.

As shown in Figure 10.13, the result given by the model shows that this student is sitting in a perfect posture and the percentage error is coming out to be 14% only. So, this is the right posture [17].

Table 10.1   Images Time and Percentage error

Image details	Processing time 1	Processing time 2	Percentage error
Image 1	6.77588	7.84454	10
Image 2	7.29488	8.47172	24
Image 3	5.45801	6.33763	4
Image 4	4.96725	5.90866	27
Image 5	5.41632	6.32576	28
Image 6	5.38586	6.12198	10
Image 7	4.33889	4.96723	27
Image 8	5.42066	6.30028	39
Image 9	5.64139	6.53608	0
Image 10	4.94698	5.88783	8

The above-mentioned table and graph illustrate how much time was taken by the model to process these images and to calculate the percentage error. While working on this model, the one thing that has been observed is the time taken. Different images take different amounts of time for processing, and, accordingly, on the basis of the different processing times, the percentage accuracy differs. Processing time is the time that the image takes to check the image for its training, comparison, and for testing the model also. The images are used two times in this model; first is the time when it is used to train the model and second is the time when it is used to test the model and to give the output on the basis of which the results are formed and the analysis is done. It

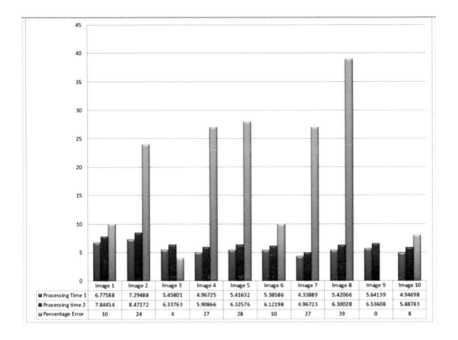

	Image 1	Image 2	Image 3	Image 4	Image 5	Image 6	Image 7	Image 8	Image 9	Image 10
Processing Time 1	6.77588	7.29488	5.45801	4.96725	5.41632	5.38586	4.33889	5.42066	5.64139	4.94698
Processing time 2	7.84454	8.47172	6.33763	5.90866	6.32576	6.12198	4.96723	6.30028	6.53608	5.88783
Percentage Error	10	24	4	27	28	10	27	39	0	8

tells us that a lot of students are suffering from the problem of sitting in bad posture.

The graph shows that the training time of the model is always less than the testing time, which indicates that it is less complicated to train the model rather than to test the model and to get the results. In this, one image is of the student who is sitting perfectly in the correct posture and his percentage error is 0 and then there is a student whose sitting posture is very bad and the percentage error is coming out to be 39. The model will match the posture with the points of the correct posture and compare them and provide us the result in a manner that tells the percentage error of the posture. If the posture is matching very similar to the points that are provided for the correct posture, then in that case, the percentage error is very low and vice versa.

10.5 Conclusion

We can draw the conclusion that machine learning is a rapidly developing field of computer science as a result of the posture information that is accurately retrieved by scanning the images using a model. Many people, especially students, will get the benefit from its assistance in developing and maintaining a good habit of sitting upright. It includes a CNN algorithm, which aids in image classification, and by calculating distance and angle, it provides information on human posture. The final accuracy achieved on this dataset was 98%. If there is no one behind the subject whose image needs to be processed and identified, as well as adequate and good lighting, we get the proper information about their posture.

References

[1] Chen, K. (2019, December). Sitting posture recognition based on open-pose. In IOP Conference Series: Materials Science and Engineering (Vol. 677, No. 3, p. 032057). IOP Publishing.

[2] Kulikajevas, A., Maskeliunas, R., & Damaševičius, R. (2021). Detection of sitting posture using hierarchical image composition and deep learning. PeerJ computer science, 7, e442.

[3] Fragkiadakis, E., Dalakleidi, K. V., & Nikita, K. S. (2019, July). Design and development of a sitting posture recognition system. In 2019 41st Annual International Conference of the IEEE Engineering in Medicine and Biology Society (EMBC) (pp. 3364-3367). IEEE.

[4] Wan, Q., Zhao, H., Li, J., & Xu, P. (2021). Hip positioning and sitting posture recognition based on human sitting pressure image. Sensors, 21(2), 426.

[5] Liu, W., Guo, Y., Yang, J., Hu, Y., & Wei, D. (2019, February). Sitting posture recognition based on human body pressure and CNN. In AIP Conference Proceedings (Vol. 2073, No. 1, p. 020093). AIP Publishing LLC.

[6] Kulikajevas, A., Maskeliunas, R., &Damaševičius, R. (2021). Detection of sitting posture using hierarchical image composition and deep learning. PeerJ computer science, 7, e442.

[7] Yu, M., Rhuma, A., Naqvi, S. M., Wang, L., & Chambers, J. (2012). A posture recognition-based fall detection system for monitoring an elderly person in a smart home environment. IEEE transactions on information technology in biomedicine, 16(6), 1274-1286.

[8] Kim, W., Jin, B., Choo, S., Nam, C. S., & Yun, M. H. (2019). Designing of smart chair for monitoring of sitting posture using convolutional neural networks. Data Technologies and Applications, 53(2), 142-155.

[9] Kim, Y. M., Son, Y., Kim, W., Jin, B., & Yun, M. H. (2018). Classification of children's sitting postures using machine learning algorithms. Applied Sciences, 8(8), 1280.

[10] Zeng, X., Sun, B., Wang, E., Luo, W., & Liu, T. (2017, June). A Method of Learner's Sitting Posture Recognition Based on Depth Image. In 2017 2nd International Conference on Control, Automation and Artificial Intelligence (CAAI 2017) (pp. 558-563). Atlantis Press.

[11] Li, Z. (2020, June). Practice on Human Posture Based on OpenCV. In International Conference on Applications and Techniques in Cyber Security and Intelligence (pp. 698-705). Springer, Cham.

[12] Liaqat, S., Dashtipour, K., Arshad, K., Assaleh, K., & Ramzan, N. (2021). A hybrid posture detection framework: Integrating machine learning and deep neural networks. IEEE Sensors Journal, 21(7), 9515-9522.

[13] Fan, Z., Hu, X., Chen, W. M., Zhang, D. W., & Ma, X. (2022). A deep learning based 2-dimensional hip pressure signals analysis method for sitting posture recognition. Biomedical Signal Processing and Control, 73, 103432.

[14] M. Pandey, M. Bhatia and A. Bansal, "An anatomization of noise removal techniques on medical images," 2016 International Conference on Innovation and Challenges in Cyber Security (ICICCS-INBUSH), Greater Noida, India, 2016, pp. 224-229, doi: 10.1109/ICICCS.2016.7542308.

[15] Aha Garg, M. Bhatia, & M. Hooda. (2021). Proposed Expert System for Controlling Obesity and Overweight Issues among Urban and Semi-Urban School going Children: An Epidemiological Study. Journal of Clinical & Diagnostic Research.

[16] Bansal A, Bhatia M, Yadav D (2016) Survey and comparative study on statistical tools for medical images. Adv Sci Lett 21(1):74–77.

[17] Monika, & Bhatia, M. (2022). Extraction of posture silhouettes using human posture feature points and spatial masks for activity recognition in public place. Journal of Engineering Research, 10(3A). https://doi.org/10.36909/jer.10803.

[18] Mehta, M., & Bhadauria, M. (2021). Performance Evaluation of Neural Network for Human Classification Using Blob Dataset. Recent Advances in Computer Science and Communications, 14(5), 1592-1602. Bentham Science Publishers.

11

Identification, Analysis, and Recommendation of the Sitting Posture of School Kids

Shikhar Pathak[1], Madhulika Bhatia[1], Arun Yadav[2], and Madhurima Hooda[3]

[1]Department of Computer Science and Engineering,
Amity School of Engineering and Technology, India
[2]Department of Computer Science and Engineering, NIT Hamirpur, India
[3]National Health Services, UK
E-mail: sk77pathak@gmail.com; mbhadauria@amity.edu;
ayadav@nith.ac.in; 10madhurima@gmail.com

Abstract

This research study aims to identify, analyze, and recommend appropriate sitting postures for school children to mitigate the risk of musculoskeletal disorders (MSDs). The investigation focuses on the correlation between prolonged periods of poor sitting postures, prevalent in classrooms, and the development of MSDs in children. Utilizing a combination of surveys, observations, and biomechanical measurements, the study seeks to pinpoint common sitting postures adopted by school children and analyze their potential impact on musculoskeletal health. Subsequently, based on the findings, the study formulates recommendations for optimal sitting postures, which are then presented to schools for implementation. The anticipated outcome of this research is an improvement in the musculoskeletal health of school children, a reduction in absenteeism attributed to MSDs, and ultimately an enhancement in academic performance.

Background

The increasing amount of time children a respending sitting in school and at home is a growing concern. With the rise of technology, children are spending more time on laptops, desktops, and mobile devices for educational and entertainment purposes, exacerbating this issue. If children, teachers, or parents do not pay attention to proper sitting posture, it can lead to various health problems.

Prolonged sitting in a poor posture can result in several musculoskeletal disorders, including back pain, neck strain, and shoulder pain. These conditions can impact a child's overall well-being, lead to decreased academic performance, and contribute to long-term health problems. Therefore, it is essential to create awareness among children, parents, and teachers about proper sitting posture.

Furthermore, schools can invest in appropriate furniture that supports good posture, such as adjustable desks and chairs that can accommodate students of different sizes. This can help reduce the incidence of musculoskeletal disorders caused by poor posture and provide a more conducive learning environment for students.

Methodology

This chapter proposes a model for monitoring students' sitting posture in the classroom using student photos as raw data. The model employs OpenPose, which provides posture features, to determine whether the student is sitting efficiently or not. Convolutional neural networks (CNNs) are trained on datasets to identify a student's sitting posture. The model calculates the percentage error of a specific image within a particular timeframe.

The accuracy achieved by the model is 98% under proper lighting conditions when there is no obstruction behind the object whose image is being scanned. The implementation of this model can provide real-time feedback to students and alert teachers to students who are sitting incorrectly, contributing to better health and academic performance. Consent from students and parents was obtained before implementing the model.

11.1 Introduction

11.1.1 Problem statement

The evolution of humans has had an impact on their ability to adapt to their environment and lifestyle. In ancient times, individuals spent their time either moving or resting, with sitting becoming more common later on. However, human anatomy is not well-suited for sitting, as the pressure on the spine and

Table 11.1 Problems reported (*n*: 186; age: 10−17 years from both sexes) [1].

Upper back pain	21%
Lower back pain	18%
Wrist & hand pain	6%
Dry eye syndrome	13%
Headache	11%
Insomnia	8%
Behavioural changes(Anger, Irritation, boredom)	6%

its attachments is much higher in a seated position than when lying down or walking.

The COVID-19 pandemic has led to an increase in the amount of time children spend sitting, whether for educational or leisure purposes. This has resulted in repetitive strain injury (RSI), cumulative traumatic disorder (CTD), and musculoskeletal problems (MSD). According to a survey (Table 11.1), 21% of children experienced moderate to severe upper back pain, 18% suffered from mild-to-moderate lower back pain, and 13% experienced eye strain. Many children also reported irregular sleep patterns, and 6% experienced behavioral changes such as inappropriate anger and boredom [1].

11.1.2 Motivation

Given the various health issues associated with improper sitting posture,particularly among children, it is crucial to address this problem and create awareness among individuals. To this end, a model has been designed to assist in educating people on proper sitting habits [2].

11.1.3 Goals and objective

The objective of this project is to highlight the different aspects of an individual's posture and how they can positively or negatively affect their health and productivity. By increasing awareness and promoting good sitting posture, this model aims to help individuals achieve better productivity and avoid health issues caused by poor posture.

This model will be made available free of charge to all educational institutions and teachers so that they can incorporate it into their curriculum and promote good sitting habits among their students [3]. Through this posture education program, individuals will learn about their own posture and adopt the proper sitting position. By making this model available to schools, it is hoped that students will develop good posture habits from a young age, which will benefit them throughout their lives. The model will focus on an individual's or student's posture and highlight ways to improve it [3].

11.1.4 Four proper sitting postures

Any sitting sample that causes any specific muscle, ligament, or tendon to be misused can adversely affect posture and lower back health.

To prevent negative posture, you must avoid:

- Sit leaning to at least one aspect with an unethical spine.
- Keep your knees, ankles, or hands crossed.
- Hanging or unsuitable foot aid.
- Sitting for a long term.
- Prolonged neck stress whilst viewing a display or any display screen or report.
- Sitting in a way that does not help the back, particularly the lower back.

Every kind of positioning or motion finished by using the frame includes or affects muscle groups and different components of frame [4].

Some guidelines to improve your posture are:

- Exercise for at least 20 minutes 3 times per week.
- Do not sit still in a single position.
- Sit directly ahead when reading.
- Placement of lumbar supports [5].

11.1.5 Tools, platform, and language

Following are the conditions for successful implementation of the model developed in this initiative:

- Operating system: Cross-platform (Windows, Linux, macOS, etc.).
- Programming Language: Python.
- Python Packages: numpy, OpenCV, TensorFlow, Keras, Pandas, Scikit-learn, Keras-Preprocessing, and Matplotlib.

11.2 Literature Review

The amount of awareness that can be caused by bad posture is really low and it is not so well-taught too; results of survey prove the same. The only

Table 11.2   Awareness of parents on ergonomics [1].

Knowledge of RSI / MSD's / CTD	0%
Sitting Posture	6%
Eye-monitor Ergonomics	1%
Keyboard & Mouse Ergonomics	0%
Breaks during Work or Study	38%
Laptop Ergonomics	3%
Contribution By teachers (ergonomics)	0%

thing known to these parents was that it was important to take breaks between studies (Table 11.2) [1].

To develop our project, learning about different ways to recognize posture was important too.

Broadly, sitting posture recognition is done in two ways:

- Sensor based
- Image based

Sensor based: It involves using specially designed chairs and/or wearables to detect the sitting posture using sensors used at a specific location to detect the joint and body placement on the said system. While sensor-based recognition is effective, the problem of accessibility arises. These systems require hardware components that are not easy to build and transport, making it challenging for widespread adoption and limiting their use to hospitals [6].

Image based: In this method, the posture is recognized by the use of raw data in the form of photos of live camera feed using the easily accessible webcams; in our project, we used sample images to detect the posture because it is more efficient to collect images of the posture of the kids and use them afterwards instead of disturbing them while studying [7].

11.3 Methodology

11.3.1 Machine learning

Machine learning is a subfield of artificial intelligence that focuses on developing algorithms that enable computers to learn from data without being explicitly programmed. It involves training machine learning models on a dataset to learn patterns and relationships in the data, and then using these models to make predictions or classify new data.

There are three main types of machine learning:

1. **Supervised learning:** This type of machine learning involves training a model on a labeled dataset, where the input data is paired with the correct output. The model learns to make predictions by generalizing from the labeled examples. Examples of supervised learning algorithms include linear regression, logistic regression, decision trees, random forests, support vector machines, and neural networks.

2. **Unsupervised learning:** In unsupervised learning, the model is trained on an unlabeled dataset, where there is no explicit output variable. The goal is to find patterns and relationships in the data, such as clusters or dimensions, which can be used to understand the underlying structure of the data. Examples of unsupervised learning algorithms include k-means clustering, hierarchical clustering, principal component analysis, and generative models such as autoencoders and variational autoencoders.

3. **Reinforcement learning:** This type of machine learning involves an agent learning to interact with an environment to maximize a reward signal. The agent takes actions in the environment, and the environment provides feedback in the form of rewards or penalties based on the actions taken. The goal is to learn a policy that maximizes the expected reward over time. Examples of reinforcement learning algorithms include Q-learning, SARSA, and deep reinforcement learning algorithms such as deep Q-networks (DQNs), and policy gradient methods.

Each type of machine learning has its strengths and weaknesses, and the choice of which type to use depends on the specific problem and available data. In practice, many machine learning applications use a combination of

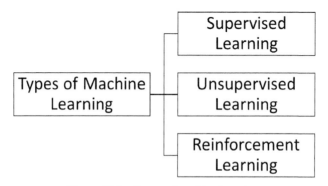

Figure 11.1 Types of machine learning.

these types to achieve the best results. For recognition of the human posture, we have used the convolution neural network (CNN) algorithm.

11.3.2 Convolution neural network

Convolutional neural networks (CNNs) are a class of neural networks that are commonly used for image and video analyses. They are inspired by the structure and function of the visual cortex in animals, which is responsible for processing visual information.

CNNs are designed to automatically learn hierarchical representations of visual data by using a combination of convolutional layers, pooling layers, and fully connected layers. The convolutional layers apply a set of filters to the input image to extract local features, such as edges, corners, and blobs. The pooling layers then downsample the output of the convolutional layers to reduce the dimensionality of the representation and increase the translational invariance. Finally, the fully connected layers combine the learned features from the previous layers to make a prediction or classification.

CNNs have several advantages over traditional machine learning models for image and video analyses. They can learn complex feature represen- tations from raw pixels, without the need for manual feature engineering. They are also highly scalable and can be trained on large datasets using parallel computing architectures. Finally, they can be used for a wide range of applications, such as object detection, image segmentation, and image classification.

Some popular CNN architectures include AlexNet, VGGNet, GoogLeNet, ResNet, and InceptionNet. These architectures vary in terms of the number of

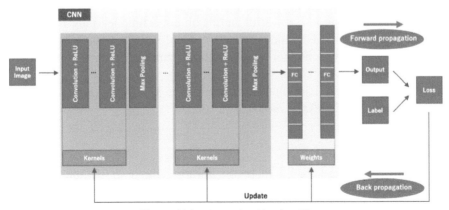

Figure 11.2 CNN classification [9].

layers, the types of layers used, and the size of the filters. They have been used to achieve state-of-the-art results on a variety of image and video analysis tasks, such as the ImageNet large scale visual recognition challenge.

CNN is highly effective for images because a feature can occur anywhere in an image, one layer feeds its output to other layers, and the extracted features can become more complex as it progresses [9].

11.3.3 TensorFlow

TensorFlow is an open-source software library for dataflow and differentiable programming across a range of tasks. It is developed by Google and was first released in 2015. TensorFlow is designed to be a flexible, scalable, and efficient platform for building and training machine learning models.

TensorFlow is based on a graph-based computation model where nodes in the graph represent mathematical operations and edges represent the flow of data between them. This makes it easy to parallelize computations and optimize performance, especially for large-scale machine learning tasks.

TensorFlow provides a wide range of tools and APIs for building and training various types of machine learning models, including neural networks, decision trees, and regression models. It also includes pre-built libraries and tools for common deep learning tasks, such as data preparation, feature extraction, and model evaluation.

In addition to its core functionality, TensorFlow also supports a range of other tools and libraries for data analysis, visualization, and deployment. For example, TensorBoard is a powerful visualization tool for monitoring and debugging machine learning models, while TensorFlow Serving is a scalable platform for serving machine learning models in production.

Overall, TensorFlow is a powerful and flexible machine learning framework that is widely used in industry and academia for a wide range of applications, including computer vision, natural language processing, and speech recognition.

It is a popular deep learning library, created by Google, free and open source. It greatly facilitates our model [10].

11.3.4 Keras

Keras is an open-source neural network library written in Python. It is designed to be a user-friendly, modular, and extensible deep learning framework that allows developers to build and train machine learning models quickly and easily. Keras was developed by François Chollet and was first released in March 2015.

Keras provides a high-level API that allows developers to easily build and train neural networks without having to worry too much about the low-level implementation details. It also supports various backends, such as TensorFlow, Theano, and Microsoft Cognitive Toolkit, which allows users to run their models on different hardware and software platforms.

Keras supports various types of neural networks, including feedforward, convolutional, recurrent, and combination models. It also includes a wide range of pre-built layers and utilities for common deep learning tasks, such as data preparation, regularization, and optimization.

Overall, Keras is a popular deep learning framework that is easy to use, flexible, and powerful, making it a popular choice for both beginners and experienced developers.

We can implement Keras for deep learning without interacting with the relatively complex TensorFlow [11].

11.3.5 OpenPose

Convolutional neural networks (CNNs) form an integral part of OpenPose – a cutting-edge deep learning framework that guarantees real-time multi-person 2D pose estimation accuracy in image or video data inputs. Developed collaboratively between Carnegie Mellon University and the OpenCV library, it enables the detection of human body position including head, torso, arms, and legs positioning. Written primarily in C++, interfacing capabilities are also available for both Python and MATLAB programming languages through bindings-enabled support within this open source software offering. By leveraging the OpenCV library, images and videos can be processed with relative ease, providing valuable inputs for the OpenPose model. A deep neural network is utilized in this model to accurately predict human poses. The two main stages involved in the process include: pose estimation and keypoint identification. During pose estimation, the image is analyzed to isolate all persons present, while keypoint identification utilizes a multi-stage CNN trained on image datasets. The OpenPose model utilizes a graphical model to improve the accuracy of keypoint detection during the pose refinement stage. The refinement process adjusts keypoint positions to enhance overall accuracy, ensuring more precise pose estimation. This graphical model takes into account the spatial relationships between keypoints, effectively refining detected poses.

Each stage in the first branch predicts confidence maps S^t, and each stage in the second branch predicts PAFs L^t. After each stage, the predictions from the two branches, along with the image features, are concatenated for the next stage.

Their architecture, as shown in Figure 11.3, allows for simultaneous prediction of both part-to-part association affinity fields and detection of confidence maps. The network is split into two branches, with the bottom branch predicting affinity fields (shown in blue) and the top branch predicting confidence maps (shown in beige). According to Wei et al. [13], each branch uses an iterative prediction architecture that refines predictions over a series of stages, $t1, ..., T$, with intermediate supervision at each stage.

To analyze the image, they use a convolutional network fine-tuned with the first 10 layers of VGG-19 [14], which produces a set of feature maps F. These feature maps are then inputted into the first stage of each branch. At the first stage, the network generates a set of part affinity fields $L1 = 1(F)$ and a set of detection confidence maps $S1 = 1(F)$, where CNN1 and CNN2 are the CNNs for inference at Stage.

To create more accurate predictions in each succeeding stage, they concatenate the original image features F and the predictions from both branches in the previous stage.

$$S^t = \rho^t(F, S^{t-1}, L^{t-1}), \forall t \geq 2, \tag{11.1}$$

$$L^t = \varphi^t(F, S^{t-1}, L^{t-1}), \forall t \geq 2, \tag{11.2}$$

where ρ^t and φ^t are the CNNs for inference at Stage t [12].

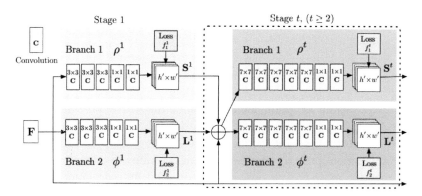

Figure 11.3 Architecture of the two-branch multi-stage CNN [12].

11.3.6 Development of the model

The development of this model required different important steps, which were very essential for this project to succeed.

These steps are:

1. Problem analysis
2. Dataset collection
3. Data preprocessing
4. Model development
5. Model evaluation
6. Further processing of the results and outputs

11.3.6.1 Problem analysis

Previously, all the problems and shortcomings of wrong posture have been discussed and it is also known that the awareness about this problem is not sufficient too. So it was clear that this project had an importance.

Now coming to the problem analysis, it was hard to understanding how this project will be going to work and how we are going to get the output and give the input. For posture detection, it was clear that we need to get the lateral view of the student as we cannot understand the sitting posture clearly without seeing the lateral view of their body while sitting, which will show their back and it will be easier to get the posture with all the keypoints that this model is going to show.

Now to find the sitting posture, we are using coordinates of ears and hips and find angle, finding if the person is in hunchback, reclined, or straight posture; here, as the condition is satisfied by using a specific method, the return value can be 1, 1, or 0, corresponding to hunchback, reclined, and straight postures, respectively.

With help of this, we found the angle and values of a correct sitting posture and used it to iňĄnd the percentage error of the posture of the student in the image used.

11.3.6.2 Dataset collection

OpenPose is one tool for extracting human posture. An open source library called OpenPose Human Body Attitude Recognition Project was created by Carnegie Mellon University (CMU) using convolutional neural networks, supervised learning, and the caffe framework [12].

It is possible to estimate attitudes using human motion, facial expressions, and finger movements.

OpenPose demonstrates excellent robustness, making it suitable for both single and multiple users [16]. This system, which operates without the need for character detectors, employs a bottom-up approach for the real-time estimation of multi-person gestures. By loading the pre-trained OpenPose model, the algorithm can efficiently extract 18 body joints and 17 lines connecting these joints. A partial dataset illustrating these features is presented in Figure 11.3.

For this model, as our focus is mainly on school kids and we have to recognize their posture, we started by going to some schools to collect images of students in their natural sitting position; thus, it will be easier to get a general idea of how their posture is naturally while studying.

In our model, we are using the CNN algorithm to fetch the features that have passed; it will locate the different parts of body like ears, eyes, shoulder, knees, hips, etc., and mark them on the photo using dots.

The distance of dots with the help of coordinates that they are plotted on will be recorded and saved in the all-peaks array. With the help of these coordinates, we will find the distance of different joints and parts of the body, which is critical for detecting the arm position, leg position, and their sitting posture. It is also important for the person to be in a lateral view for this model to work.

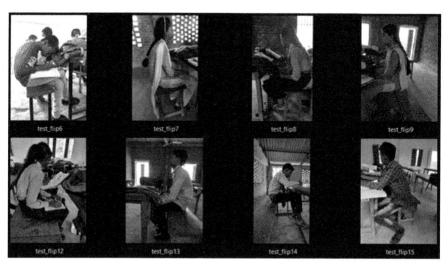

Figure 11.4   Dataset in this model.

11.3.6.3 Data preprocessing

To prepare data for machine learning models, a crucial step is preprocessing. It involves transforming the data into a format that the model can process with ease, and the choice of preprocessing techniques may vary based on the type of data and task. For instance, when working with image data, some common preprocessing techniques include normalization, resizing, cropping, and denoising using methods such as median filtering, Gaussian smoothing, or wavelet transform.

Data augmentation is another important technique that enhances the performance of machine learning models by generating new training examples from the existing data through random transformations. This increases data diversity and improves the model's generalization ability. For image data, common data augmentation techniques include flipping, rotating, scaling, shearing, adding noise, cropping, and adjusting brightness and contrast. Other data types such as text and audio data can also benefit from data augmentation techniques selected based on the data type and task.

Some of the data preprocessing steps implemented in the database collected are:

1. Normalization
2. Resizing
3. Cropping
4. Flipping
5. Denoising

11.3.6.4 Model development

With the previously discussed model of open pose and some other references [16], this model and all the other modules were created. First we need to make the convolutional neural network for predicting human body keypoints on an image. The network consists of two types of blocks: VGG blocks and stage blocks.

The VGG blocks are commonly used in convolutional neural networks for image classification tasks. The purpose of VGG blocks is to extract high-level features from the image.

The stage blocks are used to predict the location of human body keypoints. There are two types of stage blocks: stage1_block and stageT_block. The stage1_block predicts the keypoints in the first stage, while the stageT_block predicts the keypoints in the subsequent stages.

Overall, the network architecture seems to be based on the "convolutional pose machines" (CPMs) model, which is a popular model for predicting human body keypoints.

After that, we will have a configuration file, which has the box size and other information important to the model, such as start range, end range, etc.

After making all the configuration and model files, we will now make the main file that will implement the code. It loads an image, resizes it to various scales, and applies OpenPose to each resized image to detect body keypoints, including the joints, limbs, and their confidence scores. It then processes the detected keypoints to check the position of the spine, angle of the spine, whether the person is kneeling, and whether their hands are folded. It also visualizes the detected keypoints on the input image using different colors for different parts. All the data is then saved in a folder inside a specific directory and the next task of plotting and processing the data is done. This is done by combining all text output data into a single file and then the processing is done, which returns the plot of the angle with which we are finding the type of posture, the bar graph of all the different percentage error respective of image, and a graph showing how many have "reclined," "hunchback," or "straight" posture.

There are several different values that we need to find to calculate the posture and several other required information.

All the operations to find the respective values are as follows.

Finding arm position:

Here we are taking the coordinates and calculating distance between right arm joint and right palm and between left arm joint and left palm; this will help us find if the hands of the student in the image are folding or not (Figure 11.3).

```
if (all_peaks[4][0][0:2]):
    distance = calcDistance(all_peaks[3][0][0:2], all_peaks[4][0][0:2])
    armdist = calcDistance(all_peaks[2][0][0:2], all_peaks[3][0][0:2])
    if (distance < (armdist + 100) and distance > (armdist - 100) ): #
        print("Not Folding Hands",)
    else:
        print("Folding Hands",)
```

Figure 11.5   Checking the state of the arms.

Finding leg position:

```
try:
    if(all_peaks[10][0][0:2] and all_peaks[13][0][0:2]): # if both legs are detected
        rightankle = all_peaks[10][0][0:2]
        leftankle = all_peaks[13][0][0:2]
        hip = all_peaks[11][0][0:2]
        leftangle = calcAngle(hip,leftankle)
        leftdegrees = round(math.degrees(leftangle))
        rightangle = calcAngle(hip,rightankle)
        rightdegrees = round(math.degrees(rightangle))
    if (f == 0):
        leftdegrees = 180 - leftdegrees
        rightdegrees = 180 - rightdegrees
    if (leftdegrees > 60 and rightdegrees > 60): # 60 degrees is trail and error value
        print ("Both Legs are in Kneeling")
    elif (rightdegrees > 60):
        print ("Right leg is kneeling")
    elif (leftdegrees > 60):
        print ("Left leg is kneeling")
    else:
        print ("Not kneeling")
```

Figure 11.6 Checking the state of legs — whether they are kneeling or not.

Just like arms, we are using the angle of the legs by using the coordinates of hip and ankles; the angle is calculated, and using the formula, we are able to find the position of legs (Figure 11.4).

Finding the sitting posture:

```
try:
    f = 0
    if (all_peaks[16]):
        a = all_peaks[16][0][0:2] #Right Ear
        f = 1
    else:
        a = all_peaks[17][0][0:2] #Left Ear
    b = all_peaks[11][0][0:2] # Hip
    angle = calcAngle(a,b)
    degrees: int = round(math.degrees(angle))
    if (f):
        degrees = 180 - degrees
    if (degrees<70):
        return 1
    elif (degrees > 110):
        return -1
    else:
        return 0
except Exception as e:
    print("person not in lateral view and unable to detect ears or hip")
```

Figure 11.7 Checking the posture.

Now to find the sitting posture, we are using coordinates of ears and hips and find angle, finding if the person is in the hunchback, reclined, or straight posture; here, as the condition is satisïňĄed by using a specific method, the return value can be1,1, or 0, which is corresponding to hunchback, reclined, and straight,respectively.

With the help of this, we found the angle and values of a correct sitting posture and used it to find the percentage error of the posture of the student in the image used (Figure 11.5).

11.3.6.5 Model evaluation

Upon evaluation of this model, it was found that there are several ways in which this model can be optimized; these methods are:

1. Quantization: It is the process of converting 32-bit floating point weights and activations to lower bit precision formats like ITN8 or ITN4, which requires less memory and computational power [17].
2. Pruning: It is the process of removing unimportant connections or weights in a neural network. By removing redundant parameters, we can make the model smaller and faster [18].
3. Architecture optimization: Another way to improve the efficiency of this model is to optimize its architecture. This can be done by reducing the number of layers or neurons, using skip connections, or using other techniques like depth-wise separable convolutions, which can significantly reduce the number of parameters and computations required by the model.
4. Hardware acceleration: Hardware acceleration techniques like GPU, TPU, or ASIC can be used to speed up the computations required by the model. GPUs, for example, are well-suited for neural network computations and can speed up the training and inference time of the model [19].
5. Efficient data processing: Another way to improve the efficiency of the model is to optimize the data processing pipeline. This can be done by using data augmentation techniques to generate more training data, using batch normalization to speed up the convergence of the model during training or using distributed training techniques to train the model on multiple GPUs or machines.

All these tasks are reserved for future work as this is a very early version of this model, and further development and optimization are to be expected.

11.3.6.6 Further processing of the results and output

The results of this model and the observations will be discussed later in this model, but first let us understand what was done to process the data which is outputted from the python model.

These are several steps taken in order to derive some inference from the output and results:

1. Saving the output images and terminal outputs in a file inside the results directory.
2. Fetching all the data from all the text files to combine and create one combined file.
3. Using the numerical values and outputs to make the plots and graphs.

Process map

Your **name**:

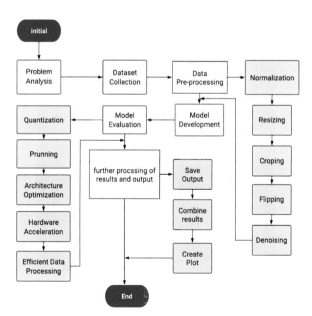

Figure 11.8   Development lifecycle of the model from the start to the end.

4. Further understanding of the graph to understand how our model can help.

With that, all the steps in the development of this model are complete; let us see what the results of this model were and understand more about the posture of kids in schools.

11.4 Results

The model worked as intended and it used the input image and returned the output image and dots corresponding to features of the body. It also returned state body parts and the posture with the percentage error.

Successful test cases:

Input image:

Figure 11.9   Input image for the model.

In this image, it is clear that the student has a straight posture and the hands are not folded too. Therefore, the expected result is to be shown as straight and it should also show that the hands are not folding [20].

Output image:

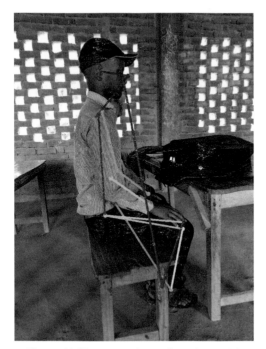

Figure 11.10 Output image from the model.

Terminal output:

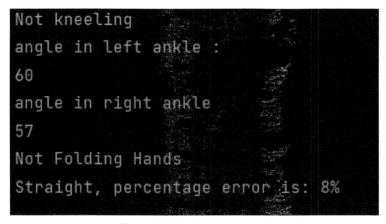

Figure 11.11 Terminal output.

Saved text output:

```
1
Straight
percentage error is: 8%
83
0
```

Figure 11.12   Output saved in the text file for further processing.

In this output, in the first line, "1" represents the index number of the image and "straight" is the type of posture that the individual is sitting in; it shows the percentage error in the next line followed by the angle between the ear point and the hip point. The value 0 shows that the posture is straight; if it was 1, it was hunchback, and if it was −1, it was reclined.

Since we can see that the individual is sitting in the same posture as the model says, the result is thus true. Now that we have seen a successful test case, let us see some test cases in which the result is not expected [21].

Failed test case 1:

Input image:

Figure 11.13   Failed input image for the model.

Output:

Terminal output:

```
Not Kneeling
angle :
53
Folding Hands
distance between right arm-joint and right palm:
Unable to detect arm joints
distance between right arm-joint and right palm:
```

Figure 11.14   Output in the terminal.

Since there is no image that can be made with the keypoints, the output will not show and there will be no output. Thus, there is no posture detection in this image.

Failed test case 2:

Input image:

Figure 11.15   Input image for the model.

Output image:

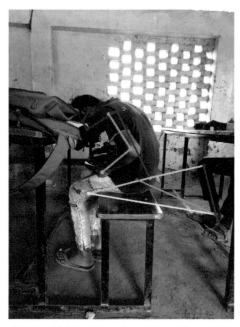

Figure 11.16   Output image from the model.

Terminal output:

```
Both Legs are in Kneeling
angle in left ankle :
154
angle in right ankle
157
Not Folding Hands
Hunchback, percentage error is: 39%
```

Figure 11.17   Wrong terminal output.

Effective data preprocessing is critical for ensuring accurate data processing and generating expected results. This is demonstrated by the image in question, where the model recorded the legs of another individual instead of the intended subject due to inadequate preprocessing [22]. Thus, attention to detail and careful consideration of preprocessing steps are essential for reliable data analysis.

All the photos are sequentially inputted in to the model, and all their outputs are saved in the ïñĄles. The outputs of some of the successful cases are shown in Table 11.3

Table 11.3 Input and output from the model showing successful test cases.

Input image	Terminal output	Output image
	1 Straight Percentage error is: 8% 83 0	
	2 Straight Percentage error is: 10% 99 0	
	3 Straight Percentage error is: 1% 91 0	
	4 Straight Percentage error is: 4% 94 0	
	5 Hunchback Percentage error is: 27% 66 1	

11.4.1 Output processing

From all the outputs after processing, the next step is to further process the output data to get a better understanding and observe the results in a much better and clearer manner [23].

These are all the different graphs that were made using the data which the model outputted.

11.4.1.1 Percentage error graph

The graph presents a visual representation of the significant number of errors observed in the sitting postures of students, particularly in junior classes. This highlights the pressing need to correct these errors to prevent any potential problems that may arise due to incorrect posture.

The high number of errors in sitting posture also indicates a clear lack of awareness among students regarding proper sitting habits and the importance of maintaining good posture. This lack of knowledge and awareness is a significant issue that requires immediate attention to prevent any long-term negative impacts on their health and well-being.

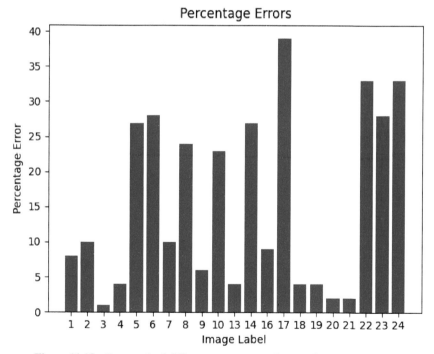

Figure 11.18 Bar graph of different percentages of error of poses of students.

It is imperative to educate students on proper sitting posture and provide them with the necessary tools and resources to develop healthy habits. Teachers play a critical role in promoting proper sitting habits by emphasizing the importance of maintaining a straight back, keeping feet flat on the ground and relaxing the shoulders [24].

Furthermore, schools should invest in ergonomic furniture that promotes good posture and supports the natural curvature of the spine. This will enable students to maintain good posture and reduce the risk of developing back pain or other related issues.

In conclusion, the graph underscores the need for concerted efforts to correct the significant number of errors in sitting posture among students. By promoting awareness and education on proper sitting habits, along with the provision of ergonomic furniture, we can prevent potential health issues and promote better academic performance.

11.4.1.2 Graph for angles

The graph provides a visual representation of the variability in the angles at which children are seated in a classroom. The data highlights the lack of consistency among students with respect to their sitting postures. It is evident from the graph that the children are sitting in a manner that suits their individual preferences, without any understanding of the potential impact

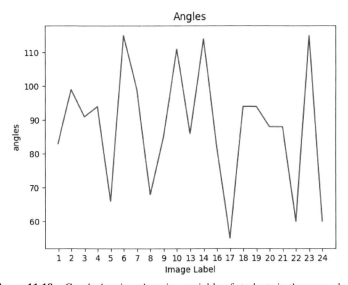

Figure 11.19 Graph showing changing variable of students in the same class.

of their posture on their health and well-being. Therefore, it is essential to educate children about the significance of maintaining a proper posture while sitting in a classroom. Teachers should encourage students to sit with their backs straight, their feet flat on the ground, and their shoulders relaxed. Additionally, classroom furniture should be ergonomically designed to promote good posture and support the spine's natural curvature.

In conclusion, the graph indicates that there is a need for increased awareness among children regarding the importance of good posture while sitting. By promoting good posture habits, we can help prevent health issues and improve the overall academic performance of students.

11.4.1.3 Graph for types of postures

The graph represents the types of poses exhibited by students in a class, with a focus on posture and angle measurements. The graph indicates that while most students have straight posture, they also have a high degree of error in their angles. This suggests that there is a need for improved ergonomics in the classroom, but also that overly strict education may not be necessary.

It is important to note that maintaining good posture is essential for overall health and well-being. Poor posture can cause musculoskeletal disorders, including back pain and neck strain, and can contribute to chronic health problems. Therefore, it is crucial for students to develop good posture habits from an early age.

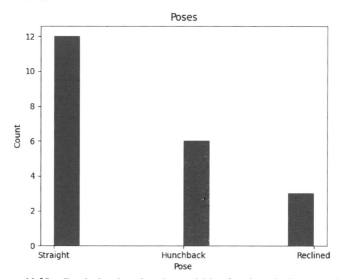

Figure 11.20   Graph showing changing variable of students in the same class.

However, it is also important to recognize that excessive emphasis on strict posture education may not be the most effective approach. Research has shown that overly strict posture instructions can be counterproductive, causing discomfort and fatigue and ultimately leading to poor posture habits. Therefore, a more balanced approach may be needed that emphasizes the importance of good posture while also recognizing the natural variations in individual postures.

Moreover, the role of school furniture in promoting good posture should also be considered. Appropriate school furniture, such as chairs and desks with adjustable heights and lumbar support, can help guide students to maintain good posture and reduce the likelihood of developing poor posture habits.

In conclusion, the graph suggests that there is room for improvement in the ergonomics of the classroom, but that a balanced approach that emphasizes good posture habits and appropriate school furniture may be more effective than overly strict posture education.

11.5 Conclusion

Based on the previous discussion, it is clear that promoting good posture among students is crucial for their health and well-being. The graph provided insights into the posture of students in a particular class, indicating that while most students exhibit straight posture, they also have high error in their angles. This highlights the need for workshops and demonstrations to teach students and teachers about better ways of sitting that promote better health.

Live demonstrations and illustrations are effective tools to help students understand the factors responsible for maintaining good posture. These workshops should also include information about the negative impacts of poor posture on health and the importance of adopting healthy habits early in life. Additionally, involving parents in these workshops can help create a supportive environment for students to practice good posture habits at home.

Furthermore, school furniture plays a critical role in promoting good posture. A seat that provides support to the back and gives students enough space to sit can make a significant difference. However, it was found that in rural areas, school furniture does not adequately support good posture, leading to a higher number of students with bad sitting posture. This highlights the need to address the disparities in school infrastructure between rural and urban areas to ensure that all students have access to appropriate school furniture.

In conclusion, promoting good posture among students is essential for their overall health and well-being. Workshops and demonstrations can effectively teach students and teachers about better ways of sitting, while appropriate school furniture can support good posture. By addressing these factors, we can help students develop healthy habits that will benefit them throughout their lives.

References

[1] Choudhary, M. S., et al. "the impact of ergonomics on children studying online during COVID-19 lockdown." J. Adv. Sports Phys. Educ (2020).

[2] Kulikajevas, A., Maskeliunas, R., & Damaševičius, R. (2021). Detection of sitting posture using hierarchical image composition and deep learning. PeerJ computer science, 7, e442.

[3] Liu, W., Guo, Y., Yang, J., Hu, Y., & Wei, D. (2019, February). Sitting posture recognition based on human body pressure and CNN. In AIP Conference Proceedings (Vol. 2073, No. 1, p. 020093). AIP Publishing LLC.

[4] Harrison, Donald D., et al. "Sitting biomechanics part I: review of the literature." Journal of manipulative and physiological therapeutics 22.9 (1999): 594-609.

[5] https://www.medicalnewstoday.com/articles/321863

[6] Matuska, Slavomir, Martin Paralic, and Robert Hudec. "A smart system for sitting posture detection based on force sensors and mobile application." Mobile Information Systems 2020 (2020).

[7] Kim, Y. M., Son, Y., Kim, W., Jin, B., & Yun, M. H. (2018). Classification of children's sitting postures using ML algorithms. Applied Sciences, 8(8), 1280.

[8] Carleo, Giuseppe, et al. "ML and the physical sciences." Reviews of Modern Physics 91.4 (2019): 045002.

[9] Yamashita, Rikiya, et al. "CNNs: an overview and application in radiology." Insights into imaging 9.4 (2018): 611-629.

[10] Manaswi, Navin Kumar. "Understanding and working with Keras." Deep Learning with Applications Using Python. Apress, Berkeley, CA, 2018. 31-43.

[11] Manaswi, Navin Kumar. "Understanding and working with Keras." Deep Learning with Applications Using Python. Apress, Berkeley, CA, 2018. 31-43.

[12] Z. Cao, T. Simon, S. -E. Wei and Y. Sheikh, "Realtime Multi-person 2D Pose Estimation Using Part Affinity Fields," 2017 IEEE Conference on Computer Vision and Pattern Recognition (CVPR), Honolulu, HI, USA, 2017, pp. 1302-1310, doi: 10.1109/CVPR.2017.143.

[13] S.-E. Wei, V. Ramakrishna, T. Kanade, and Y. Sheikh. Convolutional pose machines. In CVPR, 2016. 1, 2, 3, 6

[14] K. Simonyan and A. Zisserman. Very deep convolutional networks for large-scale image recognition. In ICLR, 2015.

[15] Kehan Chen 2019 IOP Conf. Ser.: Mater. Sci. Eng. 677 032057

[16] Qiao S, Wang Y, Jian L. Real-time human gesture grading based on OpenPose [C]// 2017 10th International Congress on Imag

[17] Joseph, Vinu, et al. "A programmable approach to model compression." arXiv preprint (2019).

[18] He, Yang, et al. "Soft filter pruning for accelerating deep convolutional neural networks." arXiv preprint arXiv:1808.06866 (2018).

[19] Shivam and Bareja, Pawan and Bhatia, Madhulika, Appearance of Machine and Deep Learning in Image Processing: A Portrayal (2018). International Journal of Computational Intelligence & IoT, Vol. 2, No. 4, 2018, Available at SSRN: https://ssrn.com/abstract=3361144.

[20] M. Pandey, M. Bhatia and A. Bansal, "An anatomization of noise removal techniques on medical images," 2016 International Conference on Innovation and Challenges in Cyber Security (ICICCS-INBUSH), Greater Noida, India, 2016, pp. 224-229, doi: 10.1109/ICI-CCS.2016.7542308.

[21] Aha Garg, M. Bhatia, & M. Hooda. (2021). Proposed Expert System for Controlling Obesity and Overweight Issues among Urban and Semi-Urban School going Children: An Epidemiological Study. Journal of Clinical & Diagnostic Research.

[22] Bansal A, Bhatia M, Yadav D (2016) Survey and comparative study on statistical tools for medical images. Adv Sci Lett 21(1):74–77.

[23] Monika, & Bhatia, M. (2022). Extraction of posture silhouettes using human posture feature points and spatial masks for activity recognition in public place. Journal of Engineering Research, 10(3A). https://doi.org/10.36909/jer.10803.

[24] Mehta, M., & Bhadauria, M. (2021). Performance Evaluation of Neural Network for Human Classification Using Blob Dataset. Recent Advances in Computer Science and Communications, 14(5), 1592-1602. Bentham Science Publishers.

12

Fatty Liver Disease Prediction: Using Machine Learning Algorithms

Devyanshi Bansal[1], Supriya Raheja[1], and Manoj Kumar[2]

[1]Amity University, India
[2]University of Wollongong, UAE
E-mail: devyanshi.bansal@s.amity.edu; supriya.raheja@gmail.com;
wss.manojkumar@gmail.com

Abstract

It has been seen that a lot of individuals nowadays are struggling with a variety of health problems. Even an infant, upon entering this world, might be subjected to the ravages of several illnesses. The prevalence of liver disease is rising faster than that of any other illness. The liver is the biggest organ located inside the human body. It assists in the digestion of meals, the storage of energy, and the elimination of toxins from the body. A condition known as fatty liver disease (FLD) occurs when there is an accumulation of fat in the liver. Every technological advancement that gives more accurate, timely, and useful analysis to provide an appropriate treatment plan in a timely manner is of immense value. At this very moment, ML is rapidly becoming the dominant force in the globe. The usage of the enormous potential offered by ML has the potential to be of help to the medical industry in several different ways. Technology based on ML enables medical practitioners to more accurately produce medication solutions that are suited to the features of specific patients. With this aim, this chapter presents several different ML algorithms, namely logistic regression, decision tree classifier, random forest classifier, KNN classifier, CatBoost classifier, and gradient boosting classifier, to perform the prediction of fatty liver diseases. This study analyzed these ML models for their degree of accuracy by using the dataset of Indian patients. ML classifiers might assist medical organizations identify and classify FLD proactively, which is important in impoverished economies.

Keywords: Machine learning, accuracy, logistic regression, boosting techniques, KNN classifier, random forest classifier, decision tree classifier, fatty liver disease.

12.1 Introduction

Fatty liver disease, which is also called FLD, is a common health problem that is linked to a high rate of both illness and death. In the long run, FLD almost always leads to different types of cancer. In the last 10 years, the biopsy has been used to sort patients into groups and has been seen as a diagnostic reference standard for figuring out if the liver has fatty infiltration. But this procedure is not only very invasive and expensive, but it could also lead to unwanted side effects and mistakes in sampling if it is used. FLD is a common and complex disorder that is characterized by an accumulation of fat within the liver.

Due to the exponential rise in the digitalization of medical information and the computer power available, ML is transforming the administration of healthcare services. A wide variety of applications and departments inside a hospital make use of predictive analytics in order to speed up workflow and enhance medical decision-making. As computer vision continues to be implemented in radiology, diagnostic procedures such as imaging are undergoing a fundamental transformation brought about by machine learning [1].

Because of the proliferation of ML in the healthcare industry, this methodology is increasingly being used to predict various illnesses. Machine learning is becoming rapidly popular for medical applications, and it has recently been applied to FLD in an effort to improve diagnosis and clinical management of this condition. Machine learning methods have been used to develop prediction models based on patient data in order to identify risk factors associated with disease progression and to categorize patients into treatment subgroups. Even though the pathogenesis of FLD is only partially understood, most people with it do not find out they have it until they have a major problem, or it comes up in tests they are getting for something else [2].

"ML," which stands for "machine learning," is a branch of artificial intelligence that uses computer algorithms to find patterns in large amounts of data [3]. These patterns may then be used to aid in making predictions about a variety of outcomes based on the data. ML approaches have only recently become a good choice for making predictions and decisions in a wide range of fields. As a result of the availability of clinical data, machine learning has played an important role in the process of making medical decisions [4]. Machine learning could be used to make a model that would help doctors figure out if someone is sick and make a good clinical decision in real time. It would also make it possible to make the best use of hospital resources by putting patients into groups quickly based on how many risk factors they have.

Many studies have been done on this subject, and the results of statistical analysis have led to the writing down of several prophecies that have come true. Several research studies have shown that some algorithms work better than others [5]. Because of this, three algorithms are used to make a model that will tell us which ML algorithm is the best.

People in the 21st century think that drinking is common and will not affect them much, but studies show that doing anything in excess is harmful, and the person with a fatty liver is starting to experience problems more frequently. One of the main causes of appetite loss, abdominal and leg edema, (inflammation brought on by the accumulation of excess fluid in the body's tissues), and weakness is this disorder [6]. Other symptoms include swelling in the legs and a weak sensation. One of the many areas of our daily lives where machine-learning-based techniques are starting to be used is in the field of medicine, such as in the process of recognizing medical illnesses. These techniques are used in this way because they have become more useful in recent years. When we have information about a patient's health and way of life, these algorithms have done a better job of predicting a stroke than experienced doctors and specialists.

The goal of this study is to use different machine learning techniques to accurately predict whether or not a patient has fatty liver disease when multiple different diseases are present. The study makes use of boosting techniques to improve the accuracy of algorithms. The study presents a comparison of the performance of these ML algorithms.

The rest of the chapter is organized as follows. Section 12.2 discusses the literature review. Section 12.3 presents the methodology adopted for the implementation of the current study. In Section 12.4, we talk in detail about the results. In Section 12.5, we come to a conclusion and discuss what we plan to do next.

12.2 Machine Learning Algorithms

a) Logistic regression

Logistic regression is a machine learning algorithm used to model the relationship between a dependent variable and one or more explanatory variables. It is used to predict a categorical outcome, such as whether a particular individual has a disease or not. The objective of logistic regression is to develop a model that assigns a probability to a particular individual having a given outcome. The algorithm is part of the supervised learning method, and it is one of the most common and widely used machine learning algorithms. The primary use of logistic regression is in categorization. When using a classification method based on logistic regression, a random set of inputs is given first. Then, a function sorts the input data into categories, which is the output of the method [7]. For example, the function output of 0 or 1 in the two classifications, respectively, shows the two classes. This makes the processing easier. As a result, it gives the probabilistic values, which may be somewhere between 0 and 1, precedence over the exact number, which could be either 0 or 1. It is an important machine learning strategy because it can use both continuous and discrete datasets to make probability values and group new

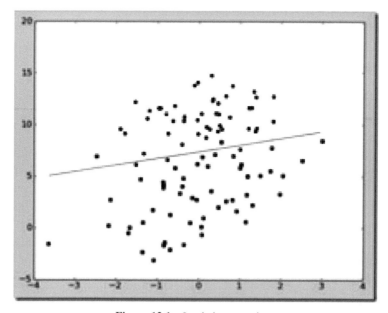

Figure 12.1   Logistic regression.

data. Because of this, it is an algorithm that has a great deal of flexibility [8]. This method can classify observations by using different kinds of data, and it is easy to figure out which things are most important when it comes to classifying observations well as shown in Figure 12.1

b) Decision tree classifier

A supervised machine learning model that may be used for classification as well as regression work is referred to as a decision tree classifier. It does this by learning basic decision rules that may be inferred from the data attributes that are presented, and then using those rules to make predictions about the value of a target variable, often known as a class label. An algorithmic technique is used to create decision trees. This approach discovers the optimal split points at which to divide data and then produces a prediction using a decision rule that takes the shape of a tree-like structure. In other words, decision trees are built using an algorithm. To train the algorithm, a decision tree classifier has to be fed instances of data (for example, a collection of records representing input data). After that, it applies a decision rule to determine which split points are optimal and constructs the decision tree, which may then be used to create predictions based on fresh data. Each decision rule relies on a feature (for example, a specific property within a data collection, such as height or weight) and a related threshold to make its determination [9].

The process of decision tree classification is to build a model of class characteristics from a dataset so that a new record can be given a class label in the most accurate way possible. A decision tree classifier is a supervised classification model that was made to group similar sets of data based on variables that can be predicted by entropy. It is a way to describe how much information an event produces. When something happens less frequently or has a lower entropy, the amount of information that can be gleaned from it increases. When something happens less often or has a lower entropy, it is easier to get more information about them [10]. The decision tree classifier is different because it uses a sequence of one or more decision functions to put an unidentified sample into a category. This is the defining feature of the decision tree classifier. A decision tree, in its most basic form, is made up of many nodes: one "root" node, several "interior" nodes, and several "terminal" nodes. The root node and the inner nodes, which are called "nonterminal nodes" as a group, are linked to make decisions. The terminal nodes, on the other hand, reflect final classifications [11].

c) **Random forest classifier**

The random forest classifier is an example of a supervised learning method that may be used for issues involving classification and regression. It does this by first building several decision trees, each of which makes use of a distinct subset of the whole data, and then averaging the outcomes of these trees. When compared to a single decision tree, this model is more reliable and less likely to suffer from the problem of overfitting. The scalability of the random forest classifier, a lower variance, and the capacity to deal with complicated nonlinear data are the primary benefits of using this method. Random forests are also simple to implement since they demand little in the way of parameter tweaking and have a small number of hyperparameters that need adjusting. In addition to this, they can be trained very quickly and can process very big datasets. In addition to this, they have a reasonable resistance to noise and can deal with missing data [12].

As a result of these factors, the random forest classifier has rapidly gained popularity in the machine learning environment of today. Random forests provide significant benefits over traditional decision trees, including higher generalization, less overfitting, enhanced accuracy, and more resilience to erroneous classifications. In addition, random forests are easier to implement than decision trees. In addition to this, they can generate predictions that are more accurate than the majority of other categorization models. Because trees may be constructed in parallel, there is also a reduction in the amount of memory used. In conclusion, most implementations of random forests make advantage of bootstrap sampling on the data that is readily accessible, which further improves accuracy [13].

Authors say that algorithms for learning in groups, like random forest, bagging, and boosting, are becoming more popular [14]. This is due to the fact that all the learning techniques are more accurate and resistant to noise than single classifiers are. The random forest classifier is made up of a collection of tree classifiers. In the random forest classifier, each classifier is made by using a random vector that is chosen separately from the input vector [15]. Also, when classifying an input vector, each tree in the random forest gives one vote to the class that has the most votes [16].

In simple terms, it is a collection of decision trees (DT) that have been chosen at random from a subset of the training set. This subset is known as the training set. The data from the training set was used to build these DTs. After that, it adds up the results of the polls that were done on each of the different decision trees to come up with the final forecast. Not only is it possible to get a better degree of accuracy when there are a larger number of trees in a forest, but it also gives a way to avoid the issue of overfitting when compared to situations in which there are fewer trees.

d) KNN classifier

K-nearest neighbor, or KNN, is a well-known technique for machine learning that is used for the solution of classification and regression issues. KNN determines an answer by computing the distance between a new data point that is input and every other point that is included in the training dataset. The model will then choose the *K* data points that are the closest together and utilize those points to create its predictions. KNN is useful for solving a wide variety of problems, including object identification, text classification, and picture classification. It can be used for both supervised and unsupervised learning, and it is often used for both purposes. KNN is superior to many other machine learning algorithms in a number of important respects. Because KNN does not make any assumptions about the data, it is possible to use it to generate predictions on any kind of data, in contrast to certain other models.

The flexibility with which the model may be used to a wide variety of contexts and forms of data helps to make it an extremely adaptable choice. In comparison to other models, KNN takes a relatively little amount of training data, and it performs very well even when the input is noisy or missing. KNN is not only incredibly efficient computationally but also does not call for a significant amount of time to be trained. In addition to this, it is a sort of model known as a non-parametric model, which indicates that the user is not required to establish any predetermined parameters in order to make it work. Because of this, the model is simple enough that anybody can utilize it. KNN is a potent tool that may be used for any kind of prediction endeavor due to its ability to perform extremely well on both supervised and unsupervised learning challenges.

The *K*-nearest-neighbor algorithm is a basic yet efficient non-parametric classification approach. It is a supervised classification machine learning algorithm [17]. A data record's *K* closest neighbors comprise its neighborhood for classification. Without distance-based weighting, majority voting among neighborhood data entries classifies to use KNN; we need to find a good value for *K*, which has a big effect on how well classification works. KNN biases an easy technique to select the *K* value is to run the algorithm multiple times with various *K* values and choose the one that performs best. The KNN method calculates the distance between the record that must be categorized and each of the records that make up the training dataset. After that, it examines the *K* data records in the training set that are the closest together.

The fact that the neighbors would focus on providing an interpretation for the categorization result is one of the benefits of making use of KNN. The downside is that it is not clear how to make metrics that show how important input subcomponents are. This is a problem because it is not clear how to come up with a criterion that can be used [18].

e) CatBoost classifier

A sophisticated machine learning technique that is specifically designed to deal with categorical data is called the CatBoost classifier. This algorithm was created by Yandex and is available as open-source software. It excels at solving classification problems that use categorical features. CatBoost is capable of accurately processing hundreds of thousands of data points simultaneously. CatBoost can automatically determine which elements are the most significant and then employ a number of methods to include that information into the model without sacrificing its ability to forecast. CatBoost also deals with missing values in an elegant manner, which is something that other machine learning algorithms sometimes struggle with. It is also capable of making accurate predictions for values that are absent for category categories, outperforming other algorithms in this regard.

In addition, CatBoost may be used in conjunction with GPU acceleration to expedite the training process, resulting in a model that is both more iterative and accurate. This method also provides a wide range of parameters, each of which has the potential to significantly improve the accuracy of predictions made using a variety of datasets. The CatBoost classifier is a good example of another system that uses machine learning to accurately predict category features.

CatBoost is a type of gradient boosting that is based on binary decision trees. The CatBoost algorithm, which is sometimes called the categorical boosting method, is mostly used to manage the categorical characteristics in a dataset. It also has a preprocessing step that is needed to change the characteristics of a category into numerical variables so that it does not appear in any other algorithm [19].

f) Gradient descent classifier

An optimization procedure known as the gradient descent classifier is used to locate the parameter configuration that will result in the lowest possible value for a certain performance function. This classifier achieves its results by continually executing a series of tiny tweaks to the values of the parameters to bring down the level of total error produced by the model. This approach makes use of a gradient, which is a mathematical notion referring to a multivariable derivative, to get an understanding of the nature of the mistakes that comprise the model as well as how these errors might be minimized [20]. The gradient descent classifier is an iterative method, which means that the parameter set is adjusted over a series of epochs; in most cases, the purpose of an epoch is to bring the total error of the model down to a lower value.

The gradient descent classifier makes use of partial derivatives to get an understanding of the nature of the mistakes and the ways in which the parameter set may be altered in order to bring this error down. This is done to make sure that the goal is reached. The parameters of the gradient descent classifier are modified to optimize their performance depending on the gradient of the loss function. The classifier learns in which direction it needs to go to get a lower total error by examining the gradient of the loss function. This procedure is repeated over the course of several epochs, with the goal of progressively reducing the overall error with each iteration. At each stage, the parameters are modified depending on the gradient of the loss function, and the model is upgraded as the errors are brought down to their lowest possible level [21].

Gradient descent is one of the most well-known ways to optimize, and it is also the most common way to improve the performance of neural networks. Different machine learning algorithms use an optimization method called "gradient descent" to get the best performance while spending less money on training data [22]. The gradient descent method is used to change the parameters of the models that are learning. When we compare the two unique optimization techniques side by side, we see that boosting a gradient has the highest accuracy.

12.3 Methodology

Our procedure consists of seven different phases. As shown in Figure 12.2.

1) The gathering of data: The data came from Kaggle and were submitted under the fatty liver patient dataset. Patients who were less than 30 years old and whose examination procedures were not finished were not included in our research.

2) Methods of machine learning: The purpose of this research was to use classification machine learning algorithms to identify prognostic indicators that may be used to predict fatty liver disease.

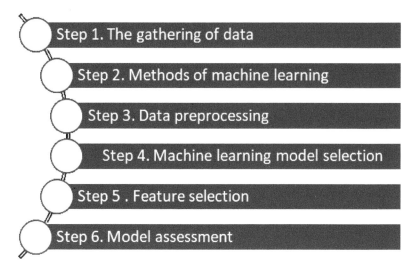

Figure 12.2   Methodology.

3) The preparation of the data consisted of erasing any variables that were missing more than half of their values. In addition, data imputation and normalization are requirements in order to get a dataset of good quality.
4) The selection of a model for machine learning includes the use of six different classification algorithms, including RF, decision tree, Cat-Boost, KNN, gradient boosting, and LR. We conducted training and assessments on the training datasets.
5) The selection of features data with an extraordinarily high dimensionality has posed significant hurdles to the various learning approaches that are now in use [8]. It may have a tendency to overfit, which would cause a decline in the model's efficiency because of the enormous number of features. The characteristic selection process for a classification algorithm involves arriving at a mildly sized subcategory that meets the following requirements: (1) there should be an improvement in the classification results; (2) the qualities for the selected features should be as similar as potential to the allocation of the classes in the beginning.
6) Evaluation of the model: A confusion matrix was used in order to establish the nature of the connection that exists between the observed values and the predictions [9]. The architecture of the confusion matrix is shown in Table 12.1.

Table 12.1 Confusion matrix.

	Positive	Negative
Predicted true (+)	TP	TN
Predicted false (−)	FP	FN

Following quality parameters were used to evaluate the results:

i. Accuracy = TP + TN/TP + FP + TN + FN
ii. Sensitive = TP/TP + FN
iii. Specificity = TN/TN + FP

12.4 Result

The volume of data relating to healthcare is growing at an exponential rate, and advances in machine learning make it possible to evaluate enormous volumes of data in a short period of time. As a result, this presents a chance for applying machine learning strategies to the treatment of specific patients in clinical settings. The most essential information for a clinician to have in order to arrive at an appropriate treatment plan may potentially be gleaned from many machine learning estimation techniques.

Our approach has the ability to diagnose FLD in its initial stages, which will assist to create medication patterns that are both precise and suitable. It is of the utmost importance for doctors to be knowledgeable about the most significant characteristics for the greatest possible result of therapy. It is possible that a patient's baseline parameters are the most accurate predictors of FLD when it comes to an analysis of a specific patient's perception. As a result, we took great effort to implement a characteristic evaluation approach and made use of accuracy in order to thoroughly test and evaluate relevant variables. In fatty liver disease, machine learning algorithms have a major influence on therapy patterns. Accurate warning with the use of this model could provide advantages like reduced need for treatments and lower overall medical costs. In this work, the prediction of fatty liver disease was made using machine learning approaches, and the results revealed that the logistic regression model performed much better than other classification strategies. This result has the possibility of assisting doctors in making choices about the evaluation and therapy of fatty liver disease that are more accurate and useful to their patients.

A pretty great accuracy in the model was accomplished, better precision relative to most of the recent research papers on prediction of fatty liver disease. After organizing the data, a confusion matrix was created for every one of the distinct algorithms. A method for analyzing and summarizing the accuracy of the classification system is known as a confusion matrix. The calculation of a confusion matrix may provide you with a clearer picture of the aspects of classification algorithms that are functioning correctly.

Count data are used to compile a summary of both the number of accurate and wrong predictions, which is then broken down by each class. The confusion matrix is unsolvable without this piece of information. It illustrates the many ways inside which the classification model might get its predictions wrong when it is used to create forecasts. It provides you with an understanding not just of the faults that your classifier is making but also, and perhaps more crucially, the categories under which those errors fall.

Accuracy in a model is measured by dividing the number of categories that a model properly predicts by the total number of classifications that are predicted by the model. It is a technique for determining how well a model has performed. There are many other metrics that may be used for

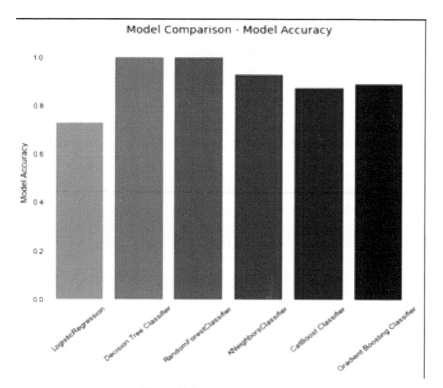

Figure 12.3   Model comparison.

assessment, such as the confusion matrix, the cross-validation, the AUC-ROC curve, etc.

When dealing with various types of issues, several metrics of assessment are used, but in this paper confusion matrix is used, and after trying out many various models on this assessment, it was found that the decision tree classifier and the random forest classifier approach were the most successful models, producing the highest possible degree of accuracy as shown in Figure 12.3.

12.5 Conclusion and Future Scope

In this work, we constructed and analyzed six ML algorithms in order to properly predict fatty liver disease. However, in comparison to other models, the gradient boosting classifier model demonstrated much better performance. In a clinical environment, the use of a gradient boosting model might assist medical professionals in stratifying individuals with fatty liver disease for the purposes of primary prevention, monitoring, early treatment, and care. In the field of study on liver illness, ML has been used for many different kinds of data, including clinical, demographic, genetic, radiographic, and pathological data. We believe that the use of ML techniques to the generation of predictive algorithms has the potential to revolutionize healthcare practice.

As a conclusion to our work, we can simply declare that ML plays a very significant part in the medical diagnostic sector, and although it does come with some obstacles, if we focus on the foundations and quality of the data that is being supplied to us, as well as eliminate the hardware restrictions that sometimes data scientists experience, then we can easily state that machine learning, together with different data analysis processes, can alter the face of medicine as we know it today. In recent years, ML has already demonstrated that it is a useful tool that simplifies the work of specialists in a variety of fields. We believe that, with the appropriate imagination and application of concepts, it has the potential to do the same for medicine as well, thereby assisting individuals in leading lives that are both better and healthier. When we compare the varying levels of accuracy that we have obtained from different ML algorithms, we are easily able to determine which ones are the most accurate and which ones may require additional application of accuracy-boosting algorithms or other optimization strategies in order to produce more desirable outcomes. It has also come to our attention that various kinds of datasets may need varied kinds of preprocessing and ML techniques. These algorithms have been tailored to the specific sort of dataset in question and may assist us in achieving better outcomes in our medical diagnosis. Because of the imbalance in the dataset that we have been working with, our accuracy has been significantly reduced. This is due to the fact that as a result of this, we are obtaining a significantly higher value of type 1 and type 2 errors. When we discuss the potential future scope of this particular work, we can absolutely work on the imbalance of the dataset that we have been working with. There are a variety of approaches that may be taken to address imbalances of this kind.

Acknowledgement

We would like to thank Prof. Manoj for his patient guidance for this research work.

References

[1] D. Anderson, M. V. Bjarnadottir, and Z. Nenova, "Machine Learning in Healthcare: Operational and Financial Impact," in Innovative Technology at the Interface of Finance and Operations: Volume I, V. Babich, J. R. Birge, and G. Hilary, Eds. Cham: Springer International Publishing, 2022, pp. 153–174. doi: 10.1007/978-3-030-75729-8_5.

[2] S. Perveen, M. Shahbaz, K. Keshavjee, and A. Guergachi, "A Systematic Machine Learning Based Approach for the Diagnosis of Non-Alcoholic Fatty Liver Disease Risk and Progression," Sci. Rep., vol. 8, no. 1, p. 2112, Feb. 2018, doi: 10.1038/s41598-018-20166-x.

[3] S. Raheja and S. Kasturia, "Analysis of Machine Learning Techniques for Spam Detection," in Applications of Machine Learning in Big-Data Analytics and Cloud Computing, River Publishers, 2022, pp. 43–62.

[4] C.-C. Wu et al., "Prediction of fatty liver disease using machine learning algorithms," Comput. Methods Programs Biomed., vol. 170, pp. 23–29, Mar. 2019, doi: 10.1016/j.cmpb.2018.12.032.

[5] X. Pei, Q. Deng, Z. Liu, X. Yan, and W. Sun, "Machine Learning Algorithms for Predicting Fatty Liver Disease," Ann. Nutr. Metab., vol. 77, no. 1, pp. 38–45, 2021, doi: 10.1159/000513654.

[6] E. M. Brunt, "Pathology of fatty liver disease," Mod. Pathol., vol. 20, pp. S40–S48, Feb. 2007, doi: 10.1038/modpathol.3800680.

[7] "Logistic Regression Model Optimization and Case Analysis | IEEE Conference Publication | IEEE Xplore." https://ieeexplore.ieee.org/document/8962457 (accessed Feb. 08, 2023).

[8] S. Raheja and A. Asthana, "Sentiment Analysis of Tweets During the COVID-19 Pandemic Using Multinomial Logistic Regression," Int. J. Softw. Innov. IJSI, vol. 11, no. 1, pp. 1–16, 2023.

[9] S. Gupta and S. Raheja, "Stroke Prediction using Machine Learning Methods," in 2022 12th International Conference on Cloud Computing, Data Science & Engineering (Confluence), Jan. 2022, pp. 553–558. doi: 10.1109/Confluence52989.2022.9734197.

[10] S. Raheja, S. Kasturia, X. Cheng, and M. Kumar, "Machine learning-based diffusion model for prediction of coronavirus-19 outbreak," Neural Comput. Appl., pp. 1–20, Aug. 2021, doi: 10.1007/s00521-021-06376-x.

[11] "The decision tree classifier: Design and potential | IEEE Journals & Magazine | IEEE Xplore." https://ieeexplore.ieee.org/abstract/document/6498972 (accessed Feb. 08, 2023).

[12] S. Raheja and S. Datta, "Analysis and Prediction on COVID-19 Using Machine Learning Techniques," in Enabling Healthcare 4.0 for Pandemics, John Wiley & Sons, Ltd, 2021, pp. 39–57. doi: 10.1002/9781119769088.ch3.

[13] M. Pal, "Random forest classifier for remote sensing classification," Int. J. Remote Sens., vol. 26, no. 1, pp. 217–222, Jan. 2005, doi: 10.1080/01431160412331269698.

[14] V. F. Rodriguez-Galiano, B. Ghimire, J. Rogan, M. Chica-Olmo, and J. P. Rigol-Sanchez, "An assessment of the effectiveness of a random forest classifier for land-cover classification," ISPRS J. Photogramm. Remote Sens., vol. 67, pp. 93–104, Jan. 2012, doi: 10.1016/j.isprsjprs.2011.11.002.

[15] "Improved Random Forest for Classification | IEEE Journals & Magazine | IEEE Xplore." https://ieeexplore.ieee.org/abstract/document/8357563 (accessed Feb. 08, 2023).

[16] A. Liaw and M. Wiener, "Classification and Regression by randomForest," vol. 2, 2002.

[17] G. Guo, H. Wang, D. Bell, Y. Bi, and K. Greer, "KNN Model-Based Approach in Classification," in On The Move to Meaningful Internet Systems 2003: CoopIS, DOA, and ODBASE, Berlin, Heidelberg, 2003, pp. 986–996. doi: 10.1007/978-3-540-39964-3_62.

[18] M. Kumar, A. Rani, S. Raheja, and G. Munjal, "Automatic Brain Tumor Detection Using Machine Learning and Mixed Supervision," in Evolving Role of AI and IoMT in the Healthcare Market, F. Al-Turjman, M. Kumar, T. Stephan, and A. Bhardwaj, Eds. Cham: Springer International Publishing, 2021, pp. 247–262. doi: 10.1007/978-3-030-82079-4_12.

[19] A. A. Ibrahim, R. L., M. M., R. O., and G. A., "Comparison of the CatBoost Classifier with other Machine Learning Methods," Int. J. Adv. Comput. Sci. Appl., vol. 11, no. 11, 2020, doi: 10.14569/IJACSA.2020.0111190.

[20] L. Mason, J. Baxter, P. Bartlett, and M. Frean, "Boosting Algorithms as Gradient Descent," in Advances in Neural Information Processing Systems, 1999, vol. 12. Accessed: Feb. 08, 2023. [Online]. Available: https://proceedings.neurips.cc/paper/1999/hash/96a93ba89a5b5c6c226 e49b88973f46e-Abstract.html

[21] A. Herschtal and B. Raskutti, "Optimising area under the ROC curve using gradient descent," in Twenty-first international conference on Machine learning - ICML '04, Banff, Alberta, Canada, 2004, p. 49. doi: 10.1145/1015330.1015366.

[22] T.-T.-H. Le, J. Kim, and H. Kim, "An Effective Intrusion Detection Classifier Using Long Short-Term Memory with Gradient Descent Optimization," in 2017 International Conference on Platform Technology and Service (PlatCon), Feb. 2017, pp. 1–6. doi: 10.1109/PlatCon.2017.7883684.

13

Computer-aided Drug Design Case Study on the Development of New Chemical Entities in the Management of HIV

Kalyani D. Asgaonkar[1], Shital M. Patil[1], and Suraj Gavande[2,3]

[1]All India Shri Shivaji Memorial Society's College of Pharmacy, India
[2]Department of Pharmaceutical Sciences, Eugene Applebaum College of Pharmacy and Health Sciences (EACPHS), Wayne State University, USA
[3]Molecular Therapeutics Program, Barbara Ann Karmanos Cancer Institute, Wayne State University School of Medicine, USA
E-mail: kalyani_a@aissmscop.com; shital_patil@aissmscop.com; ngavande@wayne.edu

Abstract

In the drug discovery process for drug repurposing, computer-aided drug design techniques such as molecular docking is one of the widely used techniques. Molecular docking is a software tool used to gauze the biological activity of different chemical moieties by their interactions with biological receptors. Similarly there are different computer-aided tools to predict pharmacokinetic and toxicity behavior of new chemical entities. The human immunodeficiency virus (HIV) invades the host cells and weakens the human immune system. Entry inhibitors, which are used in conjunction with standard anti-HIV therapy, prevent the binding of HIV protein to the chemokine receptor. These agents help to restore immunity and can, in turn, prevent HIV-TB co-infection. A study on various thiazolidinone-pyrazine derivatives as entry inhibitors targeting CXCR4 co-receptors was conducted using different *in-silico* tools. Docking studies were performed and compounds were also assessed for ADME and toxicity using SwissADME and pkCSM software, respectively. The results show the valuable contribution of such *in-silico* tools in the development of drugs for the treatment of HIV.

Keywords: Anti-HIV, entry inhibitors, thiazolidinone-pyrazine, docking, CXCR4, AutoDock Vina, SwissADME, pkCSM.

13.1 Introduction

Repurposing "old" drugs to treat diseases is increasingly emerging as an attractive proposition due to the use of already-established compounds, with potential to lower development costs and timelines. Drug repurposing along with *de novo* drug discovery definitely speeds up the new drug discovery process [1, 2]. Computer-aided drug design (CADD) is an important strategy for current drug development in which various computational methods and software tools are often combined to produce the desired results [3, 4]. Docking is one of the computational methods to predict the possible action or biological effect of new chemical entities by studying their interactions with respective targets (receptors) [5–7]. It is imperative to take pharmacokinetic behavior, viz. absorption, distribution, metabolism, excretion, and toxicity (ADMET) into consideration during the development and improvement of novel medications. Numerous machine learning (ML) platforms/software/tools such as Schrodinger, AutoDock Vina, V-life MDS, SwissADME, pkCSM, Pre ADMET, Molinsπration, TOPKAT, etc., can be used to predict these parameters [8, 9].

13.1.1 Case study of usage of different in-silico tools for drug discovery of Anti-HIV molecules

By infecting host cells, the human immunodeficiency virus (HIV) attacks and impairs the immune system of humans. Almost 33 million lives have been lost as a result, making it a serious public health concern. Moreover, due to their compromised immune system, such patients are more prone to different types of infections [10]. One of the ways of treating HIV is by highly active antiretroviral therapy, which combines many antiretroviral drugs that target various levels of the HIV life cycle. However, due to the emergence of HIV cross-resistance in recent years, their effectiveness has decreased [11]. HIV attacks CD4+ T-cells in the human body. Chemokine receptors CXCR4 and CXCR5 found on the membrane of these cells play a role in viral entrance.gp120, a component of the HIV membrane glycoprotein, and first engages with the CD4 cell receptor [12, 13]. As a result, the trans-membrane virion protein gp41 is exposed and it is able to attach to the chemokine receptors. Following this, the proteins undergo structural changes that lead to membrane fusion and the integration of genetic material of virus in the host cell [12, 13–22].

One of the strategies in the management of AIDS is by using entry inhibitors that would prevent the virus from entering the cells. When used with other medications, entry inhibitors have a synergistic impact [23]. There have been reports of several thiazolidinone compounds having anti-HIV and anti-TB effects [6, 24]. In light of rising concerns of current antiretroviral therapy, the development of chemokine receptor antagonists as entry inhibitors has provided a new direction in the treatment of AIDS. CXCR4 co-receptor antagonists prevent viral proteins from attaching to chemokine receptors by preventing the entry into the cells. By preventing the entry of viruses into the host cell, immunity can be restored and co-existence of TB and HIV can be easily prevented. To investigate the application of different CADD tools, in the current investigation, 23 variants of N-(4-oxo-2 substituted thiazolidin-3-yl) pyrazine-2-carbohydrazide were docked into the crystal structure of CXCR4. The interactions with the receptor in terms of hydrogen bonds, binding affinity, electrostatic interactions, and hydrophobicity were examined [25]. Each molecule was also examined for its ADMET characteristics [26, 27].

13.2 Computer-aided Molecular Docking and ADMET Studies

For molecular docking studies, three crystal structures for the CXCR4 receptors (3ODU, 3OE9, and 3OE6) were downloaded from Protein Data Bank (PDB) [28]. A series of 23 thiazolidinone-pyrazine derivatives earlier reported by Chitre et al. possessing anti-TB activity [12] and standard drug Plerixafor and co-crystallized ligand ITD ((6,6-dimethyl-5,6-dihydroimidazo[2,1-b][1,3]thiazol-3-yl)methyl N,N'-dicyclohexylimidothio carbamate) [16] (Figure 13.1) were used for the study. Molecular docking was carried out using AutoDock Vina software [29].

ChemDraw Ultra 8.0 and V-Life MDS software were used to draw 2D and 3D structures of the ligands [30]. These structures were further subjected to energy minimization using the Merck molecular force field (MMFF) method. Ligand optimization ensured that only the lowest energy conformer of the

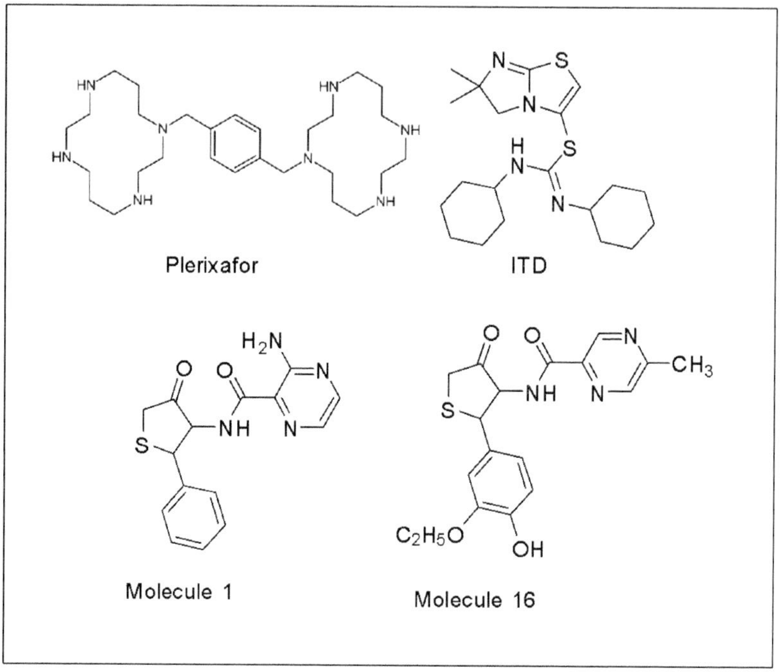

Figure 13.1 Structure of Plerixafor, ITD, Compound 1, and Compound 16.

compound binds to the receptor [6]. Ligand and protein preparation was performed using OpenBabel program, BIOVIA Discovery Studio Visualizer, and AutoDock Vina software [31–34]. With the aid of active site coordinates, a grid box was created in AutoDock Vina. The dimension of the grid box was $20 \times 30 \times 72$ A (x, y, and z) and the center coordinates were $70 \times 70 \times 78$ A (x, y, and z). The PDBQT format was used to save the protein, and active sites for favorable binding of ligands and proteins were identified. All molecules were treated as rigid during docking. Eight was chosen as the exhaustiveness value. The best posed conformer for each ligand was chosen for analysis. Various interactions including hydrogen bonds, hydrophobic, and electrostatics were examined (Table 13.1). Out of the three crystal structures, compounds showed best interactions and binding affinity with PDB 3OE6. On the basis of binding affinity (-8.0 Kcal/mol), eight compounds were selected.

From the set of eight compounds, compounds 1 (-8.0 Kcal/mol) and 16 (-8.7 Kcal/mol) showed higher binding affinity as compared to the co-crystallized ligand, ITD (-7.9 Kcal/mol). With 3OE6, compound 1

Table 13.1 Interactions of compound 1, 16, ITD, and Plerixafor with 3OE6.

Comp.	Hydrogen bond				Hydrophobic interactions				Electrostatic interactions			
	Type	Amino acid of receptor	Atom of ligand	Distance (Å)	Type	Amino acid of receptor	Atom of ligand	Distance (Å)	Type	Amino acid of receptor	Atom of ligand	Distance (Å)
1	Conventional H bond	ASP97	–H (–NH₂ of pyrazine)	2.82	π–π Stacked	TRP94	π-Orbitals of phenyl	3.82	π–Anion	ASP97	π-Orbitals of pyrazine	2.82
	–	–	–	–	π–π Stacked	TRP94	π-Orbitals of phenyl	3.80	–	–	–	–
	–	–	–	–	π–π Stacked	HIS113	π-Orbitals of phenyl	5.34	–	–	–	–
	–	–	–	–	π–Alkyl	ILE185	π-Orbitals of phenyl	5.38	–	–	–	–
16	Conventional H bond	TYR255	–O (of thiazolidi-none)	2.62	π–Sigma	TRP94	C–H (–OC₂H₅ of phenyl))	3.61	π–Cation	HIS113	π-Orbitals of phenyl	3.80
	–	–	–	–	π–Sigma	TRP94	C–H (–OC₂H₅ of phenyl))	3.81	π–Cation	ARG188	π-Orbitals of pyrazine	4.00
	–	–	–	–	π–π Stacked	TRP94	π-Orbitals of phenyl	5.41	–	–	–	–
	–	–	–	–	π–π Stacked	TRP94	π-Orbitals of phenyl	4.35	–	–	–	–
	–	–	–	–	π–π Stacked	HIS113	π-Orbitals of phenyl	3.80	–	–	–	–
	–	–	–	–	π–π T-shaped	TYR116	π-Orbitals of phenyl	4.93	–	–	–	–
	–	–	–	–	π–Alkyl	TRP94	Alkyl (–OC₂H₅ of phenyl)	4.41	–	–	–	–
	–	–	–	–	π–Alkyl	TRP102	Alkyl (–OC₂H₅ of phenyl)	4.82	–	–	–	–

Table 13.1　Continued.

Comp.	Hydrogen bond				Hydrophobic interactions				Electrostatic interactions			
	Type	Amino acid of receptor	Atom of ligand	Distance (Å)	Type	Amino acid of receptor	Atom of ligand	Distance (Å)	Type	Amino acid of receptor	Atom of ligand	Distance (Å)
—	—	—	—	—	π–Alkyl	TYR121	Alkyl (–CH₃ of pyrazine)	5.11	—	—	—	—
ITD	Conventional H bond	TYR190	–S	2.99	Alkyl	CYS186	Alkyl	5.37	π–Cation	ARG188	π-Orbitals	4.26
	π-Donor H bond	HIS113	–H	2.96	π–Alkyl	TRP94	Alkyl	4.82	—	—	—	—
	—	—	—	—	π–Alkyl	TRP94	Alkyl	4.59	—	—	—	—
					π–Alkyl	HIS113	Alkyl	4.57				
Plerixafor	Conventional H bond	VAL196	–H	3.02	π–π Stacked	TRP94	π-Orbitals	5.06	π–Anion	GLU288	π-Orbitals	4.33
	Conventional H bond	PHE199	–H	2.20	π–π Stacked	HIS113	π-Orbitals	5.22	—	—	—	—
	Conventional H bond	CYS186	–H	2.26	—	—	—	—	—	—	—	—
	Carbon H bond	GLN200	–C	3.50	—	—	—	—	—	—	—	—

(Figure 13.2) showed hydrophobic, electrostatic, and hydrogen bonding interactions with important amino acids. The hydrophobic interactions include
π-orbitals of phenyl that displayed π−π stacking interaction with TRP94
(3.82 and 3.80 Å) and HIS113 (5.34 Å), and the π-orbital of pyrazine showed
π−alkyl interaction with ILE185 (5.38A0). The amino group of pyrazine
showed conventional H-bond interactions with ASP97 (2.82A0). The π-
orbital of pyrazine displayed π−anion interaction with ASP97 (2.82A0). All
three types of interactions were displayed for compound 16 (Figure 13.3)
with 3OE6. The ethoxy group of the phenyl ring interacts with TRP94 by
two π−sigma and one π−alkyl bond (3.61, 3.81, and 4.41 Å, respectively).
Phenyl's π-orbitals displayed two π-stacked hydrophobic interactions with
TRP94 (5.41 and 4.35 Å), one with HIS113 (3.80 Å) and π−π T-shaped
bonding with TYR116 (4.93 Å). π-orbitals of phenyl and HIS113 (3.80Å) and
π-orbitals of pyrazine and ARG188 (4.00 Å) showed electrostatic π−cation
interaction. For Plerixafor, a standard drug, binding affinity was found to
be −10.4 Kcal/mol. It has three conventional hydrogen bond interactions

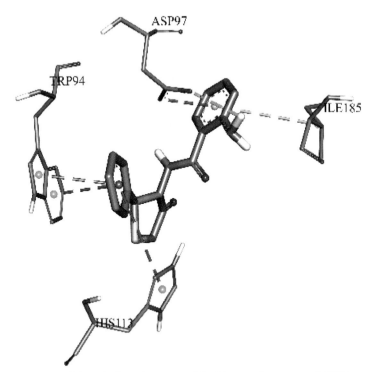

Figure 13.2 Binding of compound 1 with crystal structure of 3OE6.

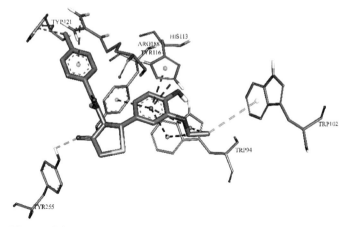

Figure 13.3   Binding of compound 16 with crystal structure of 3OE6.

with VAL196 (3.02 Å), PHE199 (2.20 Å), and CYS186 (2.26 Å) amino acids. Between the carbon atoms of Plerixafor was carbon hydrogen interaction with GLN200 (3.50 Å). π-orbitals of the Plerixafor displayed two π−π stacking hydrophobic bond with TRP94 (5.06 Å) and HIS113 (5.22 Å). Between the π-orbitals of Plerixafor and the significant amino acid residue GLU288 (4.33Å), an electrostatic π−anion binding was observed (Figure 13.4). For co-crystallized ligand, ITD (Figure 13.5) displayed one

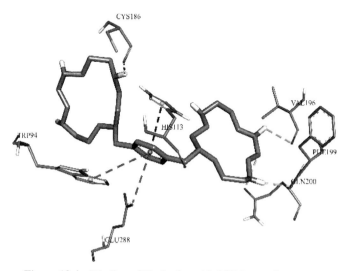

Figure 13.4   Binding of Plerixafor with 3OE6 crystal structure.

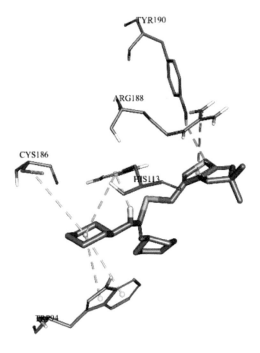

Figure 13.5 Interactions of ITD with 3OE6.

conventional hydrogen bond with TYR190 (2.99Å), one π-donor H-bond with HIS113 (2.96 Å), two π−alkyl hydrophobic interactions with TRP94 (4.82 and 4.59 Å), one π−alkyl bond with HIS113 (4.57 Å), one alkyl hydrophobic contact with CYS186 (5.37 Å), and one π−cation electrostatic interaction with ARG188 (4.26 Å).

ADME and toxicity profile using computational tools:

ADMET *in-silico* analysis was performed on all the compounds. It was carried out with the SwissADME tool [35] and pkCSM web server [36]. The Lipinski rule of five, the Veber rule, and the Muegge rule were studied. Number of rotatable bonds (NRB), molecular weight (MW), hydrogen bond acceptor (HBA), molar refractivity (MR), hydrogen bond donor (HBD), and topological surface area (TSA) are among the physicochemical variables that fall under Lipinski rules. According to Lipinski's rule, a molecule must have MW 500 Da, HBD 5, HBA 10, and log P (logarithm of octanol/water partition coefficient) 5 in order to be orally active [37]. Veber's rule takes into account polar surface area smaller than 140 Å and less than 10 rotatable bonds [38]. The molecules were additionally examined for Muegge's rule, which considers X log P -2 to 5, MW between 200 and 400 Da, TPSA below 150, number of rings < 7, number of hetero atoms < 1, number of carbons < 4, number of rotatable bonds < 15, HBD < 5, and HBA < 10 [39].

The following properties were investigated using pkCSM online tool: human intestinal absorption, Caco-2 permeability, fraction unbound, volume of distribution, P-glycoprotein inhibition ability, CYP3A4 substrate, renal OCT2 substrate, total clearance, AMES toxicity, hERG I toxicity, oral rat acute toxicity, and oral rat chronic toxicity [40]. Outcome of the ADME (Table 13.2) and toxicity prediction (Table 13.3) studies showed that all the compounds had an HBA value < 10 and the HBD value < 5. Plerixafor's HBD value was found to be higher than the prescribed limit. Lipinski's rule of five was successfully applied to all 23 molecules with no exceptions.

Brain access (blood–brain barrier) and passive gastrointestinal absorption (human intestinal absorption) are predicted by the BOILED-Egg diagram generated from SwissADME. The white zone shows a high potential of passive absorption through the gastrointestinal system, whereas the yellow region shows a high probability of brain penetration (Figure 13.6) [35]. ITD compounds 1, 9, 11, and 16 are anticipated to penetrate the gastrointestinal tract with good absorption but might not reach the brain. Compounds 4, 5, and 16 will be actively pumped up from the brain or the gastrointestinal lumen because of the P-glycoprotein (PGP+) efflux. Among all the screened molecules, analysis using the pkCSM tool revealed that compounds 11 and 16 have the highest Caco-2 permeability values (>0.90) [41]. All the molecules had very good intestinal absorption in the range 65.7%–95.8%; values less than 30% depict poor absorption. The fraction unbound value of a drug influences its distribution, efficacy, and clearance [42].

The fraction unbound values of all screened ligands were predicted to be between 0.166 and 0.285. Furthermore, compounds 4, 5, 11, 13, and 16 were found to be CYP3A4 substrates and thus can be metabolized in the liver [41]. A short-term bacterial reverse mutation assay predicts mutagenic potential using the AMES test [43]. Compounds 1, 9, 11, and 16 showed no AMES toxicity among the hit compounds. None of the 23 compounds were found to be renal OCT2 substrates or to inhibit hERG I. Inhibiting hERG can cause QT syndrome, which can lead to fatal ventricular arrhythmia [44].

Table 13.2 Drug likeness data of compounds.

Compound	Physicochemical properties						Lipophilicity	Water solubility	Drug likeness		
	MW	NRB	HBA	HBD	MR	TPSA	Consensus log $P_{o/w}$	Class	Lipinski violations	Veber violations	Muegge violations
1	315.35	4	4	2	86.02	126.51	0.72	Soluble	0	0	0
16	374.41	6	6	2	99.91	129.95	1.3	Soluble	0	0	0
ITD	406.65	6	2	1	123.17	95.22	4.63	Moderately soluble	0	0	0
Plerixafor	502.78	4	8	6	182.21	78.66	0.68	Soluble	2	0	1

Note: MW: Molecular weight; NRB: number of rotatable bonds; HBA: hydrogen bond acceptors; HBD: hydrogen bond donors; MR: molar refractivity; TPSA: topological polar surface area.

Table 13.3 Details of pharmacokinetic and toxicity profiles using pkCSM software.

Compound	Caco2-permeability (log Papp in 10^{-6} cm/s)	Human intestinal absorption (% absorbed)	P-gp substrate (yes/no)	VD$_{ss}$ (human)	Fraction unbound (human)	CYP3A4 substrate	Total clearance (log ml/min/kg)	Renal OCT2 substrate	AMES toxicity	hERG I toxicity	Oral rat acute toxicity (LD50) (mol/kg)	Oral chronic toxicity (LOAEL) rat (log mg/kg_bw/day)
1	0.583	70.992	Yes	0.41	0.285	No	0.027	No	No	No	2.619	1.866
16	1.14	73.228	No	−0.17	0.166	Yes	0.225	No	No	No	2.486	1.672
ITD	1.065	89.379	Yes	0.462	0.276	Yes	0.327	No	No	No	3.029	−0.448
Plerixafor	0.713	40.277	Yes	1.099	0.599	Yes	0.23	No	No	No	2.36	1.65

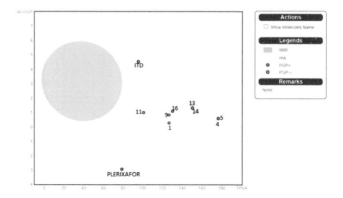

Figure 13.6   BOILED-Egg diagram.

13.3 Conclusion

In a nutshell, two molecules (1,16) were chosen from the 23 derivatives by taking into consideration the binding affinity that was comparable to the co-crystallized ligand, standard. They also demonstrated binding with important amino acids TRP94 and HIS113. They also had good pharmacokinetic and toxicity profiles. The discovery of chemokine receptor antagonists as entry inhibitors has provided researchers with a new perspective on how to treat and advance HIV disease. Various computational software used in this study such as AutoDock Vina, SwissADME, and pkCSM have been successfully used to know the binding mode and ADMET of new chemical entities for drug repurposing.

Acknowledgement

The authors would like to thank Dr. Ashwini R Madgulkar, Principal AISSMS College of Pharmacy, Pune for providing infrastructure for the project and for the free software used for the study.

References

[1] S. George, E. K. Tan, P. Sloan, M. Carl, J. I. Kirkpatrick, 'Drug repurposing using real-world data,' Drug Discov. Today, pp. 103422, Australia, Jan., 2023.

[2] F. Ruiz, A. Hoang, C. Dilmore, J. DeStefano, E. Arnold, 'Structural basis of HIV inhibition by L-nucleosides: Opportunities for drug development and repurposing,' Drug Discov. Today, pp. 1832-1846, USA, Jul., 2022.

[3] V. Sabe, T. Ntombela, L. A. Jhamba, G. Maguire, T. Govender, T. Naicker, H. Kruger, 'Current trends in computer aided drug design and a highlight of drugs discovered via computational techniques: A review,' Eur. J. Medi. Chem., Volume 224, South Africa, Nov 2021, 113705,

[4] W. Jorgensen, 'Computer-aided discovery of anti-HIV agents,' Bioorg. Med. Chem., pp. 4768-4778, US, Oct 2016.

[5] A. Berchanski, A. Lapidot, 'Prediction of HIV-1 entry inhibitors neomycin–arginine conjugates interaction with the CD4-gp120 binding site by molecular modeling and multistep docking procedure,' Biochim.Biophys. Acta (BBA) - Biomembranes, pp. 2107-2119, Israel, Sept., 2007.

[6] K. Asgaonkar, S. Patil, T. Chitre, V. Ghegade, S. Jadhav, S. Sande, A. Kulkarni, 'Comparative Docking Studies: A Drug Design Tool for Some Pyrazine-Thiazolidinone Based Derivatives for Anti-HIV Activity,' Curr.Comput. Aided Drug Des.,' pp. 252-258, India, Jun. 2019.

[7] T. Chitre, S. Patil, A. Sujalegaonkar, K. Asgaonkar, V. Khedkar, D. Garud, P. Jha,S. Gaikwad,S. Kulkarni, A. Choudhari,D. Sarkar, 'NonNucleoside Reverse Transcriptase Inhibitors, Molecular Docking Studies and Antitubercular Activity of Thiazolidin-4-one Derivatives Source: Curr.Comput. Aided Drug Des.,' pp. 433-444, India, Oct., 2019.

[8] A. Göller, L. Kuhnke, F. Montanari, A. Bonin, S. Schneckener, A. Laak, J. Wichard, M. Lobell, A. Hillisch, 'Bayer's in silico ADMET platform: a journey of machine learning over the past two decades,' Drug Discov. Today, pp. 1702-1709, Germany, Sept., 2020.

[9] D. Antoine, M. Olivier, Z. Vincent, 'SwissADME: a free web tool to evaluate pharmacokinetics, drug-likeness and medicinal chemistry friendliness of small molecules'. Sci. Rep., Switzerland, Mar.,2017.

[10] WHO Report, 17th July 2018, https://www.who.int/news-room/fact-sheets/detail/hiv-aids May 31, 2021.

[11] H. Ismail,S. Joanna, T. Alia, V. Didier, B. MenceNajdoska, B. Jane, C. Driss, 'QSAR and molecular docking studies of indole-based analogs as HIV-1attachment inhibitors,' J. Mol. Struct., pp. 429-443, Morocco, Oct., 2019.

[12] S. Virani, Z. Liang, Y. Yoon, H. Shim, S. R. Mooring, 'Synthesis and evaluation of 2, 5-diamino and 2, 5-dianilinomethyl pyridine analogues as potential CXCR4 antagonists,'Bioorg. Med. Chem. Lett., pp. 220-224, USA, Jan., 2019.

[13] Y. Ji, M. Shu, Y. Lin, Y. Wang, H. Rui Wang, L. Zhihua, 'Combined 3D-QSAR modeling and molecular docking study on azacycles CCR5 antagonists,' J. Mol. Struct., pp. 35-41, China, Aug.,2013.

[14] A. Brelot, L. A. Chakrabarti,'CCR5 revisited: How mechanisms of HIV entry govern AIDS pathogenesis,' J. Mol. Bio., pp. 2257-2589, France, Aug., 2018.

[15] T. Kobayakawa, K. Konno, N. Ohashi, K. Takahashi, A. Masuda, K. Yoshimura, S. Harada, H. Tamamura, 'Soluble-type small-molecule CD4 mimics as HIV entry inhibitors,'Bioorg. Med. Chem. Lett., pp. 719-723, Japan, Mar., 2019.

[16] M. Elsheikh, Y. Tang.D. Li, G. Jiang, 'Deep latency: A new insight into a functional HIV cure,' EBioMedicine, pp. 624-629, USA, Jul.,2019.

[17] J. Rodríguez-Muñoz, S. Moreno,'Strategies for the cure of HIV infection. Estrategias de curación de la infecciónpor VIH,' EnfermInfeccMicrobiol Clin, pp. 265-273, Spain, Apr., 2019.

[18] X. Shuang, X. Ting, Y. Z. Yuan, Y. L. Gen, F. C. Fen, 'Recent progress in HIV-1 inhibitors targeting the entrance channel of HIV-1 non-nucleoside reverse transcriptase inhibitor binding pocket,' Eur. J. Med. Chem., pp. 277-291,China, Jul., 2019.

[19] B. Chen, 'Molecular mechanism of HIV-1 entry,' Trends Microbiol, pp. 878-891, Boston, Oct., 2019.

[20] I. Lee, M. S. Palombo, X. Zhang, Z. Szekely, P. Sinko, 'Design and evaluation of a CXCR4 targeting peptide 4DV3 as an HIV entry inhibitor and a ligand for targeted drug delivery,' Eur. J. Pharm.Biopharm., pp. 11-22,USA, May,2019.

[21] M. Mirza, A. Saadabadi, M. Vanmeert, M. Salo-Ahen, I. Abdullah, S. Claes, S. Jonghe, D. Schols, S. Ahmad, M.Froeyen, 'Discovery of HIV entry inhibitors via a hybrid CXCR4 and CCR5 receptor pharmacophore-based virtual screening approach,' Eur. J. Pharm. Sci., pp. 105537, Belgium, Dec.,2020.

[22] A. Hout, A. Klarenbeek, V. Bobkov, J.Doijen, M. Arimont, C. Zhao, R. Heukers, R.Rimkunas, C. Graaf, T. Verrips, B. V. Woning, H. Haard, J. Rucker, K. Vermeire, T. Handel, T. Loy, M. J Smit, D.Schols, 'CXCR4-targeting nanobodies differentially inhibit CXCR4 function and HIV entry,' Biochem.Pharmacol., pp. 402-412, Belgium, Dec., 2018.

[23] A. A. Haqqani, J.C. Tilton, 'Entry inhibitors and their use in the treatment of HIV-1 infection' Antiviral Res, pp.158–170, United States, May, 2013.

[24] T. S. Chitre, K. D. Asgaonkar, P. B. Miniyar, A. B. Dharme, M. A. Arkile, A. Yeware, V. M. Khedkar, P. C. Jha, D. Sarkar, 'Synthesis and docking studies of pyrazine–thiazolidinone hybrid scaffold targeting dormant tuberculosis', Bioorg. Medi. Chem. Lett., pp. 2224-2228, India May,2016.

[25] T. S. Chitre, S. M. Patil, A. G. Sujalegaonkar, K. D. Asgaonkar, V. M. Khedkar, D. R. Garud, P. C. Jha, S. Y. Gaikwad, S. S. Kulkarni, A. Choudhari, D. Sarkar, 'Non- Nucleoside Reverse Transcriptase Inhibitors, Molecular Docking Studies and Antitubercular Activity of Thiazolidin-4-one Derivatives,'Curr. Comput. Aided Drug Des., pp. 433-444, India 2019.

[26] Y. Hongbin, S. Lixia, W. Zhuang, L.; Guixia, L. Weihua, T. Yun, 'ADMETopt: A Web Server for ADMET Optimization in Drug Design via Scaffold Hopping,' J. Chem. Inf. Model. pp. 2051–2056, China, Sept. 2018.

[27] S. Hatse, K. Princen, G. Bridger, E. De Clercq, D. Schols, 'Chemokine receptor inhibition by AMD3100 is strictly confined to CXCR4. FEBS Lett.,' pp. 255-262, Belgium Sept. 2002.

[28] RCSB PDB – 3OE6: Crystal structure of the CXCR4 chemokine receptor in complex with a small molecule antagonist IT1t in I222 spacegroup, https://www.rcsb.org/structure/3OE6 (Accessed June 10, 2019).

[29] O. Trott, A. J. Olson, 'AutoDock Vina: improving the speed and accuracy of docking with a new scoring function, efficient optimization and multithreading,' J Comput Chem, pp.455-461.CA, Jan. 2010.

[30] V-Life Molecular Design Suite version 4.3.[31]main protease. Bioorganic chemistry, 2021, 106, 104497.

[31] N. M. O'Boyle, M. Banck, C. A. James, C. Morley, T. Vandermeersch, G. R. Hutchison, 'Open Babel: An open chemical toolbox', J. Cheminf, pp. 33, United States, Oct. 2011.

[32] The Open Babel Package, version 3.1.1 http://openbabel.org Nov. 2021

[33] BIOVIA, Dassault Systèmes, BIOVIA Discovery Studio Visualizer, v21.1.0.20298, San Diego: Dassault Systèmes, 2021.

[34] T. S. Chitre, K. D. Asgaonkar, M.P. Patil, K. Shiva, V.M. Khedkar, D.R. Garud, 'QSAR, docking studies of 1, 3-thiazinan-3-yl isonicotinamide

derivatives for antitubercular activity', Comput. Biol. Chem., pp. 211-218, India, Jun. 2017.

[35] SWISS ADME. http://www.swissadme.ch/ Nov. 2021.

[36] pkCSM: http://biosig.unimelb.edu.au/pkcsm/predictionNov.**2021**.

[37] C. A. Lipinski, 'Lead- and drug-like compounds: the rule-of-five revolution', Drug Discov. Today Technol., pp. 337–341, United States, Dec. 2004.

[38] Y. Rohitash, Y. Imran, P. Dhamija,; D. K. Chaurasia, S. Handu, 'Virtual screening, ADMET prediction and dynamics simulation of potential compounds targeting the main protease of SARS-CoV-2', J. Biomol. Struct. Dyn, pp. 6617–6632, India, Oct. 2021.

[39] I. Muegge, 'Selection criteria for drug-like compounds', Med. Res. Rev., pp. 302-21,United States, May, 2003.

[40] D. E. Pires, T. L. Blundell, D. B. Ascher, 'pkCSM: Predicting Small-Molecule Pharmacokinetic and Toxicity Properties Using Graph-Based Signatures', J. Med. Chem., pp. 4066-72, Brazil, Apr. 2021.

[41] V. Kumar, R. Kumar, S. Parate, S. Yoon, G. Lee, D. Kim, K. W. Lee, 'Identification of ACK1 inhibitors as anticancer agents by using computer-aided drug designing', J. Mol. Struc.,pp. 1235, Korea, Feb. 2021.

[42] F. X. Domínguez-Villa, N. A. Durán-Iturbide, J. G. Ávila-Zárraga, 'Synthesis, molecular docking, and in silico ADME/Tox profiling studies of new 1-aryl-5-(3-azidopropyl)indol-4-ones: Potential inhibitors of SARS CoV-2 main protease,' Bioorg. Chem., pp.104497, Mexico, Jan. 2021.

[43] W.C.S. Faria, M. G. de Oliveira, E. C. da Conceição, V. B. Silva,; N. Veggi, A. Converti, W. M. Barros, M. F. da Silva, N. Bragagnolo, 'Antioxidant efficacy and in silico toxicity prediction of free and spray-dried extracts of green Arabica and Robusta coffee fruits and their application in edible oil,' Food hydrocoll, pp. 106004, United States, 2021.

[44] B. Hu, J. Joseph, X. Geng, Y. Wu, M. R. Suleiman,; X. Liu, J. Shi, X. Wang, Z. He, J. Wang, M. Cheng, 'Refined pharmacophore features for virtual screening of human thromboxane A2 receptor antagonists,' Comput. Biol. Chem., pp. 107249, China, 2020.

14

Detection of Brain Tumor on MRI Images using Comparison Analysis of Deep Learning Techniques

V. Sheeja Kumari[1], G. Vennira Selvi[2], I. Sudha[3], and Surender Subburaj[4]

[1]Professor / Department of Computational Intelligence-Institute of AI & ML, Saveetha School of Engineering, SIMATS University, Chennai
[2]Professor School of Computer Science and Engineering and Information Science, Presidency University, Bengaluru
[3]Professor / Department of Computer Science and Engineering, Saveetha School of Engineering, SIMATS University, Chennai
[4]Research Associate / School of Engineering, Cardiff university, United Kingdom
E-mail: sheejakumari.sse@saveetha.com; vennira@gmailcom; Sudhai.sse@saveetha.com; subburajs@cardiff.ac.uk

Abstract

The process of diagnosing brain tumors typically involves the use of scans created with magnetic resonance imaging (MRI). MRI scans have the ability to localize precisely in the brain an area that is exhibiting abnormal growth of tissue. A number of research articles have been written on the topic of locating brain tumors with the assistance of machine learning and deep learning algorithms. When combined with MRI scans, these algorithms enable a quicker and more accurate detection of brain tumors, which in turn makes it easier to treat patients who have the condition. The radiologist can more easily decide what course of action to take with the help of these projections. In the proposed chapter, self-made algorithms called Random Forest (RF) and Support Vector Machine (SVM) are used to search for brain tumors, and their performance is analyzed. Both of these algorithms were developed by the authors of the chapter. The authors are responsible for the development of both of these algorithms. The performance of these classifiers, which determine whether or not a brain image is normal, is evaluated based on a variety of criteria, including sensitivity, specificity, and accuracy, amongst others. These classifiers are responsible for determining whether or not a brain image is normal. It has a significance of 0.001, which is lower than the p value, and it has the capability of giving an accuracy that ranges between 94.1220 and 96.8940. As a direct consequence of this, its statistical significance is indisputable.

Keywords: Support vector machine, random forest, preprocessing, brain tumour segmentation.

14.1 Introduction

A person must first ensure that their brain is in good shape in order to keep their body in the best possible condition. There are hundreds of millions of people around the world who are afflicted with diseases that affect their brain health; this number will continue to rise if something isn't done. The brain is the most significant component of the human body because it regulates the activities of every other organ and facilitates the process of decision-making [9].

The brain is considered the most complex organ in the body. It controls the body and affects everything. "Brain health" refers to an individual's ability to use their cognitive, sensory, social-emotional, behavioural, and motor capacities to its utmost capacity throughout their lives, regardless of diseases [14]. Physical health, healthy environments, safety and security, learning and social contact, and lifelong access to quality services all affect how our brains develop, adapt, and respond to adversity and stress. These factors affect brain evolution, adaptation, and stress response. Optimizing these characteristics improves mental and physical health, social and economic well-being, and civilization.

However, conditions that affect the brain and nervous system in general can show up at any point in a person's development. These conditions are characterised by slowed brain development, brain injury, and/or reduced brain function. Possible manifestations of these conditions include epilepsy, headache disorders such as migraine, cerebrovascular diseases such as stroke, neurodegenerative diseases such as dementia and Parkinson disease, neuroinfectious or neuroimmunological diseases such as meningitis, HIV, neurocysticercosis, cerebral malaria, multiple sclerosis, and neoplasms [19].

The best care for these conditions can be provided by partnerships that cut across industries and disciplines, take a life-span, person-centered approach to promotion, prevention, treatment, care, and rehabilitation, and actively involve people who have lived experience, along with their families and carers.

The central nervous system, which serves as the primary command centre for the body, is responsible for controlling both the voluntary and involuntary functions that occur on a daily basis in the body. The tumour is a mesh of fibrous, unnecessary tissue that has grown inside of our brain despite our best efforts to stop its progression. This year, doctors have given the diagnosis of brain tumour to approximately 3,540 children and adolescents under the age of 15 [28]. If you want to prevent getting a brain tumour and properly treat one if you already have one, it is important to know about the different stages that it can go through.

14.2 An in-depth examination of the structure of the brain

The brain and spinal cord are the only components of the central nervous system that exist in their entirety (CNS). The brain is an organ that contains a high concentration of neurons and connective tissue, and it performs a wide variety of functions. Both the brain and the spinal cord are nerve centers that are responsible for communicating information to the rest of the body [23]. The central nervous system, also known as the CNS, is responsible for controlling and coordinating all of the body's activities.

Our very being is based on the functioning of our central nervous system. It commands everything about a person's mind, including their emotions, speech, intelligence, and memory. It also controls their level of comprehension.

Seeing, hearing, smelling, tasting, and touching are the five senses. Mechanisms essential to maintaining life include breathing, heartbeat, and blood pressure. The ability to move, maintain balance, and work together effectively are fundamental to human survival in any given setting.

There are numerous subregions within the brain, and each of these subregions performs a unique set of functions. Because of this, the location of a tumour in the brain has a significant impact not only on the symptoms it causes but also on the treatments that can be used to help alleviate those symptoms [29].

You will be better prepared to recognise the signs and symptoms of a brain tumor and to make informed decisions regarding its diagnosis and treatment if you familiarise yourself with the typical functioning of the brain and spine.

Structures of the brain that are of utmost significance: One of the three primary regions of the brain is called the cerebral cortex, and its functions include processing sensory input and directing both motor and emotional output [26]. The cerebellum is responsible for maintaining equilibrium during standing, walking, and other actions, whereas the cerebrum is responsible for reading, thinking, learning, movement, speaking, vision, personality, and emotional states. The brain stem is the part of the brain that connects the brain to the spinal cord. It is responsible for regulating many fundamental bodily functions, including breathing, sleeping, the temperature of the body, and the blood pressure.

14.2.1 The Brain's Lobes

Certain mental processes are controlled by the myriad lobes of the brain, which themselves are responsible for regulating other mental processes. The frontal lobe of the brain is responsible for helping with thinking and reasoning. The temporal lobe of the brain is where our senses of hearing and vision, as well as our actions and emotions, are all born [5]. If a tumour or the treatment for the tumour were to develop in any of these lobes, the distinctive capabilities of those lobes might be impaired. In addition, because the various parts of the brain are connected to one another, a tumor in one area of the brain may influence a brain function that is located in another area. In addition to the brain itself, tumours can also develop in other parts of the skull, including the spinal cord, the pituitary gland, the cranial nerves, the base of the skull, and other regions.

14.3 The Importance of Research in the Basic Sciences

If we have a more in-depth understanding of how a machine operates, we have a greater chance of being able to get it back into working order in the event that it breaks down. If our car were to break down, we would take it to a trustworthy mechanic who would be able to explain how it works and make any necessary repairs. When one of us develops a neurological condition, we look for a doctor who we believe has a solid grasp on the neurobiology that is driving our condition in the hopes that she will be able to recommend a treatment that will alleviate our symptoms. In the first place, we need to have a better understanding of the brain system; if we don't, it's likely that all of our efforts to treat the condition will be in vain or extremely expensive. Knowledge, on the other hand, is neither static nor staticly lacking; rather, it grows and develops over the course of time. If you or a loved one has ever struggled with a condition that affects the brain, you are well aware that the majority of contemporary medical practise is conducted in the dark. The responsibility of illuminating the way falls on the shoulders of basic science [10].

Fundamental research has influenced clinical treatment. Say you have trouble reading. Your eye doctor will test your reading speed and steadiness. She believes your eyes are healthy yet unstable, which is producing vision problems. She must then determine the root cause of her eye movement issues [13]. Now that she knows this, she can consult 50 years of fundamental studies on monkey brain circuits that control vision and eye movement. These research examined vision and eye movement brain networks. She pinpoints the patient's brain neural circuits that cause eye movement problems. If she knows this, she may be able to fix your eye movement error by altering brain activity. This makes reading easier.

This illustration shows how knowledge of the brain circuits underlying reading is necessary for treating even the most basic complaint, such as "Doc, I can't read." Instead of trying to figure out "why I can't see," researchers were more interested in answering the question, "How can we comprehend the brain circuits essential for seeing, and how are they organised?" This endeavour has required hundreds of scientists.

Basic research, which is essential for all other scientific endeavours, seeks to comprehend a system by analysing it rather than fixing or building it. Brain research is a young field. We only started comprehending the brain 150 years ago. Nonetheless, the Copernican concept of a solar system that revolves around the sun has been widely accepted for hundreds of years, and the first human landing on the moon was just commemorated. The brain has 80 billion neurons, 10 times the global population. At least 100 trillion neurons link, hundreds of times the number of stars in our galaxy. Brain research is difficult.

To help readers understand this chapter, SVM and RF algorithms distinguish between a normal brain and a brain with a tumour. Support Vector Machine (SVM) supervised learning is popular. It solves classification and regression issues. Its main use is machine learning categorization. The Support Vector Machine (SVM) technique finds the best line or decision boundary to divide n-dimensional space into classes for future data classification. Choosing here is best. SVM selects points and vectors at both ends to generate the hyperplane. Support vectors are severe examples, and support vector machines solve them. Random Forest uses many decision trees to analyse subsets of the data set to increase data prediction accuracy. Average these analyses. The random forest approach uses the forecasts of each tree to decide the outcome. More trees in the forest prevent overfitting and higher accuracy.

14.4 Types of Brain Tumors

14.4.1 Benign vs. Malignant Brain Tumours

Benign brain tumours are not linked to the development of cancer, despite the fact that they can be very problematic. This indicates that their growth is slow and that they typically do not spread to other areas of the body. In addition, their margins are typically clearer, which makes surgical removal simpler, and once they have been eliminated, they typically do not return. On the other hand, malignant brain tumours have the potential to metastasize, or spread, to other regions of the brain or the central nervous system. They pose a threat to your life due to the fact that they are carcinogenic and rapidly proliferate. Consider Figure 14.1 for the types of tumours.

14.4.2 Primary Brain Tumour

Brain tumours are cancers that originate and grow in the brain. They can originate from the cells in your brain, the meninges (which are the membranes that cover your brain), the nerve cells in your body, or glands like the pituitary and pineal. Primary tumours have the potential to be either benign or malignant. The types of brain tumors known as gliomas and meningiomas are the ones that affect people the most frequently mentioned in Figure 14.2.

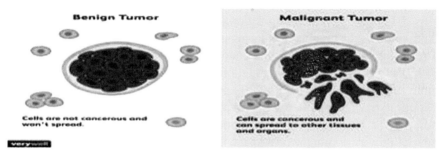

Figure 14.1 Benign vs. Malignant Brain tumour.

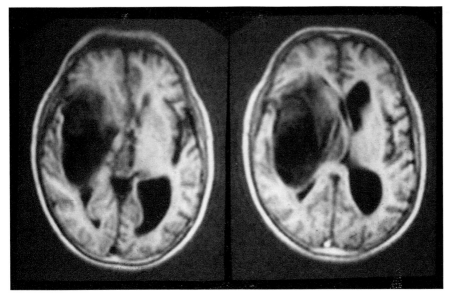

Figure 14.2 Gliomas MRI image.

GLIOMAS: Cancers that begin in glial cells are referred to as gliomas. Typically, these cells are responsible for maintaining the structure of your central nervous system, feeding it, clearing waste from the system, and destroying dead neurons. Gliomas can originate in a variety of glial cells throughout the body. Oligodendroglial tumors are prevalent in the frontal and temporal lobes, and frontal and temporal lobe astrocytomas and glioblastomas are the most aggressive types of brain tumors that originate in glial cells. Astrocytomas originate in the cerebrum. Glioblastomas originate in the brain's supporting tissue. Some types of brain tumors begin in glial cells.

14.4.3 Secondary Brain Tumour

Secondary brain tumours account for the vast majority of cases of brain cancer. They start in one part of the body and eventually spread to the brain through a process known as metastasis. The following are some of the things that can cause an infection in the brain: cancers of the breast, lungs, kidneys, and skin are included in this category.

It is always the case that secondary brain tumours are cancerous. Malignant tumours, on the other hand, can spread to other parts of your body, but benign tumours cannot as mentioned in Figure 14.3.

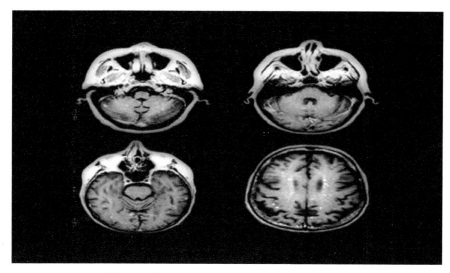

Figure 14.3   Secondary Brain tumour MRI Image.

14.5 Literature Survey

Preprocessing, segmentation, postprocessing, and image fusion were the techniques that were utilised in order to deconstruct the MR images of the cerebrum and locate the tumour. In order to give the image a more professional look, the preprocessing stages included the use of a 2-D adaptive filter. In a similar manner, Otsu's segmentation method was utilised on MR images of the brain in order to differentiate between normal tissue and tumour tissue. At the stage of post-processing, morphological procedures were utilised in order to remove the additional noise that was produced as a result of segmentation. Menze et al. (2015) investigated the Dice score and developed the BRATS benchmark for the segmentation of brain tumours. Image fusion that was based on overlay was utilized so that a distinct visual segmentation of the tumour area could be obtained. The new piece of work has an error rate of 7% and a detection rate of 93% (Li et al., 2015). Kumarganesh et al. (2016, 2018) devised an effective method to determine the location of a picture of a tumor and to evaluate the sensitivity, specificity, and accuracy of various brain tissues.

The authors of the study, Dumpuri et al. (2010), proposed a new framework, local binary patterns, and levels of fusion in order to extract the characteristics. When piecing together the findings from the classification ensemble, the soft-decision fusion rule is a useful tool to have at your disposal. Fully Convolutional Neural Networks (FCNNs) and Dense Micro-block Difference Feature were used in the novel system that was proposed by Deng et al. (2019) in order to differentiate between Different Types of Brain Tumours (DMDF). In this section, the texture feature was analysed with the help of the Fisher vector encoding method. After that, precise boundary segmentation was accomplished by combining non-quantifiable regional characteristics with FCNN. The findings of the trials demonstrated that segmentation was accurate and stable, as well as the fact that image segmentation of a brain tumour could be completed in about one second [14].

A strategy for intelligently diagnosing Brain MRI tumours was developed by Wu et al. (2020). In order to complete this chapter, a deep convolutional neural network and the SVM method, which consists of three phases, were utilised.

At first, a deep convolutional neural network was trained to figure out how to move from image space to the space occupied by tumour markers [9]. After that, the SVM classifier is fed the anticipated labels that were generated in the previous stage. In the final step, the outputs of a deep convolutional neural network and a support vector machine are combined in order to train a deeper classifier that is more accurate.

Because of this, reviews of the research on MR brain imaging have shown the various segmentation approaches that can be used to locate tumours and divide them up. These strategies can be found in the previous sentence. Thus, researchers from all over the world are focusing their attention on the process of segmentation in medical images, although their work is not yet complete. With all of the information in mind, the purpose of the current research is to develop new methods that can be utilised to better segment MR brain pictures and locate specific features [10].

It was claimed that T1 magnetic resonance images may be used to extract the brain in a programmed manner. This could be accomplished through the use of area-based tagging and morphological activity (Chinnathambi et al., 2014; Devi and Asokan, 2014).

In the beginning, the binary picture was created from MR images by employing a method called adaptive intensity thresholding. This method was unsupervised and relied on the individual's prior knowledge. Anatomical data were used by Periyasamy and Ramasamy (2018) in order to identify the binary image, and a rudimentary brain mask was created with the help of a run-length technique. After that, morphological functions were applied to the most connected region of the MR images in order to obtain a more detailed portion of the brain.

When doing the performance analysis, the following factors were taken into consideration: specificity, execution time, and the amount of false positives. Hence, the specificity is 0.992, the execution time is 1 second for each slice, and the false positive rate is 0.075. These findings are based on the outcomes of the studies (Krishnamoorthy and colleagues, 2016).

14.6 Proposed System

Here, unlike many other modern deep learning approaches, which use the entire image, you shouldn't. Instead, zero in on a specific region of the image to isolate specific details. The negative impacts are mitigated significantly by omitting the irrelevant details. Moreover, if you employ this tactic, you won't need a deep convolutional model [10].

To provide the highest quality final segmentation, we employ four distinct brain imaging modalities (T1, FLAIR, T1, and T2). To standardize the MRI data and eliminate the impact of anisotropy, particularly in the FLAIR mode, we employ Z-score normalization across all employed modalities. The method yields an image with a mean of zero and a variance of one when applied to a medical image of the brain [12]. We did this by dividing the average by the standard deviation for each brain area (not the background). Each patient's brain capacity required a unique approach at this stage [10].

In this chapter, it was discovered that the tumor grew and morphed consistently from one tissue section to the next. The tumor is visible from the very first slice and can be seen clearly from any angle. The tumor will be located in the same relative position on the image throughout successive slices, but it will grow in size. After the tumor has reached its maximum size, it will gradually decrease in size until it disappears [9]. The premise behind our pre-processing methodology is this.

These four brain scans are employed mostly because they each have their own unique technique of detecting certain aspects of a tumor. The three components of a tumor must be located in each of the four imaging

Figure 14.4   Block Diagram of the Proposed System.

modalities, and then assembled. The primary objective is to localize the tumor using information from all available modalities.

14.7 Architecture

The algorithm for this classifier is based on a random forest. A vast collection of binary decision trees can be generated using the random forest classifier with the use of two separate random processes [8]. To begin, parts of the training set are chosen at random, and then those parts are used to create the bootstrap set. Next, by introducing an element of chance into the process of creating trees, we may make it more intriguing. In order to determine the most effective method for splitting the tree, random features are used. Images generated by Bootstrap and those generated by the training set have the same dimensions.

The difference between the training sets and the bootstrap set is two thirds. A bootstrap set is created when training sets are combined. The remaining samples from the training set are taken from the bootstrap set. In conclusion, the Out-of-bag set is comprised of these individual cases. It is possible to put the tree through its paces using an out-of-the-bag set even as the bootstrap set is being utilized to construct it. The following task is to determine the error by calculating the total out-of-bag set error, which is equal to the average classification mistake made on the sets that were not contained within the bag. The mistake in generalizing about the upper bound has

$$GE = \Omega(1/s^2 - 1). \tag{14.1}$$

"In this equation," "represents the "mean value of correlation," while "s" represents the "ensemble strength." When the strength is increased while the correlation is decreased, the amount of error that occurs is kept to a minimal. A single model can be created by using the predictions of several decision trees and a random forest classifier is used to do this. The usage of this one model of the random forest classifier yields more accurate findings, which are then put to use in the process of locating faults in images of tumours.

14.8 Support Vector Machine Classifier

One of the methods that fall under the category of binary linear classification is the Support Vector Machine [12]. Its purpose is to clearly demarcate the border in order to reduce the amount of inaccuracy that can be introduced

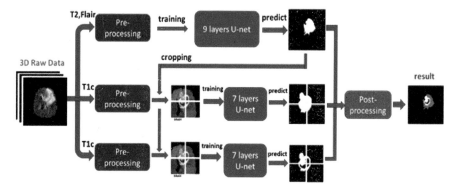

Figure 14.5   Architecture.

through generalisation. This strategy is utilised rather frequently while dealing with linear as well as nonlinear classification issues. In addition to that, it can perform regression, and it can even perform the process of finding outliers. In support vector machine (SVM) analysis, the goal is to construct a hyperplane that sorts vectors into a variety of classes in the correct sequence [9].

The pixels of an image need to be segmented in order to achieve the goal of creating groups of pixels that are highly resemblant to the objects that are depicted in the image. The picture is divided into a number of distinct subregions, and each of those subregions has its own unique set of pixels that have a grayscale level that is comparable to and consistent with that of the rest of the subregion. A number of different methods that focus on regions have been used to collate these pixel values into the same region. Approaches that concentrate on regions can recognise repeating patterns by analysing the pixel intensities in their immediate surroundings. This is done in order to find the patterns. The term "cluster" is sometimes used interchangeably with the term "region," and the categorization of regions into groups is determined by the functions that they perform [10]. The process of segmenting an image involves doing exactly this kind of thing from start to finish. The relative strength of the individual pixels that comprise an image is the second method that can be used to establish the threshold for an image. By utilising this method of thresholding, it is feasible to turn the image that was provided as input into a binary image. After this phase, edge detection algorithms are employed in order to discover cracks in the grey level images. This step is the last step in the process. The objective of this technique, which is known as a "boundary-based method" [10], is to pinpoint the areas of the image in which the intensity values of the pixels vary. Using this method of edge detection is something that is done. The manner in which the segmentation process operates can be found above in this paragraph. This method of data segmentation can be applied to the data that has been supplied in order to gain varied degrees of return on investment. In order to carry out the task of segmentation that was outlined in this chapter, the technique that is commonly referred to as the Principal Component Analysis Method was utilised. The following directions are provided with this package.

Collect the data collection that consists of pictures of tumours in their various stages.

Create a pixel-based representation of the images that are contained in a data set by transforming the photos.

You can figure out what the mean value is by performing a subtraction calculation.

Construct Co-variance matrix. Calculate Eigen value by using the common formula.

You need to pick the major component that has the highest Eigen value in order to proceed.

The regular principal component analysis (PCA) is a factual method that focuses on the direct projection of multivariate high-dimensional information onto a low-dimensional subspace by employing the least square deterioration while maintaining the biggest difference [10]. This method is known as the principal component analysis (PCA). The principle component analysis (PCA) is an approach that looks for symmetrical headings that are buried deep inside data that is severely discordant. After segmentation, normal tissues and aberrant tissues are partitioned off from one another so that they can be studied separately.

14.9 Data Set

The dataset was obtained by downloading it from the platform known as Github. This dataset contains MRI scans of a brain tumour that were performed on a patient. The normal structure of the human brain is photographed in one folder, while malignant growths are depicted in the other. These two folders include a combined total of 2065 images in their contents. Figure 14.2 provides an illustration of a normal brain as well as an image of a brain tumour. There are a total of 1085 shots taken of tumors and 980 photographs taken of normal tissue. The photographs have been resized to 256 by 256 pixels and are available in a variety of formats. There are 1672 photographs

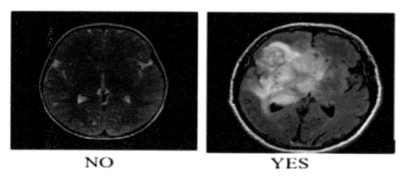

NO   **YES**

Figure 14.6 Normal Brain and Brain with tumour.

taken for the purpose of training, 186 for the purpose of validation, and 207 for the purpose of testing. 795 out of the 1672 training shots, don't depict any tumours, while 877 of the training photos do. The 92 tumor images and the 94 non-tumor images were both created using a total of 186 validation photos.

14.10 Results and Discussion

Table 14.1 Comparison of Prediction Accuracy between SVM (Support Vector Machine) and RF (Random Forest) algorithm. The Support Vector Machine Accuracy 96.89% compared to Random Forest algorithm having 94.12%

Samples (N)	Support Vector Machine(SVM) Algorithm Accuracy in %	Random Forest(RF) Algorithm Accuracy in %
1	91.22%	90.12%
2	91.65%	90.45%
3	92.55%	91.55%
4	92.65%	91.88%
5	92.45%	91.65%
6	93.45%	92.55%
7	93.88%	92.89%
8	94.10%	93.45%
9	94.55%	93.88%
10	96.89%	94.12%

Table 14.2 Group Statistics of SVM and Random Forest by grouping the iterations with Sample size 10, Mean = 96.89, Standard Deviation = 0.3393, Standard Error Mean = 0.1517.

	Group	N	Mean	Std.Deviation	Std.Error Mean
Accuracy	SVM	10	96.8940	0.3393	0.1517
	Random Forest	10	94.1220	0.3737	0.1671

Table 14.3 Independent sample T-test.

		Levene's Test for Equality of Variances		T-test for Equality of Means						95% Confidence Interval of the Difference	
		F	Sig.	t	df	One-sided p	Two-sided p	Mean Differ-ence	Std. Error of Dif-ference	Lower	Upper
Accuracy	Equal vari-ances assumed	0.400	0.545	7.848	8	0.001	0.001	1.772	0.225	1.251	2.292
	Equal vari-ances not assumed			7.848	7.927	0.001	0.001	1.772	0.225	1.250	2.293

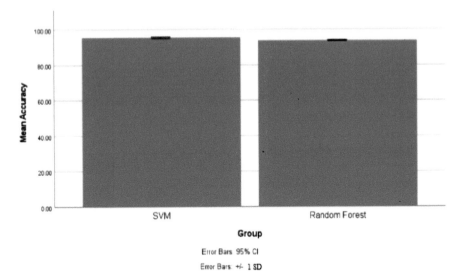

Error Bars 95% CI

Error Bars +/- 1 SD

Figure 14.7 Comparison of SVM and Random Forest in terms of mean accuracy. It explores that the mean accuracy is slightly better than random Forest and the standard deviation is moderately improved compared to random Forest.

14.11 Conclusion

SVM is thought to be one of the best ways to study a group of images. The SVM makes the prediction by reducing the size of the image without losing any of the information it needs. By adding more image data, the RF model can be used to test more accurately. The same thing can be done by using picture enhancement techniques and figuring out how well the RF and SVM work. Here, the model is made through a process of trial and error. In the future, techniques for optimization will be able to tell which is best. As of now, the SVM is the best way to predict whether or not a brain tumour is present in the given dataset.

Acknowledgement

We would like to express our sincere gratitude to the Saveetha School of Engineering, SIMATS University, Chennai, India that have given full support to the publication of this research paper. We would also like to thank our colleagues for their feedback and support throughout the research process.

References

[1] S. R. Telrandhe, A. Pimpalkar and A. Kendhe, "Brain Tumor Detection using Object Labeling Algorithm & SVM", in International Engineering Journal For Research & Development Vol. 2, special issue, pp. 2-8, Nov 2015.

[2] SobriMuda and M. Mokji, "Brain Lesion Segmentation from Diffusion-Weighted MRI Based On Adaptive Thresholding And Gray Level Co-Occurrence Matrix", J. Telecommunication Electronic and Computer Engineering, Vol. 3, No. 2, 2011.

[3] S. Cha et.al, "Review Article: Update on Brain Tumor Imaging: From Anatomy to Physiology", Journal of Neuro radiology, Vol.27, pp.475-487, 2006.

[4] R. Adams and L. Bischof, "Seeded region growing," IEEE Trans. On Pattern Analysis and Machine Intelligence, vol.16, no.6, pp.641–647, 1994.

[5] J. Selvakumar, A. Lakshmi and T. Arivoli, "Brain tumor segmentation and its area calculation in brain MRIs using k-mean clustering and fuzzy c-mean algorithm" in Proceedings in IEEE-International Conference

On Advances In Engineering, Science And Management, pp. 186-190, 2012.

[6] R. Muthukrishnan and M. Radha, "Edge Detection Techniques for Image Segmentation" in International Journal of Computer Science & Information Technology, Vol 3, No 6, Dec 2011.

[7] M. Saritha and K. Paul Joseph, "Classification of MRI brain images using combined wavelet entropy based spider web plot and probabilistic neural network" ELSEVIER, pattern Recognition letters 34, pp. 2151-2159, 2013.

[8] P. N. Gopal and R. Sukanesh," wavelet statistical feature based segmentation and classification of brain computed tomography images" IET Image Prosess Vol. 7 pp. 25-32 2013.

[9] Sheejakumari V, Gomathi S. Healthy and pathological tissues classification in MRI Brain Images using Hybrid Genetic Algorithm-Neural Network (HGANNA) Approach. European J Sci Res 2012; 87: 212-226.

[10] Sheejakumari V, Gomathi S. MRI Brain Images healthy and pathological tissue classification with aid of Improved Particle Swarm Optimization and Neural Network (IPSONN). Comput Math Methods Med. 2015; 2015: 1-12.

[11] A. Laxmi and P. Samata, "Optimization of visual presentation of MRI image for accurate detection of tumor in human brain using virtual instrument" in The Biomedical Engineering International Conference 2012.

[12] G. Hamerly and C. Elkan, "Learning the k in K-Means" in Proceedings 7th Annual Conference on Neural Information Processing Systems (NIPS), pp. 281-288.

[13] Kumarganesh S and Suganthi M (2018) An enhanced medical diagnosis sustainable system for brain tumor detection and segmentation using ANFIS classifier. Current Medical Reviews 14(2): 271–279.

[14] Li W, Chen C, Su H, et al. (2015) Local binary patterns and extreme learning machine for hyperspectral imagery classification. IEEE Transactions on Geoscience and Remote Sensing 53(7): 3681–3693.

[15] Menze BH, Jakab A, Bauer S, et al. (2015) The multimodal brain tumor image segmentation benchmark (BRATS). IEEE Transactions on Medical Imaging 34(10): 1993–2024.

[16] Periyasamy N and Ramasamy A (2018) A novel edge preserving improved adaptive wavelet filter (EPIAWF) for speckle removal in ultrasound images. Current Medical Imaging Reviews 14(4): 521–532.

[17] Hassabis D, Kumaran D, Summerfield C, Botvinick M. Neuroscience-inspired artificial intelligence. Neuron 2017;95:245-58. 10.1016/j.neuron.2017.06.011 [PubMed] [CrossRef] [Google Scholar]

[18] Poo MM, Du JL, Ip NY, Xiong ZQ, Xu B, Tan T. China Brain Project: basic neuroscience, brain diseases, and brain-inspired computing. Neuron 2016;92:591-6. 10.1016/j.neuron.2016.10.050 [PubMed] [CrossRef] [Google Scholar]

[19] Chen R, Cui Z, Capitão L, Wang G, Satterthwaite TD, Harmer C. Precision biomarkers for mood disorders based on brain imaging. BMJ 2020;371:m3618. 10.1136/bmj.m3618 [PMC free article] [PubMed] [CrossRef] [Google Scholar]

[20] Chen W-J, Cheng X, Fu Y, et al. Rethinking monogenic neurological diseases. BMJ 2020;371:m3752 10.1136/bmj.m3752. [CrossRef] [Google Scholar]

[21] Doody RS, Thomas RG, Farlow M, et al. Alzheimer's Disease Cooperative Study Steering Committee. Solanezumab Study Group Phase 3 trials of solanezumab for mild-to-moderate Alzheimer's disease. N Engl J Med 2014;370:311-21. 10.1056/NEJMoa1312889 [PubMed] [CrossRef] [Google Scholar]

[22] Gauthier S, Feldman HH, Schneider LS, et al. Efficacy and safety of tau-aggregation inhibitor therapy in patients with mild or moderate Alzheimer's disease: a randomised, controlled, double-blind, parallel-arm, phase 3 trial. Lancet 2016;388:2873-84. 10.1016/S0140-6736(16)31275-2 [PMC free article] [PubMed] [CrossRef] [Google Scholar]

[23] Shi J, Sabbagh MN, Vellas B. Alzheimer's disease beyond amyloid: strategies for future therapeutic interventions. BMJ 2020;371:m3684. 10.1136/bmj.m3684 [PMC free article] [PubMed] [CrossRef] [Google Scholar]

[24] Henstridge CM, Hyman BT, Spires-Jones TL. Beyond the neuron-cellular interactions early in Alzheimer disease pathogenesis. Nat Rev Neurosci 2019;20:94-108. 10.1038/s41583-018-0113-1 [PMC free article] [PubMed] [CrossRef] [Google Scholar]

[25] Sweeney MD, Kisler K, Montagne A, Toga AW, Zlokovic BV. The role of brain vasculature in neurodegenerative disorders. Nat Neurosci 2018;21:1318-31. 10.1038/s41593-018-0234-x [PMC free article] [PubMed] [CrossRef] [Google Scholar]

[26] Pan Y, Li H, Wardlaw JM, Wang Y. A new dawn of preventing dementia by preventing cerebrovascular diseases. BMJ 2020;371:m3692.

10.1136/bmj.m3692 [PMC free article] [PubMed] [CrossRef] [Google Scholar]

[27] Zhang L, Li D, Xiao D, Couldwell WT, Ohata K. Improving brain health by identifying structure-function relations in patients with neurosurgical disorders. BMJ 2020;371:m3690. 10.1136/bmj.m3690 [PMC free article] [PubMed] [CrossRef] [Google Scholar]

[28] Chen Z, Rollo B, Antonic-Baker A, et al. New era of personalised epilepsy management. BMJ 2020;371:m3658. 10.1136/bmj.m3658 [PMC free article] [PubMed] [CrossRef] [Google Scholar].

15

Biomedical Applications of Footprint Recognition: Harnessing Artificial Intelligence and Machine Learning for Footprint Image Monitoring

Aditya Bhardwaj[1], Madhulika Bhatia[1], and Lata Nautiyal[2]

[1]Amity University, India
[2]University of Bristol, UK
E-mail: bhardwajaditya0204@gmail.com; mbhadauria@amity.edu;
lata.nautiyal@bristol.ac.uk

Abstract

The research chapter explores the biomedical applications of footprint recognition, focusing on the utilization of artificial intelligence (AI) and machine learning (ML) techniques for image monitoring. Footprint recognition offers a non-intrusive approach to individual identification and authentication in healthcare settings. By leveraging AI and ML algorithms, valuable insights can be extracted from footprint images, enabling advancements in various biomedical and healthcare domains. This work highlights the potential of footprint recognition in biometric identification and authentication, enhancing security and convenience in hospitals and healthcare facilities. Gait analysis and rehabilitation benefit from footprint analysis, aiding in the diagnosis of musculoskeletal disorders and neurological conditions, as well as the design of personalized rehabilitation programs. Furthermore, footprint recognition, AI, and ML techniques contribute to disease detection and monitoring by identifying patterns or markers in footprints. This allows for the early detection of conditions like peripheral vascular diseases, diabetes, or foot ulcers. The continuous monitoring of footprints enables disease progression tracking and facilitates timely interventions and personalized treatment plans. Additionally, the design of prosthetics and orthotics benefits from footprint analysis, ensuring optimal fit and functionality through AI and ML algorithms. Overall, this chapter highlights the potential of footprint recognition, AI, and ML in biomedical applications, paving the way for improved healthcare and personalized treatments.

Keywords: Footprint recognition, classifying footprint, new-born footprint recognition, biometrics, footprint-based security, footprint recognition in crime scenes.

15.1 Introduction

15.1.1 Problem statement

In many big hospitals, maternity institutions where babies are born every day, swapping of babies is a big problem. Many parents and even doctors do not get to know this even after several years. Footprint recognition is useful technique in such situations and already being used in many countries and their hospitals for recognizing infant using footprints of the new-born baby. Every large organization or security system uses biometric systems for the identification of their employees. Places like banks or parliament house needs high- level security systems. Fingerprint recognition is currently used for security in such places, but they do not provide the required security. But because of the practice of wearing socks and shoes, it can be considered more secure.

15.1.2 Motivation

The motivation is to develop a footprint recognition model for recognizing the footprint, which matches with the footprints available in the database. The model will be a single solution for both security and identification problems.

15.1.3 Uniqueness of footprints

All people have some inimitable set of elevations that make their prints unique from others. One of the ways to obtain footprints can be by using a pressure sensing mat [2]. As with prints, the footmark's shape and pattern is a distinguishing feature that can identify any one specific individual. Footprint sign is found at many crime scenes and subsequent to DNA. Both footprints and fingerprints have the capability of recognizing someone's identity. Just like the fingerprints, footprints also have the unique features and no two footprints can be similar to each other even if they are two different feet of the same person. Another footprint type is when someone is walking on the floor with both his feet dry; in this situation, latent prints are formed, which cannot be seen with naked eyes. The last type is when footprint is extracted from some soft surface like clay. In such a situation, footprint is visible with naked eyes and can be used for identification purposes but after some modifications. Such prints obtained on soft materials and are partially clear are called plastic prints. One of the problems faced while taking footprints of new born is that he/she moves a lot and is difficult to take prints as discussed in a research paper [3].

15.1.4 ML concepts used

Deep learning – A sub-concept of ML is deep learning. It uses many artificial intelligence concepts and functions for improving the computerization process. It tries to copy the thinking process and behavior of humans for taking decisions. It learns from large amount of data provided in the form of images or text or audio files. A large dataset of footprint images has been used in the paper for recognition purposes. It drives many AI services and features to improve the decision-making process. It is used in different situations in real life such as TV remotes with voice recognizing features and face recognition and many more. The major difference between deep learning and machine learning is that in ML, predictions are made with the help of data that is labeled and properly structured while in deep learning, some pre-processing steps are removed, which are necessary in ML. It can work on unstructured data image files and text files. Both concepts use different learning processes like supervised, unsupervised, and reinforcement learning for learning from the dataset provided.

Supervised learning – Also a subset of machine learning that uses data with labels for making predictions accurately. When data is put into the model as input, it adjusts the weight of data for fitting the model. Training set is used for teaching purpose and to get the desired output. This training dataset provided includes both inputs and their outputs. The model uses the loss function for measuring its accuracy. It is subdivided into two types, of which one is classification and the other is regression. Classification algorithm distributes test data into different classes based on their features, while regression is for understanding the relationship between independent and dependent variables. Different algorithms used with supervised learning are discussed in the following.

Neural networks: These are used in deep learning for processing the trained data. It copies the human behavior and the way of thinking with the help of different nodes. Different nodes have different weights, a threshold, output, and input. Supervised learning is used for learning the mapping function. Model accuracy is considered good if the cost function for the model is close to zero.

Linear regression: It uses the concept of finding the relationship between independent and dependent variable. It is divided into simple and multiple linear regression depending on the number of independent and dependent variables provided. If only one dependent and one independent variable are provided, it is called simple linear regression and if the number of variables increases, then it is called multiple linear regression.

15.1.5 Background information

The Figure 15.1 shows how the revenue of biometric systems globally is going to increase in the upcoming years.

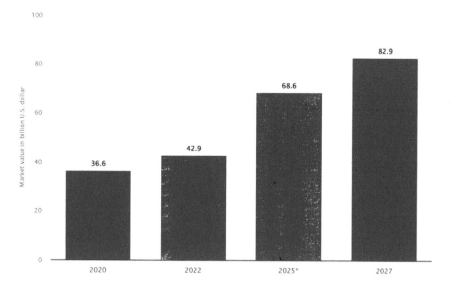

Figure 15.1   Global biometric systems revenue from 2020 to 2027 [15].

15.2 Literature Review

As the concept of footprint recognition has a lot of real-life applications and uses, a lot of research work and studies have been conducted on this. Most of the studies have focused on using convolutional neural networks for the tasks like image recognition and image classification. As discussed in a research paper, minutiae point is the point that provides important information about a footprint image [4].

Object detection is the most useful service for the perspective of computer vision. The research by Rawat and Wang has discussed the usage of deep convolutional neural network in image classification [10]. One of the studies discussed about some popular algorithms used in convolutional neural networks, such as RCNN, SPP-Net, and SSD [5]. Single-shot detector is a well-known detection algorithm made my Google, which uses VGG-16 architecture. Its development is easy. A number of default boxes are passed to the different feature maps. When it is in the training state, the matching is done between the two types of boxes, of which one is the default box and the other is the training box.

When the provided dataset is not very large or the model does not have enough images to recognize, a popular concept used is data augmentation. Research by Mikolajczyk and Grochowski discussed how data augmentation is used to solve image classification problems [9]. How a model is going to perform, its accuracy, and predictions are dependent on the amount or size of the dataset provided to the model. It is costly and difficult to find a big dataset, which satisfies the need. To solve all these problems, data augmentation is used. It is a method by the use of which the size of a dataset can be increased by adding a greater number of images. Different operations are performed on an image, and this image is then converted to multiple images by making small changes in all the images. It is about making small changes in the data using different OpenCV tools to generate new images. The usage of machine learning is increasing day by day especially in the field of deep learning. It is a good solution for the problems faced by developers in the AI world. It is very helpful in increasing the performance of a model by making unique and new data to train the models. It is very difficult for anyone working with machine learning or deep learning models to collect and label the data. Using data augmentation reduces the project cost by removing the operational costs. A very crucial step while making a deep learning model is to clean the data for obtaining highly accurate model. But if while cleaning the data the representability of the data is reducing, then it is very difficult for the model to provide high accuracy and predict correctly. The different changes that are possible to the images when doing data augmentation are rescaling the image. In rescaling, the height and width of the images get changed and all other features remain the same. Another change that can be made in the image is cropping. In this, some portion of the image will be removed. The portion that is not necessary or does not have a lot of descriptor features is removed. Another important change is converting the colored image into a grayscale image [11]. In a grayscale image, all the pixels have their intensity as either zero or one. The next important change that can be made in an image is zoom-in the images where a particular portion of the image, which is enough to explain the image, is used. The next important factor is making changes in the noise of the image. Removing random portions from the image, also called random erasing, is another very important change that can be made in an image. When some portion is removed from an image, then, because of the other samples of the same image present in the dataset, it is not impossible for the model to know what was present in that removed portion. Change in the contrast of image can also be made. Last is the translation of the image for creating a new image. In this, the image is moved in the x- and y-direction. Different advantages of using data augmentation are that it increases the deep learning model accuracy by adding more training data in the model. It helps in reducing the overall cost of the project because it is not easy to find a dataset of our choice.

Problems while using data augmentation:

A lot of problems can arise in the model when using data augmentation. Some of these are:

- Businesses must create measures for judging the effectiveness of augmented datasets. An estimation of the result quality of data augmentation technologies will be needed as their use grows.
- It is very difficult to generate the images that have high resolution and are generated with GANS. A lot of research and studies need to be conducted to generate synthetic data.
- If there is favoritism in the real dataset, then data generated from data augmentation will also have biases. Therefore, it is very important to identify the optical augmentation.

Research by Licheng Jiao and Fan Zhang [7] has discussed the ways to achieve object detectors with high efficiency and accuracy. One of the research projects conducted on footprints highlights the important features that make a footprint unique. Deep learning has a lot of applications in the field of object detection as mentioned in research [6]. Some of the features highlighted are the features of a person's toe. There are differences between the toes of different persons because of the differences between the shape and size of the feet. Different people have different shapes of toes, such as round, oval, or asymmetrical shapes. As explained in Table 15.1, the present population can be classified into four types of footprints based on the morphological length of the toes. The four types are shown in Figure 15.2.

Table 15.1 Types of feet based on the morphological length.

Sl. no.	Types	Description
1	T-type	This is when the length of first toe is greater than the length of the third toe.
2	F-type	When the length of toe 2 is greater than the length of toe 3, then it is of F-type.
3	M-type	When the length of toe 3 is greater than the length of toes 1 and 2, then the type is called M-type.
4	O-type	When the lengths of all three are the same.

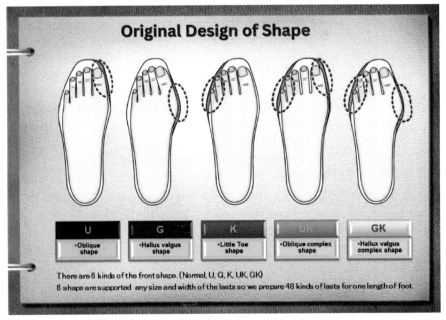

Figure 15.2 Different shapes of the human feet.

15.3 Methodology

This chapter aims to study and develop a deep-learning-based convolutional neural network model for recognizing persons' footprints. A large dataset of 7920 samples has been used for recognizing the matching footprint out of 220 footprints available in the dataset. Different layers used in the model include conv2d and maxpool2d layers. A two-dimensional convolution is applied on the users' input when using the conv2d layer. A convolution kernel winded with layers is created through this layer, which is useful in producing the tensor of outputs. One of the most important parameters of this layer is the number of filters from which the layers are going to learn. In this chapter, 16 filters have been used. To choose the correct number of filters, a good practice is to choose the filters in power of 2. Another way of doing recognition is by using PCA and ICA by taking help of a distance algorithm [1].

Another most used layer in convolutional neural networks is the max pool layer. Some of the important parameters used by this layer are stride, kernel size, and padding. Stride is used for specifying the number by which the kernel will move when sliding through different images. If stride value is 1, then it will mean that the kernel will move through the image from one pixel to another. That means no pixel will be skipped, while if the value of the stride is 2, then it will mean that the kernel will access alternative pixels. The size of the kernel is another important parameter in max pooling, which specifies the height and width of the filter mask. This layer is used to get rid of overfitting as it provides a less complicated version of the actual representation. The maximum value of the neurons is used in this layer. The reason for using convolutional neural networks is their superior image recognition features. To improve accuracy in deep learning, data augmentation can be used as mentioned by Perez and Wang in their research [8].

15.3.1 Convolutional neural networks

Mainly three layers are used in convolutional neural networks, out of which the first one is the convolutional layer. This layer is the topmost or the first layer of convolutional neural networks. This layer is followed by other different layers like max pooling. Each added layer upgrades the complexity of the model and neural networks. The starting layers have more attention on color and boundaries.

The central component of a convolutional neural network is the convolutional layer, which is also the place where majority of the calculation takes place. It needs input data, a filter, and a feature map, among other things. Assume that the input will be a color image that is composed of a 3D pixel matrix. As a result, the input will have three dimensions — height, width, and depth — that are analogous to RGB in an image. Additionally, we have a feature detector, also referred to as a kernel or filter, which will move through the image's receptive fields and determine whether the feature is there. Convolution describes this process. A two-dimensional array with weights serving as the feature detector is used in representing a portion of the images [14].

15.3.2 Changing the volume size of the output

1. The depth of the output is influenced by the number of filters. Three different filters, for instance, would result in three different feature maps, giving a depth of 3.
2. The kernel's stride is the number of pixels it travels over the input matrix. Despite the rarity of stride values of 2 or higher, a longer stride results in a lesser output.
3. In cases where the filters do not fit the input image, zero-padding is typically utilized. This results in a larger or equally sized output by setting any elements that are not part of the input matrix to zero.

This is sometimes referred to as valid padding or no padding. In this situation, if dimensions do not line up, the final convolution is dropped. In the same padding, the output layer will be of the same size as the input layer. Complete padding enlarges the output by padding the input border with zeros.

A CNN performs a rectified linear unit transformation on the feature map following every convolution operation, adding non-linearity to the model. The first convolution layer may be followed by another. When this occurs, the CNN's structure may become hierarchical because the later layers will be able to view the pixels in the earlier layers' receptive fields. Let us use the case of trying to ascertain whether a bicycle is there in an image as an example. The bicycle can be viewed as a collection of components. A feature hierarchy is created within the CNN by the bicycle's component pieces, each of which represents a lower-level pattern in the neural network and the bicycle as a whole a higher-level pattern. In the last step, the image is converted into numeric values for rendering. Downsampling, sometimes referred to as pooling layers, does dimension reduction, lowering the number of parameters in the input. The pooling operation distributes a filter across the whole input identical to the convolutional layer, with the exception that this filter lacks weights. Rather, the kernel populates the result array by applying an aggregation function to the values in the receptive field. There are principally two forms of pooling.

Max pooling: The filter chooses the pixel that has the maximum value to send to the resultant array as it progresses toward the input. As a side note, the method discussed is applied more frequently than average pooling.

Average pooling: In this, the filter calculates the average value inside the receptive field as it passes across the input and sends that value to the output array.

The pooling layer loses a lot of information, but it also offers the CNN a number of advantages. They lessen complexity, increase effectiveness, and lower the risk of overfitting.

15.3.3 Languages, tools, and platform used

The important tools and environments used for the development of model are as follows:

- Programming language used is Python.
- Python packages used are Opencv, Keras, Tensorflow, Numpt, Matplotlib, and Pandas.
- Environment used: Jupyter was used for running and executing the Python programs.

Depending on the features that were retrieved from the preceding layers and their various filters, this layer conducts the classifying operation. FC layers often utilize a softmax activation function to categorize inputs suitably, generating a probability ranging from 0 to 1. Convolutional and pooling layers typically used ReLU functions. Convolutional neural networks give power to image recognizing ability and computer vision abilities. It is an area of AI, which gives power to the computers to extract important and necessary information from the images. It is used in a lot of places, such as in radiology technology, where it helps the doctors finding the tumor [17].

15.3.4 Dataset used

A dataset of 220×6 images provided for free use by IEEE data port has been used. Since the dataset provided only have six images for each foot, it is very difficult to develop a model. To solve this problem, data augmentation was used to generate more images and increase the size of the dataset [12]. The dataset used has been created using a simple PSC machine EPSON 5500

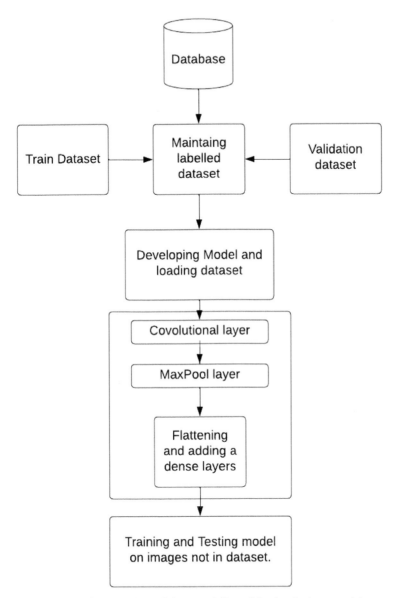

Figure 15.3 Flowchart of the steps followed for developing a model.

Scanner. Figures 15.4 and 15.5 show samples of footprints used in the dataset. The dataset provided was first labeled and distributed into folders with the help of an automated Python program as shown in Figure 15.3.

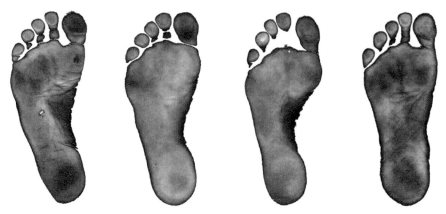

Figure 15.4 Sample footprint images used in the dataset.

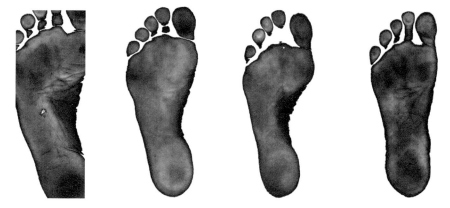

Figure 15.5 Corresponding augmented images generated by the model.

15.4 Results and Discussion

The convolutional neural network for footprint recognition was successfully implemented using deep learning and Python techniques. The model was able to achieve a good accuracy. One of the other techniques used for recognition was by normalizing the input footprints and using Euclidean distance and geometric information between the prints provided in the dataset. The model used Adam optimizer and categorical_crossentropy as loss for achieving the present accuracy.

Table 15.2 Summary of the model created.

Layer (type)	Output shape	Param #
conv2d (CONV2D)	(None, 254, 254, 16)	448
max_pooling2d (MaxPooling2D)	(None, 127, 127, 16)	0
Conv2d_1 (Conv2D)	(None, 125, 125, 32)	4640
max_pooling2d_1 (MaxPooling2D)	(None, 62, 62, 32)	0
conv2_2 (Conv2D)	(None, 60, 60, 64)	18,496
max_pooling2d_2 (MaxPooling2D)	(None, 30, 30, 64)	0
Flatten (Flatten)	(None, 57,600)	0
dense (Dense)	(None, 512)	29,491,712
dense_1 (Dense)	(None, 220)	112,860

Table 15.2 shows the summary of the model created in this report.

Training and validation loss shown in Figure 15.6 are two important parameters for analyzing a model. An indicator of how well a trained model fits the data for training is the training loss. In other words, it evaluates the model's error on the training dataset. The training set is a subset of the dataset that was initially used to train the model. The total of errors for each sample in the training set is used to computationally determine the training loss. It is also crucial to remember that each batch ends with a measurement of the training loss. Typically, a training loss curve is plotted to show this. On the other hand, a model's performance on the validation set is evaluated using a statistic called validation loss. A section of the dataset designated as the validation set was used to examine the model's effectiveness [17]. Similar to the training loss, the validation loss is determined by adding the errors for each sample in the validation set.

Training accuracy and validation accuracy are two important factors that show the accuracy given by the model while training and validating.

The graph of accuracy depicted in Figure 15.7 shows that the model successfully solves the problem of overfitting and underfitting. Whenever the model fits the training set too well, overfitting occurs. The model, therefore, finds it challenging to generalize to fresh samples that were not part of the training set. As an illustration, as opposed to recognizing broad patterns, the model detects particular photos from the training set [18]. The accuracy during learning will be greater than the accuracy during validation/testing. This could be because the model needs more training time, more input features, or less regularization.

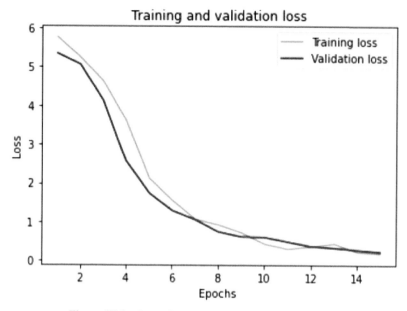

Figure 15.6   Graph for training and validation loss of model.

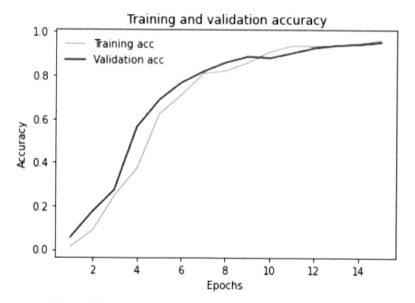

Figure 15.7   Graph for training and validation accuracies of the model.

15.5 Conclusion

The biomedical applications of footprint recognition, along with the integration of artificial intelligence (AI) and machine learning (ML) techniques, showcase significant advancements in healthcare and image monitoring. The rapid evolution of deep learning and AI has led to the development of new tools and techniques that enhance the accuracy and effectiveness of footprint recognition systems.

The utilization of convolutional neural networks (CNNs) in deep learning for recognizing footprints, particularly in newborns, has demonstrated remarkable accuracy rates exceeding 90%. This robust model effectively identifies and matches footprints from extensive datasets, offering promising potential for reliable identification and authentication.

The integration of AI and ML techniques in image monitoring enables healthcare professionals to leverage valuable insights derived from footprint analysis. This aids in the diagnosis of various conditions such as musculoskeletal disorders, neurological impairments, and vascular diseases. Additionally, continuous monitoring of footprints facilitates early detection, disease progression tracking, and personalized treatment planning, leading to improved patient outcomes.

The advancements in footprint recognition, AI, and ML techniques offer significant contributions to personalized healthcare, rehabilitation programs, and the design of prosthetics and orthotics. These technologies enhance the accuracy, efficiency, and convenience of individual identification, gait analysis, and disease monitoring, ultimately improving the overall quality of healthcare services.

As deep learning and AI continue to evolve, it is expected that further advancements will be made, leading to even more sophisticated tools and techniques in the field of biomedical applications. The integration of footprint recognition with AI and ML holds great promise for transforming healthcare practices, enhancing diagnostics and enabling personalized treatment strategies for individuals in need.

15.6 Future Scope

Recognition models are playing a very important role in different sectors. Some of the examples are the entry of students in colleges using face recognition and hand recognition systems being used at various security sectors. For future work, the aim will be to explore more in the field of image classification using convolutional neural networks and develop a model that can tell more about a person by knowing his footprints and fingerprints.

References

[1] Khokher, R., Singh, R. C. & Kumar, R. (2015, January)."Footprint recognition with principal component analysis and independent component analysis." In Macromolecular symposia, vol. 347, no. 1, pp. 16-26. 2015.

[2] Nakajima, K., Mizukami, Y., Tanaka, K., & Tamura, T.(2000).Footprint-based personal recognition. IEEE Transactions on Biomedical Engineering, 47(11), 1534-1537.

[3] Jia, W., Cai, H. Y., Gui, J. Hu, R. X., Lei, Y. K., & Wang, X. F. (2012). New-born footprint recognition using orientation feature. Neural Computing and Applications, 21(8), 1855-1863.

[4] Liu, E. (2017). Infant footprint recognition. In Proceedings of the IEEE international conference on computer vision (pp. 1653-1660).

[5] Zhou, X., Gong, W., Fu, W., & Du, F. (2017, May). Application of deep learning in object detection. In 2017 IEEE/ACIS 16th International Conference on Computer and Information Science (ICIS) (pp. 631-634). IEEE.

[6] Pathak, A. R., Pandey, M., & Rautaray, S. (2018). Application of deep learning for object detection. Procedia computer science, 132, 1706-1717.

[7] Jiao, L., Zhang, F., Liu, F., Yang, S., Li, L. Feng, Z., & Qu, R. (2019). A survey of deep learning-based object detection. IEEE access, 7, 128837-128868.

[8] Shivam and Bareja, Pawan and Bhatia, Madhulika, Appearance of Machine and Deep Learning in Image Processing: A Portrayal (2018). International Journal of Computational Intelligence & IoT, Vol. 2, No. 4, 2018, Available at SSRN: https://ssrn.com/abstract=3361144.

[9] Mikolajczyk, Agnieszka, and Michal Grochowski, M. (2018, May). Data augmentation for improving deep learning in image classification problem." In 2018 international interdisciplinary PhD workshop (IIPhDW) (pp. 117-122). IEEE.

[10] Rawat, W., & Wang, Z. (2017). Deep convolutional neural networks for image classification: A comprehensive review. Neural computation, 29(9), 2352-2449.

[11] Kunar, V. A., & Ramakrishnan, M. (2010). Footprint recognition using modified sequential haar energy transform (MSHET). IJCSI International Journal of Computer Science Issues, 7(3).

[12] DeVries, Terrance, and Graham W. Taylor. "Dataset augmentation in feature space." arXiv preprint arXiv:1702.05538 (2017)

[13] Kumar, V. A., & Ramakrishnan, M. (2013). Employment of footprint recognition system, Indian J. Comput. Sci. Eng. (ICJSE), 3, 774-778

[14] Albawi, S., Mohammed, T. A., & Al-Zawi, S. (2017, August). Understanding of a convolutional neural network. In 2017 international conference on engineering and technology (ICET) (pp. 1-6). Ieee.

[15] https://www.statista.com/statistics/1048705/worldwide-biometrics-market-revenue/

[16] Bhatia, M., Poojitha, V., & Verma, N. V. (2018). Review on Biometric Identification Using Lip Prints. MR International Journal of Engineering & Technology, 9(1), 26-30.

[17] Soni, Rahul and D., Tanmay and Twinkle, Twinkle and Bhatia, Madhulika, Digital Twin: Intersection of Mind and Machine (March 27, 2019). International Journal of Computational Intelligence & IoT, Vol. 2, No. 3, 2019, Available at SSRN: https://ssrn.com/abstract=3361029.

[18] Mishra, P., Mann, S.S., Sharma, M., Bhatia, M. (2022). Design of Facial Recognition Based Touchless Biometric System. In: Singh, P.K., Kolekar, M.H., Tanwar, S., Wierzchoń, S.T., Bhatnagar, R.K. (eds) Emerging Technologies for Computing, Communication and Smart Cities. Lecture Notes in Electrical Engineering, vol 875. Springer, Singapore. https://doi.org/10.1007/978-981-19-0284-0_19.

Index

About the Editors

Dr. Poonam Tanwar has 21 years of teaching experience working as professor in Manav Rachna International Institute of Research & Studies, Faridabad. She has published more than 100 research papers in various international journals and conferences, 40 are indexed in Scopus. She has one copyright and filled six patents. She has edited books and was guest editor for special issues of for International Journal of Recent Patents in Engineering (UAE) and one more is in process. She has been awarded a woman researcher award by VDGOODS Academy Chennai, International Inspirational Woman Award 2020. She has organized various science and technology awareness programs for rural development. She received a Certificate of RECOGNITION (Silver Category) for outstanding contribution to the Campus Connect Program for all academic years since 2011 to 2017 by INFOSYS, Chandigarh. She is convenor and coordinator of many technical events like IEEE international conference COM-IT-CON 2019, 2022, International symposium on Computational Intelligence, International Hackhthon (Hack the Mountain), etc. Beside this she is Technical program committee member for various International Conferences Like ICIC 2018, ICFNN, Rome (Italy), European Conference on Natural Language Processing and Information Retrieval, Berlin(Europe), etc.

Dr. Tapas Kumar holds a Ph.D. degree in Engineering (2013), gained at Dept. Of Computer Sc. & Engineering, Birla Institute of Technology, Mesra, Ranchi, (Jharkhand). He received his master's degree in Computer Science from Guru Jambeshwar University of Science and Technology, India, and a B.E. from Amravati University, Amravati. He has supervised 10 M.Tech theses and guided more than 200 students of B.E/B.Tech in their research-based and application-based projects. Prof. Tapas Kumar has published almost 45 research articles in refereed international journals and15 research papers presented and published in various international and national conferences and scholarly meetings. He has also successfully guided six Ph.D. scholars.

Dr. K. Kalaiselvi received her doctoral degree from Anna University, Chennai, India in 2013 under the Faculty of Science and Humanities. Currently she is working as Professor in the Department of Data Analytics, Saveetha College of Liberal Arts and Sciences (SIMATS), Chennai, India. She completed a mini project entitled "Mobile Tracking System for Preventing the Propagation of Feminine Victim" funded by VISTAS Project, developed e-content for the Database Management Systems course, SAP. She has published more than 60 articles in the Scopus indexed journals, Web of Science and UGC Journal and presented more than 20 research papers at international conferences. She filed and published a patent based on Internet of Things applications and has published around five monographs which includes Springer, Emerald publisher. She has acted as reviewer and editorial board member for reputed journals. She received a "Senior Woman Educator & Scholar Award" in the 11th Teachers Day Awards 2020, a "Young Woman Educator & Scholar Award" in the 6th National Women's Day Awards 2019, and a"Best Researcher Award" from DK International Research Foundation, 2018.

Dr. Haider Raza received a Ph.D. in Computer Science from University of Ulster, Northern Ireland, UK, a master's degree in Computer Engineering from Manav Rachna International University, India, and a bachelor's degree in Computer Science and Engineering from Integral University, India. He completed his primary and secondary education in 1991–2003 from Colvin Taluqdars' College in Lucknow, which is one of the oldest private schools in India. He was born in the city of Lucknow and spent nearly 24 years there. He has previously worked at Swansea University, Wales, UK, University of Ulster, Northern Ireland, UK, Dilla University, Ethiopia, and Manav Rachna International University, India. He is a Fellow of the Higher Education Academy (FHEA) and a Senior Member of the Institute of Electrical and Electronics Engineers (SMIEEE). His research interests focus on the artificial intelligence machine learning for decision making, non-stationary learning, brain-computer interface, EEG/MEG signal processing, computer vision, and computational intelligence methods for healthcare, businesses, and environment.

Dr. Seema Rawat is an Associate Professor, Amity School of Engineering and Technology, Amity University Tashkent, Uzbekistan with around 15 years of teaching experience. Her research areas are cloud computing, data mining, artificial intelligence, and big data. She has a lot of research experience and has published more than 100 research papers in international journals and conferences (Scopus indexed) and book chapters, and holds 12 Patents. She is the Placement Head of the Department of Information Technology, Head of the Entrepreneurship cell, Advisor of Amity IEEE student chapter (AICSC) and manages the funding and consultancy. She is a member of many international journals and conferences like Elsevier, IGI, Wiley, Inderscience and has reviewed many technical articles. She is a member of IETE, ACM, WEC (Women Entrepreneurship Cell), and other renowned technical societies and committees. She is a technical advisor at Deetya-Soft Pvt. Ltd. Noida, Ennoble Pvt. Ltd., MyDigital360, MSME Technology incubators, etc. She received government funding from the Ministry of Skill and Development for her project. She was awarded the "Faculty Innovation Excellence award 2019" on World Intellectual day by the secretary of the Department of science and technology, Government of India.

For Product Safety Concerns and Information please contact our
EU representative GPSR@taylorandfrancis.com Taylor & Francis
Verlag GmbH, Kaufingerstraße 24, 80331 München, Germany